*Between the Human and the Divine*

# Between the Human and the Divine

## The Political Thought of Simone Weil

*Mary G. Dietz*

Rowman & Littlefield
PUBLISHERS

ROWMAN & LITTLEFIELD

Published in the United States of America in 1988
by Rowman & Littlefield, Publishers
(a division of Littlefield, Adams & Company)
81 Adams Drive, Totowa, New Jersey 07512

**Library of Congress Cataloging-in-Publication Data**

Dietz, Mary G.
   Between the human and the divine.

   Bibliography: p. 197
   Includes index.
   1. Weil, Simone, 1909–1943—Political and social
views. I. Title.
JC261.W45D54   1987      320.5'092'4      87–20569
ISBN 0-8476-7574-2
ISBN 0-8476-7575-0 (pbk.)


90 89 88
5 4 3 2 1

Printed in the United States of America

For my mother,
and in memory of
my father

# Contents

# Abbreviations

**HP**   "Human Personality." *Selected Essays 1934–1943*. Richard Rees, trans. London: Oxford University Press, 1962b.

**LGA**   "The Love of God and Affliction." *On Science, Necessity, and the Love of God*. Richard Rees, ed. London: Oxford University Press, 1968.

**RLO**   "Reflections Concerning the Causes of Liberty and Social Oppression." *Oppression and Liberty*. Arthur Wills and John Petrie, trans. Amherst: University of Massachusetts Press, 1973.

**SS**   "Reflections on the Right Use of School Studies With a View To the Love of God." *Waiting for God*. Emma Craufurd, trans. New York: Harper, 1951b.

**TNFR**   *The Need for Roots*. Arthur F. Wills, trans. Boston: Beacon Press, 1952b.

**TPF**   *The Iliad or The Poem of Force*. Mary McCarthy, trans. Wallingford, Pa: Pendle Hill, 1956a.

**P**   Pétrement, Simone. *Simone Weil: A Life*. Raymond Rosenthal, trans. New York: Pantheon, 1976.

**W**   For a list of Weil's works, see the bibliography at the end of this volume.

To make an inventory or criticism of our civilization—what does that mean? To try to expose in precise terms the trap which has made man the slave of his own inventions . . . the spirit and the world in the very civilization of which we form a part. But it is a task which is beyond our power on account of the shortness of life and the impossibility of collaboration and succession. That is no reason for not undertaking it. The situation of all of us is comparable to that of Socrates when he was awaiting death in his prison and began to learn to play the lyre. . . . At any rate we shall have lived.

Simone Weil

# Acknowledgements

THIS BOOK has been long in the writing, and many hands have helped to guide its way. I wish, first, to thank Hanna Fenichel Pitkin and Norman Jacobson at the University of California, Berkeley. Both of them gave me invaluable advice and wise counsel in the thesis stage, and helped me to define and refine my purpose. Ann Smock provided helpful criticism, and Michael Rogin's response to the first chapters encouraged me to press on. Many friends in Berkeley also provided insightful commentary and support; I am especially grateful to Robert Arseneau, Michael MacDonald, and Jennifer Ring. In 1979, I met Andreas Teuber and Larry Blum; their respective writings on Simone Weil set standards of scholarship and sensitivity that I can scarcely hope to approximate. I owe a special debt of thanks to Larry Blum, whose close and perceptive reading of the revised manuscript saved me from numerous errors.

Other friends and colleagues have been most helpful in the later stages of this book as well. My thanks to Joan Tronto and Annmarie Levins, who provided intellectual and spiritual reinforcement, friendship, and good humor over the years. Thanks also to Harry Boyte, who offered both his friendship and a forum for some of my thoughts-in-progress. Terence Ball has been an inimitable friend and supportive colleague whose gentle prodding to finish the book I (now) appreciate in full. The deepest debt of all I owe to James Farr, whose love and friendship continue to be a source of inspiration and lend joy to my work.

Financial support for the research and writing of this book came through the assistance of a faculty grant and a McMillan Travel Grant from the University of Minnesota. My research was also substantially aided by Professor André Weil, who granted kind permission to use the Simone Weil archives at the Historical Studies Library at Princeton University. Finally, I should like to thank Arthur Hamparian for his editorial support, and Jerri McDermott and Mary Simmons for their valuable assistance in the production of this manuscript. My thanks also to Mary Ellen Otis, at the University of Minnesota, for her patient and efficient labors on the word-processor; they greatly facilitated the completion of this book.

Mary G. Dietz
*Minneapolis, Minnesota*

# Introduction

W ITHIN THE CONFINES OF ACADEMIA, unstudied thinkers seem to fall into at least two categories. On the one hand, there are those authors whose writings, regretably, fail to issue any great masterpiece, memorable achievement, or even an intriguing possibility. In such cases, academic dismissal (although always properly open to reconsideration) is understandable. What is less comprehensible, on the other hand, are those writers who remain widely unexamined, perhaps even ignored by their academic counterparts, despite thought-provoking, masterful, even extraordinary work.

Scholarly neglect of the writings of Simone Weil (1909–1943), the French theorist, political activist, and mystic, would appear to belong to the latter, less comprehensible category. Although Weil's writings have been admired and cited by a generation of thinkers and writers as diverse as Albert Camus, Martin Buber, T.S. Eliot, Dwight MacDonald, Hannah Arendt, and Czeslaw Milosz, they have been largely ignored by the academic community. Her life has been chronicled in numerous biographies and biographical essays, but her thought has not been subjected to the same detailed exploration that distinguishes many of her contemporaries—Sartre, for example, or Aron, Camus, de Beauvoir, and Orwell (to whom Weil has often been compared).[1] The lack of attention to Weil is made all the more puzzling if one considers Sir Richard Rees's observation that, by 1939, "Simone Weil had developed a social and political awareness which it took the war and the German occupation to awaken in many French intellectuals and beyond which many of them, including Sartre, have never progressed" (Weil 1962b: 8). Rees's judgment is not an isolated one. Weil's contribution to political and social thought has been widely noted, and she has even been called "one of the most brilliant and original minds of twentieth-century France." Yet her political thought has not been examined in any systematic way, and therefore stands only partly appreciated.

One reason for this neglect is that Weil has not generally been considered, first and foremost, a political thinker but rather a mystic whose demanding and austere personal theology set her apart from almost all other thinkers of her time. Accordingly, most of her commentators, both admirers and detractors alike, have focussed upon her uncompromisingly ascetic doctrine and her spiritual otherworldliness. Depending upon how her mystical writings are assessed, Weil has been characterized as either "akin to the saints" or as "supremely deluded." Exaggerated claims have not been lacking on either side. Thus, Eliot deems her "a woman of genius" (1952:vi); Angelica Krogmann reveres her "sublime spirit" (1973:v); Camus offers her as "the only great spirit of our time" (1969:1699). But Leslie Fiedler has found her a "tragic buffoon" (1951:38); Joyce Carol Oates sees her as a "sick, desperate, broken woman" (1977:39); Buber comments upon her "far-reaching negation of life" (1952:33). All of these diagnoses are based upon the image of a mystical ascetic who rejects the human in pursuit of the divine. The debate then centers around the meaning of Weil's withdrawal and the contribution of her spirituality. What both sides ignore, however, is the degree to which Weil's withdrawal from the world is simply the other side of her deep involvement in it, ambivalent although it was. She once wrote, "we have to struggle against the world as a swimmer does against the water . . . but we have to love it as the swimmer loves the water that bears him up" (W1978:180). The task she set herself, of simultaneously struggling against and loving the world, was not resolved as easily as those who find her a "saint" or a "tragic buffoon" would imply. Neither her life nor her thought reflect an utter abandonment of worldly things; within both a perpetual struggle takes place between attachment and withdrawal, worldliness and worldlessness, the human and the divine. Thus, to understand Weil fully we need to attend not only to those writings that have already made her famous—her theological and mystical tracts—but also to those political writings that capture the "other side" of her intellectual and practical life. To do so is not only to become aware of how Weil's political ideas are bound up with her spiritual impulses, but also to recognize how much she has to contribute, as critic and theorist, to the political discourse of our time.

Weil's "social and political awareness" is the subject of this book. My intention, in focusing upon her involvement in the world as well as her withdrawal from it, is to offer both an interpretive framework for understanding her political ideas, and an assessment of the strengths and weaknesses of the ideas themselves. By way of introduction, I want to suggest what both of these aims entail and the form they will take in what follows.

Coming to terms with Weil's ideas is not an easy task. As a whole, her writings are extremely varied, unsystematic, and diffuse, certainly impossible to summarize as a "theory." They are open to no ready categorization. As G.L. Arnold (among others) has noted: "to class Simone Weil is not a simple matter . . . she may serve as a catalyst of opinions cutting across traditional lines of thought. In the end she is likely to become . . . one of those lonely figures belonging to no party, yet claimed by all" (Arnold 1951:336–37). Her resistance to categorization is one of the things that makes Weil such a fascinating thinker to study, but it also places demands upon the interpreter who wants to organize and situate her work without compromising its originality and eclecticism. With this in mind, I want to offer an interpretive framework that attempts both to accept the unreconcilable strains within Weil's ideas and to address them in a unified way.

The framework I establish in Part I takes its inspiration from an observation made by Simone Pétrement, Weil's friend and biographer. "To write of [Weil's] life," Pétrement observes, "means to deal with her work, for the bond between her life and her thought was inconceivably close" (Pétrement 1976:viii). Just as Pétrement incorporates Weil's thought into her account of Weil's life, so I propose to integrate Weil's life or, more specifically, certain events in her life, with specific themes in her work. The events I focus upon are not, of course, raw, "external" data that leap out and demand the observer's attention. Rather, they emerge from a particular interpretation that informs their selection. Keeping Pétrement's comment in mind, I propose to offer some psychoanalytic insights, with specific attention to identity theory, as the basis for the organization of my analytical commentary on Weil's political writings.[2] The interpretive framework takes its impetus from the methodological presumption that deep interrelationships exist between early conflicts in a thinker's life and later themes and ideas in his or her work. Thus, Part I of this study establishes the early conflicts; Parts II to IV are analytical investigations of substantive ideas the psychoanalytic argument helps us uncover. Before proceeding farther, however, I want to lodge a brief disclaimer and a clarification, directed particularly toward those readers who may doubt the legitimacy and the usefulness of psychoanalysis in the history of ideas.

My appropriation of psychoanalysis to study Simone Weil should be taken neither as a blanket endorsement of its validity for any and all such studies, nor as an interpretation in and of itself. Clearly, some individuals in the history of ideas are more suitable subjects for this sort of enterprise than others: those for whom we have little biographical information—Aristotle, for example,—would seem questionable candidates, while those who have written self-reflective memoirs or autobiographies—like John Stuart Mill—would seem *prima facie* to be more promising ones. Even more importantly, although all thinkers, at least as individuals in the modern age, go through some form of identity crisis in the movement from child to adolescent to adult, some surely have crises that are far more dramatic and fraught with difficulties than others'.[3] We need only think of Augustine as compared to Thomas Aquinas, for instance, or Rousseau as compared to Locke, or Nietzsche in contrast to Marx. This is not to say that Thomas, Locke, or Marx are inappropriate subjects for psychohistorical examination, but simply to suggest that Augustine, Rousseau, and Nietzsche may be more telling ones because they themselves acknowledge (in very different ways) the impact of their personal "selves" upon their public and political thought.

Simone Weil, too, is an especially appropriate candidate for a psychoanalytic study, and for at least three reasons having to do with the above. First, extensive information is available (both from Weil herself and from others) concerning her passage from "child to adult." Second, that passage, and her adulthood itself, was by all accounts difficult, complex, and rife with inner conflicts. The sheer number of biographical books and essays attests to this, although few have pursued the psychological dimension I will explore here. Finally, Weil's early identity crisis brought with it a unique and especially intriguing confluence of dilemmas concerning gender, sexuality, personality, family, ethnicity, religion, and nationality that makes it, even as identity crises go, unusually compelling and complex. She was a clear example of what Erik Erikson has termed "a contradictory bundle of identity fragments": a woman who did her best to obliterate what was feminine about her, yet who found masculinity a suspect category, a Jew who rejected the Hebrew tradition and professed Christianity while refusing to join the church, a defender of the working class who found all political collectivites suspect, a mystic who renounced this world, yet died literally identifying with France, while denouncing French nationalism. These identity fragments contain both personal and collective elements; that is, Weil's confusion rested not only on an inner sense of who she was, but also on an outer sense of where she belonged. As J.M. Cameron has written, "everything connected with Simone Weil, her life of study and teaching and political agitation, her beliefs in religion, philosophy, and politics, her mysticism, and the claim made, not unreasonably . . . for her sanctity, is enormously complicated and often hard to put together in a consistent way" (White 1981:35).

Accordingly, by carefully reconstructing the elements of her identity crisis, we might discover clues that will help us arrange, or at least sort out, some of the prevailing and inconsistent "impulses" and themes in Weil's thought. Or, to put this otherwise, if we can succeed in uncovering the major psychological conflicts that mark Weil's early life, we might gain a deeper understanding of the theoretical tensions that emerge in her later work.[4] With this in mind, what I will suggest in Part I is that two different but related "tensions" dominate Weil's life and appear thematically in her writings. The first is the "worldly" tension between individual autonomy and collective belonging. The second is a tension that subsumes the first, and pits "worldliness" against "worldlessness," or involvement in the world against withdrawal from it. When we turn to Parts II through IV, we will find that individual autonomy, worldly belonging, and withdrawal from the world are three discernible themes in Weil's political writings, and that the psychological insights gleaned in Part I allow us to understand her writings in a richer and more complex way than hitherto imagined.

What I wish to make clear, however, is that the psychoanalytical element of this study is not intended *as* interpretation. Although psychoanalysis can help expand our insights into a theorist's constructions, it is not, in the end, a substitute for comprehending the nature and meaning of the ideas themselves, or for assessing their contribution to our understanding of political life. Thus, my aim in this study is not to reduce Weil's "apparently" political ideas to their "true" psychological meaning, but rather to draw upon Weil's unique identity crisis to help illuminate the concepts, themes, ideas, and ambiguities in her thought. The interrelationship I want to posit between her personal crisis and her social and political ideas is meant to serve as a prolegomenon to, and not as a substitute for, the study of the ideas themselves.

In turning to Weil's ideas in Parts II through IV, we will focus on three works that stand out as central to her political thought. They are, in essence, "hubs" from which a diffuse array of ideas radiate. Part II centers on the early (1934) essay, "Reflections Concerning the Causes of Liberty and Social Oppression," which Weil once called her "magnum opus." Part III takes its starting point from *The Iliad, or The Poem of Force*, written in 1940, and perhaps Weil's most famous work. Finally, in Part IV we will examine her only systematic book-length work, finished shortly before her death, *L'Enracinement*, translated as *The Need for Roots*. Weil called it her "other magnum opus." Not only do these writings give us starting-points from which to engage her wide-ranging ideas; they also give dramatic expression to the tensions that dominate Weil's life. Most importantly, however, all of these writings are important contributions to the dialogue of Western political thought, and deserve to be better known and more widely discussed.

Thus, my overall aim in Parts II through IV is to examine and clarify the arguments in some of Weil's central writings and to assess their merits, in order to understand Weil as a political thinker of our time. As the reader will soon notice, in the course of undertaking this assessment of Weil's work, I will refer often to Hannah Arendt, whose political thought has influenced much of my own thinking, and whose ideas on work, politics, action, and the "public realm" serve in certain places as conceptual "signposts" for this study.[5] To set Weil against Arendt in theoretical agonal contest, or to recover Weil's political thought only to sacrifice it to Arendt's, is not my aim. Rather, I will invoke some of Arendt's concepts and categories in order to emphasize and illuminate the strengths and weaknesses of Weil's. Wherever it occurs, the "imaginary dialogue" between these two very important women will be put, first and foremost, to the task of retrieving and revitalizing the political significance of Weil's work, in the hope that we might finally move beyond the debate that pits the glories of the "saint" against the absurdities of the "tragic buffoon."

## Notes

1. For biographical studies see, among others, Cabaud (1957), Pétrement (1976) and McFarland (1983). Book-length works that address Weil's thought in a general expository manner include Tomlin (1954), Rees (1956), Hellman (1982), and Dunaway (1984).

2. Because I focus upon identity, and the crisis of identity that surrounds the passage from childhood to adulthood, my approach to Weil's life is most indebted to the writings of Erik Erikson (1958, 1968, 1978). See also Dinnerstein (1977).

3. Although I am somewhat sympathetic to (a watered-down) claim that identity crises are incredibly varied, historically and culturally, but (in some sense) "universal"—something Erikson often appears to presume—I think I can legitimately evade agument on that score here. Because we are investigating a thinker in the post-Freudian age, we do not have to face the historical problem of whether such a phenomenon as an "identity crisis," or even "childhood" itself can be said to have had meaning for previous ages or cultures. For a psychohistorian's defense of the universality argument, see Kohut (1986). For an alternative view, see Bainton (1971) and Spitz (1973). For a historical study of the changing concept of "childhood," see Ariès (1962).

4. This logic works the other way as well. By focusing on Weil's adult political and theoretical writings, which in many instances give direct expression to her personal conflicts, we can learn more about the latter—about, that is, the "theoretical essence" of her personality.

5. I am especially indebted to Arendt's argument in *The Human Condition* (1958), but also to *On Revolution* (1963), and to many of her essays in *Between Past and Future* (1968).

# Part I

## *The Crisis of Identity*

# 1

# The Dilemma of Worldliness

SIMONE ADOLPHINE WEIL was born February 3, 1909 in Paris, the second child and only daughter of Bernard and Salomea Reinherz Weil. Her father, a physician, was born in Alsace in 1872, into a family of highly pious Jewish merchants. Her mother was born in Rostov-on-Don in 1879, into a family of cultured, musically gifted, liberal Jews who did not observe any of the religious practices. According to Simone Pétrement, the Weils had "the happiest and most united of marriages" and the family itself was united by "a delicate, attentive tenderness," marked especially by Mme. Weil's "passionate love of her dear ones," André (né 1906) and Simone.[1] The appreciative words are not merely those of a loyal biographer. Pétrement was a personal friend of Simone's, and she remained in close contact with Mme. Weil after Simone's death in 1943. Nevertheless, we know that a child's early "identifications" depend upon that hierarchy of roles that surround her in some form of family. And we also know that Simone Weil's identity appears to have been unusually filled with conflict. Hence, Pétrement's appreciation notwithstanding, we need to look more intently at the context within which Simone's early development took place, to see if we might discern some clues to the formation of her identity.[2]

## "I": The Problem of Personal Identity

About Simone's father, Bernard, we know little. As a young man, he deviated from family tradition in both in his profession and in his professed agnosticism, which came close to atheism. He seems to have been something of a traditional, bourgeois, French father—an aloof and removed authority figure. Yet the extent of his authority is itself questionable, considering that he was entirely absorbed by his profession as, first, a family physician and then as an army medic during World War I. These duties kept him absent from his wife and children much of the time. Pétrement describes the doctor as kind and modest, but also anxious, and sometimes taciturn, even tormented (P5). Sensitive to

3

hurts, he allowed minor problems to plague him, and it appears that he was completely devastated when "circumstances made it impossible for him to practice medicine" in France and the family finally left the country for the United States in 1942.[3] What seems certain is that there was a distance—although an affectionate one—between the doctor and his children. André and Simone were reared primarily by their loving, possessive, and indomitable mother.

Salomea Reinherz was raised in a sophisticated, bourgeois household and from all indications never lacked any of the comforts of nineteenth-century life in Belgium, where her family moved when she was twelve. However, hers was an age in which determined and ambitious young women were severely limited by social practices. Salomea (Selma) wanted to study medicine but her father would not permit it—so instead she studied voice and piano. It was not until 1905, when she married Dr. Bernard Weil, that she finally found an outlet for her ambitions, through a kind of vicarious participation in her husband's work (against strict military orders, she followed him everywhere during World War I), and later through her children. As a wife and mother, Mme. Weil was a vigorous, aggressive woman, completely devoted to her children, whom she believed were exceptional. She seemed the perfect example of what Nietzsche once called "smother love." As Pétrement notes, "Her affection and her ability to organize were so overpowering that one was tempted to submit to her" (P6). And her son later acknowledged that his mother was "in some ways a possessive character" (W1974:149). Quite obviously, Mme. Weil had a "passion for life," and life's pivot was her family. Nothing was neglected in furthering her children's education, a matter upon which Mme. Weil placed the highest importance. This was particularly so with regard to André, who received the best tutors and was sent to the finest and most rigorous lycées.

Mme. Weil's most striking characteristic, however, was her extreme protectiveness of Simone. Her daughter's early infancy was marred by serious illness and a disastrous weaning (after which Simone refused for many months to eat anything not in a bottle). Although she was born a perfectly healthy baby, and developed well until she was six months old, Simone's health deteriorated rapidly after her mother contracted appendicitis and was confined to bed but still continued to nurse her daughter (P7). In psychoanalytic terms, Simone did not suffer an early "separation anxiety" in a direct physical sense, but was confronted with something much more complicated: a continuing love and nurturance that, literally, threatened her life. From her eleventh to her twenty-second month, the infant was not expected to survive. Thus, the initial mutuality between mother and child that "provides a safe pole of self-feeling from which the child can reach out" was severely jeopardized in Simone's case (Erikson 1968:159). At the least, we might expect that her early loss of her mother as a "comfort" contributed to her later sense of personal isolation and aloneness.[4] This jeopardized "mutuality" might also, partly, explain Simone's lifelong and deep affection for the mother who protected and nursed her, and also her persistent need to escape the mother who threatened her autonomy and independence.[5] Whatever else it did, the disastrous nursing helped set the stage for the child to make some connection between her personal sense of unworthiness and her mother's power over her. Simone herself seems to have revealed as much, for as Pétrement notes: "Years later she used to joke about this precocious decline . . . with a smile, she would complain that she had been poisoned in infancy. 'That's why,' she would say, 'I am such a failure' " (P7).

In general, her childhood growth and development were slow, particularly in comparison to those of André, who was far more active and robust. Throughout her life Simone was encumbered by weak and awkward hands; her clumsiness, which was often attributed to her absent-mindedness, was rather a physiological problem that severely inhibited her. Very few recognized this, however. Even her mother tended to attribute Simone's slowness to mental and not physical causes. She frequently wrote of André's prowess and self-assuredness and Simone's timidity and backwardness (P16). Mme. Weil viewed her daughter in this way, it seems, throughout her life, and never abandoned her role as Simone's protectress and nurse.[6] For whatever reasons (but quite possibly including guilt over the disastrous nursing of her daughter), the mother sought, unconsciously enough, to keep Simone in a prolonged state of infantilism.[7] Her concern was for Simone to have those things which all babies need—food, warmth, and comfort. Even as an adult, Simone was followed almost everywhere, occasionally surreptitiously, by her mother. Mme. Weil would check on her lodgings, her diet, and her wardrobe. This was not an entirely obsessive or irrational behavior since, from an early age, Simone was a committed ascetic, and later was adamant about spurning any form of the comfortable bourgeois existence that marked her childhood.[8] She regularly gave away her salary, roomed in unheated flats, subsisted on rice and potatoes, and dressed in makeshift attire. When she spent nearly a year engaged in back-breaking factory work, often sick and exhausted, she had only her mother to thank for tending to needs that she otherwise would have ignored.

The complexities of this mother-daughter relationship cannot be fully understood in isolation, however. There was another central figure in this interaction, one who contributed deeply to the nature of that relationship itself. This was André. Simone once wrote, "A brother is like a tooth; it is a good thing provided one is not forced to become aware too often that it exists." That remark should serve notice on the complicated mix of feelings she had for her elder brother.

If there is a central theme in Simone Weil's early life, it is probably her simultaneous admiration for and (repressed) resentment of André, who served as her model, her master, and her teacher in their childhood. As a very young child, Simone totally surrendered her identity to her brother; she followed him everywhere and imitated all that he did.[9] When he decided he would brave the cold and no longer wear socks, she did the same; his life was dominated by books and so was hers. According to a governess, Simone never played with a doll, nor, it seems, with other children. André was her world. He taught her to read and brought her into his universe of literary allusions and intellectual games (P14). Although he was only three years older than she, in later years Weil often spoke of her brother as if he were a third parent: "I was brought up by my parents and my brother in a complete agnosticism," she says in her "Spiritual Autobiography" (W1951b:94). In a sense, he *was* a third parent to her. In the place of an absent father, it was André who became the symbol of masculinity and authority in Simone's life.

The total identification with and subordination of one sibling to another is a psychological time bomb. For awhile, one child might flourish under another's tutelage but the ultimate realization that only one fully possesses the identity can be devastating. Simone differed from André in two important ways: she lacked his masculinity, and his genius in mathematics. On both counts—as female and as intellectual—she believed herself the inferior. And on both counts—as male and as "genius"—André found himself at the advantage. Intellectual success offered the key to being treated as an adult, and the promise of full belonging in the Weil family. André was accorded this status and, whether legitimately or not, Simone felt relegated to the lonely outpost of second-best, female, child. In truth, however, Simone did not arrive at this outpost solely on her own. In considering the development of her personal identity, we must not only account for André, but also for Mme. Weil's attitude toward both masculinity and genius that had so much influence on the daughter.

For the mother, masculinity denoted more than gender. It was indicative of worldly achievement, success, and "advancement" in both personal and social terms. (We might recall Selma Weil's own early ambitions, which were thwarted because she was female). In a letter to a friend, Mme. Weil once wrote:

> I shall always prefer the good little boys, boisterous and sincere as I see them coming out of the Lycée Montaigne. And I do my best to encourage in Simone not the simpering graces of a little girl but the forthrightness of a boy, even if this must at times seem rude (P27).

The playfulness with which the Weils referred to their only daughter as "Simon" and "our *cagne* boy" had predictable effects. While still a young girl, Simone preferred tailored, masculine clothes and for a period of time actually signed letters to her parents "your respectful son" (*P27*). Pétrement also recounts an occasion when Mme. Weil induced Simone to accompany her to the opera and, "Simone agreed to have made for her not an evening gown but a tuxedo—a jacket and suit in black cloth, the jacket being quite similar to that of a man's suit" (*P28*).

Without doubt, the mother encouraged the attitude toward masculinity that her daughter assumed. This attitude was reinforced in a society in which girls were less valuable than boys because they represented greater prestige risks and because their marriage required a large divestment of property, at least among the bourgeoisie (Pitts in Hoffman 1963:296). At work as well was the more time-honored practice of the West in which women are socialized to view the world and humanity's achievements in the world through the eyes of men. Whatever the core of these attitudes, however, they took firm root in the young Simone, who soon came to prefer masculine dress and shunned all things feminine. As Pétrement points out:

> As for the plans she had already formed . . . it was—as she herself later said—a great misfortune to have been born a female. So she had decided to reduce this obstacle as much as possible by disregarding it . . . by giving up any desire to think of herself as a woman or to be regarded as such by others, at least for a set period of time. It was perhaps this that made many people consider her in some way inhuman. . . . But Simone wanted to express [her femininity] as little as possible (*P27*).

Her "disregard" for her womanliness took on different form as she developed, as least in the matter of dress. Sometime during her adolescence, Simone moved from masculine dress to clothes more akin to those of a monk, as Pétrement describes them. In particular she favored a large cape, baggy pants and shirt.

If the tension between the female she looked like and the male she thought it better to be was ultimately resolved by an androgynous, monk-like appearance, then the problem of Weil's sexuality was ultimately resolved by an ascetic turning away from sexuality altogether. As we shall see in more detail in Chapter 2, it was Christianity that provided her with not only with a style of dress, but, more crucially, with a rationale for asexuality. As she suggests in her "Spiritual Autobiography": "The idea of purity, with all that this word can imply for a Christian, took possession of me at the age of 16, after a period of several months during which I had been going through the emotional unrest natural in adolescence" (*W1951b:65*). Hence, it seems that at a crucial moment in her transition from adolescent to adult, Simone resourcefully avoided the choice of "masculine or feminine" by choosing a "Christian purity" that avoided both (and finessed her mother as well).

The adoption of androgynous dress and sexual "purity" may have eased the masculinity dilemma that André represented and Mme. Weil reinforced, but the "genius" André embodied and the "adult" status conferred upon him and denied to Simone were more difficult problems for her to surmount. Here we arrive at what is perhaps the pivotal point of her childhood crisis of "identifications"—the question of her worth in terms of intellect and her belonging in the family. Naturally enough, she contrasted her own abilities to André's and always came up short. And again, Mme. Weil contributed to the situation. She once wrote to her husband after worrying about Simone's halting advancement in her studies: "How different André is! For him interrogations or compositions are a real joy and without the slightest vanity [sic] for he's sure of himself when he has learned something" (P16). Simone, her mother reported, wrote too slowly, had trouble catching up, and was "always inclined to doubt and mistrust herself" (P16).[10]

André's intellectual ability was apparently the topic of conversation and praise outside the family as well. One commentator makes much of an incident in which Simone overheard a family friend say to Mme. Weil, "One is genius, the other beauty" (W1951b:15).[11] In a family where the intellect was paramount, such a remark could have only a deleterious effect on the beauty, and no doubt reinforced her distaste for her femaleness. It was not by chance that throughout her life Simone went out of her way to appear as unattractive as possible, believing perhaps that some antithesis existed between physical attractiveness and mental ability and, at the same time, reinforcing her conviction of her own "disgustingness" and inferiority.

In general, and without doubting that Mme. Weil had only the best of intentions toward her daughter, we might suspect that a great deal of Simone's inferiority was brought about by a mother who held her son in something close to awe, and transmitted that feeling to the "baby" she wanted to care for and protect. Perpetually hovering over Simone, Mme. Weil persistently reinforced her daughter's nonadult status, just as her far less protective and nuturing treatment of André was a reminder of his intellectual independence and autonomy. Although both children were surely loved, they were also treated in profoundly different ways, with life-long effects for the one who found herself the "child" to her brother's "adult."[12]

Little wonder, then, that Simone conceived of herself as the outsider in a family of full-fledged "parents," (i.e., "superiors") and viewed herself as the "child" (i.e., "inferior") under their tutelage. As we shall see, when she was fourteen she fell into a "bottomless despair" and thought seriously of dying because she thought she was completely unworthy of notice—"the color of dead leaves," she once said (W1951b:101). When she later wrote of the oppression of the workers, and then of the nature of affliction, she betrayed a sense of complete identification with her subjects and, in essence, gave theoretial expression to her personal identity. So, for example, of the workers she wrote:

> It seems to those who obey that some mysterious inferiority has predestined them to obey from all eternity and every mark of scorn—even the tiniest—which they suffer at the hands of their superiors or their equals, every order they receive, and especially every act of submission they themselves perform confirms them in this feeling (W1973:145).

And, later, of "affliction" she says: "Affliction hardens and discourages because, like a red-hot iron, it stamps the soul to its very depths with the contempt, the disgust, and even the self-hatred and sense of guilt and defilement which crime logically should produce but actually does not" (W1968:173).[13]

As pervasive as Simone's sense of inferiority was, it would be mistaken to conclude that this was the only identification that emerged from her early family life or that she reacted in a simple, predictable way, by ultimately rejecting the family to which she felt she did not fully belong. She was a naturally gifted and also an immensely resourceful child. Consequently, her identity formation was a mélange of the most extreme tensions, and these tensions might be understood as attempts to reconcile—or at least hold in equilibrium—the various inner conflicts she faced. (She was distinguished, for example, by both a sense of inferiority and a fiercely independent intellect). Before we examine these tensions in full, however, we must turn to a reciprocal set of influences upon her, in addition to her family. Only by considering the nature of collective identity—the "We" that absorbs the "I" of the newly emerging individual—can we gain a full understanding of the tensions that marked Simone Weil's life.

## "WE": The Problem of Collective Identity

Although immensely difficult, a situation in which childhood identifications are unsatisfactory or problematic need not prove psychologically fatal. A great deal of strength may be found in some kind of collective, larger community, or what Erikson calls the "absorption" of childhood identifications into a "new configuration" wherein the community recognizes the individual and gives his or her "self" a sense of purpose and meaning.[14] Put more simply, the "We" can provide support for a weak and uncertain "I." From what we know of Simone's later childhood, it seems that she did indeed turn outward, to the larger community, to find some locus of "belonging." As one of her friends observed, "She had a desperate desire for tenderness, communion, friendship, and she didn't always discover the secret of how to obtain what she desired so deeply" (P23). But perhaps this was because what she desired was something her "communal culture" not only could not, but would not provide. To understand how this was so, we need to look more closely at the "group identities" Simone encountered and determine the social demands that influenced her sense of personal identity.[15]

We might begin by way of ethnicity and religion. Although the Weils were both of Jewish origin, they raised André and Simone in agnosticism and never mentioned to them the difference between Jew and gentile.[16] It was not until she was ten that Simone learned of the distinction. This situation was not particularly unusual. In France, the participation and assimilation of Jews in bourgeois and intellectual circles was fairly extensive. As one historian has put it, "In the country of Voltaire, an attitude of doctrinaire 'enlightenment' was the rule rather than the exception" (Hughes 1958:56). But regardless of how politically assimilated they might have felt, the Weils were still social "outsiders." The aim of first generation "enlightened" Jews was to erase their collective ethnic ties and merge into the nation of France. Yet the merging was never complete, as the vitriolic anti-Semitism of post-Dreyfus France signified. Even the much touted political emancipation of the Jews in mid-nineteenth century France did not change the cultural reality that they were a distinctively homogeneous people. Indeed, the very emancipation effort itself testified to the "otherness" of the Jewish community, and in an age marked by the rise of the nation, that community was perceived as alien, dangerous, and threatening. The perception was fated to return and worsen in France with the collaborationist policies of the Vichy regime. Even before that time, however, many French Jews who "escaped" from their original collectivity found themselves in a strange position. Neither fully accepted (i.e., gentile) participants in a predominantly Catholic society, nor any longer members of an inherited spiritual and ethnic community, these people lived in a kind of social and cultural limbo, or what Howard Brotz has called a "demi-monde" (Bendix and Lipset 1974). Bernard and Selma Weil were in exactly this position, and the tenuous nature of their collective identity becomes even more apparent if one remembers that neither of them was a French national by birth. Nationally, culturally, and spiritually, they were uprooted souls. Not surprisingly, their strongest bonds were familial—to each other and to their children—and their existence, although comfortably bourgeois, was an insulated one.

The children of these first generation assimilated Jews found themselves in an even more difficult situation. First, they were born and raised in a cultural atmosphere that was becoming increasingly hostile to Jews. Anti-Semitism spread in France before World War I, fueled by publicists for such organizations as the *Action Française*. With regard to professional anti-Semites, the historian Eugen Weber notes: "They provided the theoretical arguments that made base prejudice socially acceptable and even, in a sense, defensible" (Weber 1962:200). Second, in the face of this rising tide of prejudice, children of assimilated families had no immediate place to turn for protection, psychological or otherwise. The parents who had hoped for a new, more fully integrated and nonalien identity for themselves and particularly for their children, left the children with no collective identity at all. The only alternative for the second generation was to "adopt" a collectivity and make it their own. And often, the more extreme the identification the better. Perhaps this partially accounts for the phenomenon of French Jews in the early twentieth century converting to Catholicism, demanding dangerous service at the front during the war, and even joining such organizations as *Action Française*.

These circumstances might also shed some light on why a young Jewish girl raised in a secular household would claim Christianity as her heritage. Consider Simone Weil's rather mysterious assertion in her "Spiritual Autobiography," "I always adopted the Christian attitude as the only possible one. I might say I was born, I grew up, and I always remained within the Christian inspiration" (W1973:62). Here Alain, Simone's extraordinarily influential teacher at the Lycée Henri IV, cannot be underestimated. Simone first encountered him in 1925, and he without doubt had much to do with her "discovery" of Christianity. As Pétrement notes, Alain was not religious in the usual way. In his lectures he spoke little of religion in any explicit sense, but "he manifestly believed in the soul as distinct from the body," and he sometimes evoked, "with visible admiration, the images that Christianity had rendered popular: the Crucified One, the Virgin and Child, and the saints" (P34). He found them an inexaustible source of truth, and Simone came to do the same. With her turn to the Christian inspiration, it seems that she might have found the locus of belonging that her (conflicted) Jewish heritage denied. But the substitute was not wholly fulfilling.

In order to understand why Christianity was not fully adequate as a source of identity formation, we might note the educational culture in which Simone was reared. The environment she knew well was the austere intellectualism of the French lycée (of which Alain's classroom was exemplary) and a corresponding home life in which playthings were books, not toys, and where scholarly achievement and reason were highly praised. If there was any prevailing religion in the Weil family or in the French secondary schools, it was faith in reason and in intellect.

And, in fact, the "Christian inspiration" to which Simone paid homage had more in common with Cartesian rationalism than with religious dogma. She seems to have equated Christianity, at least in her early years, with a kind of "openmindedness," not with any sort of theology. The problem of God, for example, was a problem of "data" or "postulation" as Alain had it, so she chose neither to affirm nor to deny anything. And Christianity was a matter of adopting the "best attitude with regard to the problem of this world," more a matter of philosophical method than of theological doctrine. The Cartesian strain in Simone kept her from submitting to any dogma; the idea of such a submission was completely alien to her, and incidentally, to her notion of Christianity. As she later wrote:

> to add dogma to this Christian conception of life, without being forced to do so by indisputable evidence, would have seemed to me like a lack of honesty. . . . I have an extremely severe standard for intellectual honesty, so severe that I never met anyone who did not seem to fall short of it . . . (W1951b:66).

In her early years, then, rationalism was apparently the better part of her Christianity, and her "Christian inspiration" seems to have come more from Alain's lectures (and from his favorite thinker, Descartes) than from the Gospels.

In the end, instead of being a means of buttressing her membership in a close and organic community of believers, Weil's Christianity was to become the foundation of a self-directed and lonely calling. Her Christian inspiration was hardly the stuff of collective identity; indeed (as we shall see) it was in opposition to it. Even though her conversion experiences in 1938 rid her "religious vocation" of much of its austere rationalism, the elements of Christianity to which she felt most drawn remained decidedly noncollective: "the instant of death itself," the call to a vocation, the spirit of poverty, purity, and the "acceptance in all that concerns the will of God" (W1951b:65). This emphasis on asceticism, duty, obedience, selflessness and death as opposed to brotherhood, community, fellowship, and the redemption of humankind points to a highly individualistic conception of Christian life. Ultimately, she used it to reinforce her sense of exile, not to ameliorate it. Indeed, her concept of Christianity seems to have been a way of rationalizing her "escape" from Judaism, while still "punishing" herself by disallowing any solidifying coherence with a social group. Her lifelong refusal to become a member of the Catholic Church, among other things, attests to this.[17]

If Simone Weil sought Christianity as a substitute for Judaism, then belonging to France became a substitute for belonging to family. At the age of eight, she took up patriotism with a passion and projected all her needs for acceptance and membership, normally accorded to one's family and friends at this age, onto her country. According to Pétrement, this ardent patriotism began at the same time that André was discovering his genius for mathematics. One assumes that he must have been receiving great attention and praise from both his awestruck parents and relatives. Perhaps at this time the little girl sensed that her brother's genius made him more accepted, more a part of the family than she was. Hence her resourceful turn to a larger family, the nation, where she too could enjoy the security and warmth of belonging. One of Mme. Weil's letters from this time refers to "Simonette's" preoccupation with patriotic poems and her attachment to an "adopted" soldier to whom she would send candy and letters.[18] But, in the end, Simone's patriotism was to prove another inadequate means of achieving a positive sense of belonging. The soldier she had "adopted" and later met was killed in action (*P*16). And her own perceptions of World War I, what she heard from her father and saw in the medical encampments where he worked, destroyed early dreams of a glorious and just nation. Almost twenty years later, she recalled in a letter to Georges Bernanos:

> I was 10 years old at the time of Versailles and up to then I had been patriotically thrilled as children are in wartime. But the will to humiliate the defeated enemy which revealed itself so loathsomely everywhere at that time (and in the following years) was enough to cure me once for all [sic] of that naïve sort of patriotism (*W*1965:109).

For the young Simone, the word "France" came to be associated with the carnage, brutality, and destruction of war. Perhaps the violent anti-Semitism of French "patriots" of the time had its effects as well, but on a far less conscious level.[19] In short, Simone had put her trust and found security in something that had betrayed her. Her reaction to this betrayal took the form of antimilitaristic and antinationalistic sentiments during her years at the Ecole Normale, but it did not result, as her later work proves, in the wholesale rejection of the idea of belonging to country.

One final aspect of Simone Weil's problematic collective identity must be considered. In late childhood and adolescence membership in a peer group and acceptance by one's age mates is a crucial determinant of any human being's eventual outlook on social life, not to mention his or her sense of self. The embarrassment and threat of the public exposure of one's personality is mitigated by peer groups, which provide, in Erikson's words, a protective "group certainty." At the same time, these initial public engagements with others are tests of firm self-delineation (Erikson 1968:183–84). A youth who enters the world outside the family with a confused sense of identity is apt to isolate himself or herself from personal relations with others, being perpetually unsure of where that identity begins and ends in terms of those relations. The isolation is likely to be reinforced by a peer group that finds the outsider "different" from itself, both a threat to its own group image and a foil against which that image can be reaffirmed.

Simone Weil entered school with just this sort of confused identity, and with respect to her peer groups she was again denied the security of belonging.[20] Simone Pétrement (who was one of her few close friends) reports that Simone's schoolmates at Lycée Henri IV made fun of her and even engaged in "malicious mockery" (P24). They thought she was exceedingly odd, an "intellectual monster," and it seems she was never fully accepted as a schoolmate. Part of this rejection stemmed from Weil's own uniqueness. "She was truly different," Pétrement says, "in the sense that she was already well above the common level, owing to the purity of her emotions and the strength of her character even more than to her intelligence" (P24–30). This rejection was further fostered by Simone herself who was, as another acquaintance complained, "completely aloof and unsociable" (P24). An aloof and unsociable nature is an understandable attribute in a child who found all collectivities, family and neighborhood, school and country, threatening. She had learned to rely upon herself alone for "purity and strength of character." But as we should now recognize, that individual "self" was also beset with difficulties.

In short, what Erikson calls "the identity of both identities,"—both the core of the individual and the core of her communal culture—were deeply compromised in Simone Weil (Erikson 1968:22). And this conflict gave rise to what we might call "the dilemma of worldliness" she faced throughout her life: the tension between individual autonomy and collective belonging, between "I" and "We." We might conceive of her dilemma in this way: As we have seen, the other side of her personal sense of worthlessness and inferiority was her desire to find strength and support in some sort of collectivity. But virtually all of the alternatives, including her family, were inadequate and more importantly, rejecting of her. It might be ventured that the seeds of her later revulsion for "collectivities" of any sort were sown in a childhood denied the enveloping warmth and security of belonging to anything. Thus, the other side of the unsatisfactory communal identity was the "self," an "I" that could remain independent of all collectivities and survive. For Simone, that sort of "self" could only be the rational, autonomous, intellect, which from early childhood she had learned to admire and respect. Yet there lay another obstacle: in the end she could not find that intellect within her own (inferior) self. That "exceptional gift" was the province of her brother, and Simone felt her "I" was no match for his. So we are back to the other side of the dilemma—the need to "belong" to some "We" that will shore up the fragile self, and the rejection that comes along with it.

To put all of this quite simply, Simone Weil's childhood confusion rested not only on an inner sense of who she was, but also on an outer sense of where she belonged. And what was most denied her in the world—a strong "I" and an enveloping "We"—she also perceived as most valuable, although always in tension and incapable of being reconciled. In short, if the locus of identity is found in the core of the individual and in the core of communal culture, then it can be said that Simone Weil's identity was deeply problematic on both counts. The dilemma of worldliness consumed her.

## Notes

1. The information on Simone Weil's life is drawn primarily from Pétrement's biography (1976) hereafter cited as (*P*). All references will be to it, unless otherwise noted. Despite numerous errors by the translator. Pétrement's is still the definitive biography in English. Also see Cabaud (1957, 1967), Weil's first biographer, and McFarland (1983) for an especially sensitive treatment. I make no attempt here to present a full-blown biographical account of Weil's life, but rather draw upon only those events and experiences I find instructive in the formulation of the interpretive framework that structures this study of her thought.

2. In this formulation, I am accepting the framework Erikson offers in *Identity, Youth, and Crisis* (1968). He draws a distinction among "introjection," "identification," and "identity formation" in his discussion of the ego's steps to maturity. Introjection involves the satisfactory mutuality of the mother-child relationships; identifications depend upon the satisfactory interaction "with trustworthy representatives of a meaningful hierarchy of roles as provided by the generations living together in some form of family," and identity formation arises from the assimilation and absorption of the former into a new configuration, the larger society (1968:159). As I will suggest (without belaboring the technical details of Erikson's framework), Simone Weil's "ego" was compromised on all three levels.

3. The words are André Weil's, who was interviewed by Malcolm Muggeridge in 1973 (*W*1974:148–59).

4. Dinnerstein (1977:31) notes, "Separation from the touch, smell, taste, sound, sight of [the mother] is the forerunner of all isolation, and it eventually stands as the prototype for our fear of the final isolation." Since all infants must experience such separation eventually, the issue is not whether, but how, we deal with it. But, as Dinnerstein and others have emphasized, a premature separation from the mother poses the most problems for the infant. Exactly what sort of problems attend the kind of experience Simone faced—a "separation" brought on *through* nurturance—is less well discussed, but it seems that a prolonged nuturance accompanied by serious illness would lead to at least a profound distrust of intimacy, if not an outright abhorrence of it, as well as the isolation Dinnerstein discusses.

5. Another event that further complicated her already ambivalent feelings toward her mother occurred in 1912 when Simone went through her own

(traumatic) operation for appendicitis. Her recovery was slow and she had to stay hospitalized for three weeks. Upon arrival at the hospital, her mother had carried her to the operating room, telling her that she would see a Christmas tree. As Pétrement reports, "Simone later reproached her mother in a grave, sad voice for having tricked her" (P8–9). The experience also gave rise to a horror and fear of doctors, as Pétrement notes: "When she saw a stranger enter the room she did not want to stay there, fearful that he might turn out to be a doctor" (P9). Within this one incident we might find both a new ambivalence toward her father (another doctor), and a deepening anxiety about the trustworthiness of the family itself, and her place within it.

6. It appears that Simone thought it important to allow her mother this role as well. As André Weil notes, "except where she considered it an essential duty, my sister tried her best to entertain the illusion in her mother that she, my sister, was my mother's thing in a way, and certainly this caused a certain amount of strain on her, which, joined with many other strains, eventually led to her death" (W1974:149).

7. This infantilism seems to have been reinforced by French culture itself. Jesse Pitts (Hoffman 1963) notes that the sheltered education women received in France promoted an "official" infantilism. In her early childhood at least, Simone Weil seems to have had just such a sheltered education.

8. Perhaps some of Simone's asceticism can also be traced to her mother's early influence. As André Weil reports, "my mother . . . had some views about natural living, and we [i.e., he and Simone] took those views up with a vengeance" (W1964:151). Mme. Weil's views on "natural living" included at least a passing conviction that walking in bare feet or sandals, even in the most bitter weather, was good for the health. Even more significantly, however, Mme. Weil had an extreme fear of microbes. Pétrement reports that Mme. Weil did not want her children to be kissed by strangers, and before all meals their hands had to be rigorously cleaned. If they had to then open a door, they were instructed to use their elbows (P11). In short, this obsession about cleanliness sounds more extreme than a mother's usual concern about germs. And, accordingly, we can find in both the young and the adult Simone something close to a fanatical revulsion for any form of physical contact, including with certain foods. The revulsion extended to herself as well. "She spoke of her 'disgustingness.' " Pétrement writes, "When it was a question of doing certain things, she would say, 'I can't, because of my disgustingness' " (P11). To what extent this childhood feeling of disgust for herself was exacerbated by an already developing sense of weakness and unworthiness born of her infant experience is difficult to say. But both attitudes are predominant features of the adult Simone's negative sense of identity.

9. André himself seems to have taken this as a sign of their close intimacy. When Muggeridge asks him if he and his sister had an intimacy between them, he replies, "Very much so. My sister as a child always followed me, and my grandmother, who liked to drop into German occasionally, used to say that she was a veritable *Kopiermachine*" (W1974:148).

10. In a later letter, written in 1932 when she was staying for a few days with Simone in Le Puy, Mme. Weil wrote to her husband referring to a discovery André had apparently just made in mathematics. She said that she had "cried with joy" upon hearing of it, then added (referring to Simone by a revealing nickname that André had given her and the parents used as well), "By a kind of seesaw action that is no doubt quite natural, I am less enchanted with the trolless at this moment . . . she really is too unreasonable when it comes to the

necessities of everyday life" (P93). No doubt the "seesaw action" that so often accompanied news of André's discoveries was not unfamiliar to the "trolless," who had come to expect that her accomplishments would not meet with the same sort of awe and tearful joy as her brother's.

11. The visitor's perception, at least of André's genius, was not misguided. At fourteen he passed his first university entrance examination, or *bachot*. At sixteen, he presented himself for the competitive examination for the Ecole Normale in the department of sciences and was accepted. In elementary mathematics, Pétrement notes, "he had a point total that is rarely attained" (P21). Today, he is one of the preeminent mathematicians in the world, and affiliated with the Institute for Advanced Study at Princeton University.

12. In the interview with Muggeridge, André Weil says that Simone's reputed inferiority complex "has been to some extent exaggerated by some of her biographers. She mentions that at one moment in her early life she was in complete despair because she thought I was so far ahead of her and therefore . . . much closer to the truth. But I don't suppose that this was a constant mood with her" (W1974:150). Depending upon what a "constant mood" entails, Professor Weil may be correct. But what we might consider is whether and, if so, how, this "complete despair" about her abilities manifests itself in her later, adult thought, if not in her day-to-day, conscious moods.

13. Connections between her theoretical expressions and her personal sense of self can be found throughout Simone Weil's writings. Her account of affliction, for example, a significant part of her mystical thought, has an analogue in a commentary she offers of herself in her "Spiritual Autobiography" (actually a letter written in 1942). There, she speaks of her year in the factory as a "contact with affliction [that] had killed my youth" (W1951b:66). In the factory, she continued, "I received forever the mark of a slave, like the branding of the red-hot iron the Romans put on the foreheads of their most despised slaves. Since then I have always regarded myself as a slave" (W1951b:67). But she also acknowledges that she had had "contact with affliction" before the factory experience, although of a "partial, biological" not a "social" nature. And she admits her "obsession" with the idea (W1951b:66). What I am suggesting here is that this "obsession" took hold very early on in her life, and was born of both the illnesses she experienced from the age of 6 months, and with the way her family treated her, especially in relation to André.

14. More specifically, Erikson argues: "The community supports [identity] development to the extent that it permits the child, at each step, to orient himself toward a complete "life plan" with a hierarchical order of roles as represented by individuals of different ages. Family, neighborhood, and school provide contact and experimental identification with younger and older children and with young and old adults. A child, in the multiplicity of successive and tentative identifications, thus begins at an early age to build up expectations of what it will be like to be older and what it will feel like to have been younger— expectations which become part of an identity as they are, step by step, verified in decisive experiences of psychosocial 'fittedness' " (Erikson 1968:161).

15. Although I have separated the discussion of Weil's personal growth from that of communal change for analytical purposes, it is important to note that in reality, the two are in close reciprocal relationship. As Erikson writes, "the two help to define each other and are truly relative to each other. In fact, the whole interplay between the psychological and the social, the developmental and the historical, for which identity formation is of prototypal significance, could be conceptualized only as a kind of *psychosocial reality*" (Erikson 1968:23).

16. Pétrement reports: "It was about [1919] that she learned of the existence of Jews and gentiles. Her parents had not told her about this. When she was younger and read Balzac, she had thought that the word Jew was the name given to usurers" (P19). And André Weil tells Muggeridge: "I even remember that during the war someone told me I was Jewish and I just didn't know what that meant" (W1974:153). Although we might assume he refers to sometime around 1919, from the context of the interview it is not entirely clear.

17. Nowhere is the subject of Weil's Jewish identity and her conflicted response to it brought up more directly than by the writer herself, in a letter written to the French Minister of Education in 1940. For many reasons, the letter is painful to read and difficult to fathom. Those who would consider Weil a "saint" usually gloss over it or ignore it completely. Those who find her "supremely deluded" make it fuel for this charge, and worse. Weil wrote the letter in response to a racist statute instituted by the Vichy government, denying the rights of Jews to teaching positions. She had been denied such a position in 1940, after applying for one following a two-year leave of absence. Among other things, she questions the statute's "designation" of the word Jew, as it applies to her, and she denies three times—on the matter of religion, race, and heredity—that she is a Jew. She ends by asserting: "mine is the Christian, French, Greek tradition. The Hebraic tradition is alien to me, and no Statute can make it otherwise. If, nevertheless, the law insists that I consider the term, 'Jew,' whose meaning I don't know, as applying to me, I am inclined to submit, as I would to any other law. But I should like to be officially enlightened on this point, since I myself have no criterion by which I may resolve this question" (Panichas 1977:80–81).

In a rather convoluted sentence that attests to the uncomfortable nature of the subject, Pétrement suggests that Simone's intention was merely to "demonstrate the difficulty of defining the word "Jew" and "mock" the statute and the confused ideas on which all anti-Semitic racism rests (P392). MacFarland and Van Ness (1987:17), however, acknowledge the "Jewish antisemitism that was an altogether involuntary reflex of her psychology." Others have found the letter, and the attitude the letter represents, quite voluntary on Weil's part and a sign of her own self-hatred and an overt anti-Semitism.

Some partial truths exist in all of these interpretations, and perhaps we can better understand (though not resolve) them if we acknowledge the psychosocial reality of Simone Weil's early identity. As we have seen, she grew up "a Jew but not a Jew,"—within a culture that identified her Jewishness and therefore rejected her, and within a family that denied their Jewishness yet also rejected her, while rewarding her brother (as Muggeridge puts it) for "something of a Jewish trait," his education and learning. One of the keys here seems to be that because, or in spite of, her ethnicity, Simone was denied "belonging" in two very important collectivities, the family and the nation. Hence she attempted to escape her Jewishness and even came to associate the Jews with "the idolatry of the We." Many of her writings—where she explicitly condemns "the Hebrews" (as well as the ancient Romans) for their "idolatrousness"—confirm how thoroughly she transferred a personal conflict into a theoretical position. Thus, it should not be surprising that when she is (once again) rejected because she is declared a Jew, she responds by challenging the very coherency of that identity itself.

This interpretation notwithstanding, there is still a none too admirable, "self-consumed" tone to her letter that reads less as a mockery of Vichy than a desperate and opportunistic attempt by the writer to regain a teaching post. On this, I think the best we can do is remain attentive to (though not absolve) the writer herself, and recall that her wholly conflicted identity was a pervasive part of her life, and her life itself a struggle, both personally and theoretically, to resolve what it means "to belong." If that dilemma gave issue to writings of an objectionable nature, then we might remember that it also surfaced in writings of great profundity and sensitivity for the oppressed and afflicted who are subject to the manifold evils of the modern world and denied "belonging" in it.

18. André Weil downplays this attachment in his interview. Referring to the *filleuls de guerre* he and Simone both had, he notes, "We were encouraged [by Mme. Weil] in the idea of saving up on our sugar ration and our chocolate . . . in order to be able to send packages to our soldiers. My mother told the story to some of my sister's biographers, who made much more of it than it deserved" (W1974:152). Perhaps "out of context" this is true, but as part of Simone's overall "psychosocial reality" the experience takes on deserved significance.

19. As a youth Simone Weil was sharply aware of anti-Semitism in France. Although she was raised in an agnostic home and was, in conscious behavior at least, "non-Jewish," in a deeper sense her Jewishness remained very real to her. Pétrement writes, "My father one day absent-mindedly called her Mlle. Levy, which made her blush . . . on another occasion . . . some students in the Latin Quarter were shouting the name of the newspaper they were selling and added, "Anti-foreigner and anti-yid." I hadn't heard them clearly and asked her what they had said. She told me and explained, "It's a name they give the Jews," and then blushed. I hope that was the only time I hurt her by such thoughtless behavior," (P43–44). The embarrassment indicates that she was not unaware that she was, after all, Jewish, and perhaps somehow "foreign"—an outsider—as well.

Perhaps it was this conflict between her inescapable ethnicity that made her "unFrench" and her need for belonging to (a Catholic) country, that led to her later extraordinary comment on the *statut des minorites*: "The central idea is valid," she wrote, including the notion that "the Jewish minority . . . has as a bond a certain mentality, corresponding to the absence of Christian heredity." On the other hand, she thought the Jewish minority should not be given official recognition, "for that would crystallize it. . . . The existence of such a minority does not constitute a good in itself; the objective must be to prompt its disappearance." To that end, she encouraged "mixed marriages" and a "Christian education for future Jewish generations . . . the inculcation . . . of an authentic spirituality" (Marrus and Paxton 1981:190). Yet Weil herself, it should be remembered, refused baptism into the Catholic church or any "formal" institutionalization of her "Christianity."

20. School life in France had an unusual character. The school was viewed not as an alternative center of loyalty in competition with the family (as in Germany or America) but as a facility where knowledge was procured, nothing more. Likewise, the French peer group received no official recognition and no legitimacy from school authorities or the students' family. Consequently, peer groups functioned *sub rosa*, but their lack of collective legitimacy resulted in an emphasis on the individual and his or her private interest. As Jesse Pitts notes, "The peer group operates above all as an organ for defending the interests of the individual member—the integrity of his personality in its entirety and particularly those aspects of the self which find no outlet in the roles encompassed by the legitimate group activities" (Hoffman 1963:256). Simone Weil's exclusion from that group left her without any external source of personal reinforcement and without a haven from the hierarchial authority of a family

that denied her own worth. This exclusion worked in two ways; it reinforced her resentment of collectivities and it confirmed their value as well. Hence Weil could later view "belonging" as both dangerous and desirable and envision both an evil "collectivity" and a warm and nourishing "culture-bed" or "country."

# 2

# The Effort of the Mystic

U P TO NOW, we have been considering the "crisis" of Simone Weil's identity in something like the ancient Greek sense of the term, *krisis*, meaning a general condition or ailment that persists over time. But we might also understand her identity in terms of our more ordinary sense of the word "crisis," meaning a "moment" or "turning point" upon which other events or consequences hinge. For Weil, that moment or "turning point" arrived when she reached the age of fourteen.[1]

There is no doubt that Simone Weil's adolescence brought with it a full blown "crisis." The account she later gave of it in her "Spiritual Autobiography" is worth quoting in full:

> At fourteen I fell into one of those fits of bottomless despair that come with adolescence, and I seriously thought of dying because of the mediocrity of my natural faculties. The exceptional gifts of my brother, who had a childhood and youth comparable to those of Pascal, brought my own inferiority home to me. I did not mind having no [sic] visible successes, but what did grieve me was the idea of being excluded from that transcendent kingdom to which only the truly great have access and wherein truth abides. I preferred to die rather than live without that truth (W1951b: 61).

The genius of her brother, it seems, had finally become too much to bear, and the burden of living some fourteen years in the shadow of the "truly great" had led her to consider death. At fourteen, she was at the point of imminent collapse. But then she found a spiritual solution.[2]

The phrase "born-again," although over-used in contemporary vocabulary, nevertheless has a literal connotation that is helpful in understanding the psychic rebirth of an individual like Simone who has experienced some sort of mental collapse or paralysis. Such a collapse can be the individual's way of dealing with a desire to "die," and the recovery, the reentry into the world, can be viewed as an attempt, literally, to begin again and to attain a sense of self that was denied in the first birth. Such is the case with Weil. The breakdown and its aftermath were a crucial part of her life—from them emerged the foundation of her later more fully articulated conversion experiences. Put simply, the breakdown resulted in the attainment of an adequate alternative to her immensely complicated struggle to belong, and it provided a substitute for (her brother's) "genius" as well. Or, in Erikson's arresting phrase, this crisis forced her to "mobilize capacities to see and say, to dream and plan, to design and construct, in new ways" (Erikson 1958:15).

In order to understand what Weil's breakdown wrought, we should notice what was truly at stake in her temptation to die—not just her sense of worthlessness (as intense as that was), but her exclusion from a "transcendent kingdom," to which André, but not she, had access. What she "mobilized," however, in the midst of this crisis, was an alternative "kingdom" and a new way of belonging all her own. Thus, she reports:

> After months of inward darkness, I suddenly had the everlasting conviction that any human being, even though practically devoid of natural faculties, can penetrate to the kingdom of truth reserved for genius, if only he longs for truth and perpetually concentrates all his attention upon its attainment. He thus becomes a genius, too, even though for lack of talent his genius cannot be visible from outside (W1973:64).

On its face, Weil's revelation seems to have had much to do with the recognition that truth can be attained through attention. This concept was to become of paramount importance in her later spiritual writings. But clearly it is not just attention and truth that concerned her. What she was really talking about was genius. That is, attention was important to her precisely because it was the key to genius, not just the way to truth. By becoming a genius through attention rather than through the "natural faculties," which she believed she did not possess, Weil achieved a status equal to her brother's. Moreover, this was a kind of genius that could not be determined "externally" (i.e., by those who had granted André the honor), but was rather made legitimate through an internal revelation. It appeared, then, that the "everlasting conviction" that came to Weil substituted an esoteric and authentic "genius" for the more conventional, intellectual (and collectively idolized) variety of André's.

Another vital feature of Weil's account has to do with the direction taken in the attainment of truth. She described it as though she were moving to another place, a "kingdom" which was not earthly. The Christian implications were not fully apparent to her at the time of the breakdown, but there was nevertheless a sense of moving out of the world, or at least of penetrating into a realm not wholly of the world of "mortal" geniuses. Thus, through attention and concentration she moved "beyond" this world to another. As a result, "the dilemma of worldliness" was no longer a problem; she had escaped it by creating a different world, beyond both "I" and "We."

The resourcefulness of Weil's adolescent "escape" from both "I" and "We" becomes even more apparent in one other dimension of attention, or rather in a state she later associated with attention, and elevated above all others. She called this state "impersonality," and in essence, it was the erasure of both personal and collective identity.

> Impersonality is only reached by the practice of a form of attention which is rare in itself and impossible except in solitude. This is never achieved by a man who thinks of himself as a member of a collectivity, as a part of something which says "We." . . . The man for whom the development of personality is all that counts has totally lost all sense of the sacred; and it is hard to know which of these errors is the worst (W1962b:14).

In one dramatic moment, then, not only was the "sacred" made attainable through the destruction of both "I" and "We," but a nonexistent or invisible "self" became a spiritual blessing, not an earthly curse. As Weil noted elsewhere, "The whole effort of the mystic has always been to become such that there is no part left in his soul to say 'I.'" (W1978:117). Accordingly, by discovering this "transcendent kingdom," she found a way to move beyond André's intellect, legitimize the destruction of her "worthless" self, and remove the pressing burden of worldly belonging all at once. In this other "worldless" kingdom, who she was and where she belonged was no longer problematic.

Or so it may seem. In actuality, of course, neither the problem of communal nor personal identity were eliminated in the aftermath of Weil's adolescent crisis or even after the conversion experiences in 1938. Indeed, her "rebirth" simply brought those problems into sharper focus. Or, to put this in terms of human psychology: a preoccupation with the rejection of self signifies, though in a negative way, a preoccupation *with* self. In this sense, Weil's turn to "impersonality" was simply the other side of her need to accept herself *as* a "self," a whole and valuable person, and to be so accepted by the "collectivity." Her friend Gustave Thibon expressed this perfectly when he observed that Weil's "terrible preoccupation with herself, her *ego*, as it were, was like a word that she may perhaps have succeeded in obliterating but that was still underlined" (Perrin and Thibon 1953:119). Hence, her denial of self was not the resolution of her identity problems, nor was "impersonality" a final and static state, a mystical alternative to the nagging dilemma of worldliness. Indeed, if we can conclude anything about her adolescent crisis, it appears that in its aftermath the conflicts in Weil's life were not resolved, but became ever more complex. For now another dilemma emerged alongside the dilemma of "worldliness": the need to choose between "the human and the divine" became a controlling impulse in her life, and in her thought.

## Worldliness and Worldlessness: A Tension Unresolved

In the immediate aftermath of Weil's discovery of the other kingdom, however, the tension between worldliness and worldlessness did not appear to trouble her. It was not by chance that her interest in philosophy coincided with her emergence from that "bottomless despair" and her subsequent entrance into Lycée Henri IV where she spent three years. As we have noted, Alain's influence upon her was extremely significant. He transmitted his admiration for Plato, Descartes, and Kant to his students, and Weil's later work reflected his impact. The mysticism of Platonic philosophy, Kant's moral absolutism, the implications of the Cartesian split between subject and object for the "detachment" of self, all surface in her writings. So, too, does Alain's negative view of the state, and his convictions about the corrupting influence of power. Alain also valued perception over reason, and stressed the importance of work and judgment in the attainment of knowledge. In this way he introduced the faculty of attention, that form of meditative thought that would become so crucial in Weil's work and which she says is achievable only through arduous apprenticeship.

The real psychological value of Weil's studies at the lycée and later at the Ecole Normale Supérieure, however, was that they temporarily delayed the conflict between worldliness and worldlessness, and they also seemed to allay the dilemma of worldliness as well. Philosophy, with both its logical rigor and its metaphysical concerns was the perfect path in her search for a discipline that approximated the demands of mathematics and provided a "warrant of veracity," to paraphrase William James, for her more spiritual quest. It may be that she found in philosophy a way to articulate that other order of truth that she had discovered, and at the same time it offered an acceptable, even distinguished, profession that made her more a "genius" rather than a "beauty," an adult rather than an inferior, helpless child. Hence, through philosophical work she could both intellectualize and legitimize mystical attention (i.e., reconcile "being in" and "outside" the world) and receive parental "attention" (i.e., individual worth and collective belonging *in* the world) as well.

But this happy "balance" did not last.[3] We know, for example, that she was not content to remain a teacher of philosophy in various girls' lycées.[4] Her philosophical ideas provided a basis for much of her later thought, but her increasing politicalness during the 1930s was also crucial to her thinking and, furthermore, it interfered with her job assignments. Quite clearly, the vocation of teaching and the life of the academician did not erase a desire that emerged early on in her life—to be a part of the struggle of the workers and the unemployed and to engage in political action in the world. Yet her ambivalent views about the nature of collective action in politics simply reinforced the tension between worldliness and worldlessness until, finally, a recurrence of something like her adolescent breakdown led to her spiritual experiences of 1937–1938. But before we turn there, it is necessary to mention briefly two significant events in Weil's life—the workers' movement in France in the early 1930s, and the Spanish Civil War. Both exacerbated the dilemma of worldliness, and opened the door to her spiritual epiphany in Solesmes.

In the early to mid-1930s, workers' demonstrations erupted throughout France, and Weil was in the midst of both organized and spontaneous activities. She was, as Pétrement notes, "a resolute advocate of trade union activity," and worked intensely to effect some rapprochement among the various factions and organizations of the French working class (P79).[5] She was also a regular contributor to the revolutionary syndicalist magazines *la Révolution prolétarienne* and *Le Cri du peuple*. All of these activities coincided with her early teaching career at the girls' lycée in the small town of Le Puy. She gained no little notoriety among the "respectable" citizens as the school teacher who was active in the "committee of the unemployed" and given to agitating for the rights of men and women out of work.

But despite her deep involvement in working-class politics, Weil was never inclined to identify too deeply with any organized political party or regime, not even with those who professed themselves to be defenders of the working class. As her first "magnum opus," "Reflections on the Causes of Liberty and Social Oppression" (written in 1934) revealed, her support for a working class revolution was decidedly ambivalent. Writing of her reaction to the General Strike of 1936, she defended her expression of approval and support of the workers to M. Bernard, a factory manager. She said her relationship with Bernard would be one of the "worst hypocrisy" if he were to believe that she approved of the "oppressive power" that he represented (W1965:52). But this militant position was altered considerably in another letter in which Weil asserted that although a worker's revolt would have her sympathy she would not want to encourage anything of the kind (W1965:52). And later she repeated that she did nothing "to promote or prolong" the strike occurring in Bernard's own factory. Perhaps her most telling remark to Bernard was, "It occurs to me that very possibly my position, somewhere between you and the working class organizations, may appear to you ambiguous" (W1965:40).[7] Her reluctance to support a worker's revolt rested partly on a pessimism concerning the probable and permanent alleviation of oppression, especially by means of revolution. But even had she been able to accept the idea of revolution on a theoretical level, she would have remained aloof and unwilling to "promote or prolong" an uprising because she was suspicious of political organizations, whether they were interest groups, trade unions or workers' cells. Her doubts revolved around the integrity of such associations: "How can one make sure that the leaders of this organization will not turn into oppressors?" Yet she continued to participate in collective movements, often to the perplexity and distress of more radical adherents.[8]

The tension Weil felt between "I" and "We" was perhaps most dramatically realized in her experience in the Spanish Civil War. In 1936, she left France to join with the Republican forces. Using the credentials of a journalist to get to the front, Weil joined the Durruti column, an anarchist group that operated along the Ebro River. She quickly came face to face with the horror and bloodshed of the war however, and recoiled, disgusted and disillusioned. "One sets out as a volunteer, with the idea of sacrifice" she wrote, "and finds oneself in a war which resembles a war of mercenaries, only with much more cruelty and with less human respect for the enemy" (W1965:109). Eventually, the war became for her (as for George Orwell), not one of peasant against proprietor but an amoral "no man's land" in which both sides acted without restraint: "As soon as men know that they can kill without fear of punishment or blame, they kill, or at least they encourage killers with approving smiles" (W1965:108). In her passionate but dispirited letter to the royalist Bernanos, written two years after her civil war adventures, she observed:

> I recognize the smell of civil war, the smell of blood and terror, which exhales from your book; I have breathed it too. I must admit that I neither saw or heard of anything which quite equalled the ignominy of certain facts you relate, such as the murders of elderly peasants or the *Ballillas* chasing old people and beating them with truncheons. But for all that, I heard quite enough. (W1965:106).

She went on to relate a number of cold-blooded killings her comrades committed against fascists ("the latter being a very elastic term") and members of the *Falange*, some of them only peasants, including a boy of fifteen. Once people are labelled, she added, "placed by the temporal and spiritual authorities outside the ranks of those whose life has value," then murder comes very naturally. And she concluded, "The very purpose of the whole struggle is soon lost in an atmosphere of this sort. For the purpose can only be defined in terms of the public good, of the welfare of men—and men have become valueless" (W1965:108).

The great significance of the Spanish experience, so it seems, lay in the effect it had upon her vision of the world. The civil war, even more than the intransigent sloganeering of unions and management during the days of General Strike, seems to have left her with a feeling about the futility—and the baseness—of engagement in the political world. Upon her departure from Spain, she disassociated herself from the anarchists, and after that time she remained apart from all political organizations and collectivities, finding solace and solidarity in a moral disengagement that distanced her from all sides.

This time in her life paralleled her entrance into adolescence in many ways—again there was the heightened, unresolved tension between personal autonomy and collective belonging, the almost naïve desire to be a part of a just collectivity, the disappointment in finding the "ideal" to be all too human and, in fact, dangerous for the threat it posed to one's own self. And there was also the reaction to this entire sequence, the temptation to reject this dilemma of worldliness altogether. This time, however, the crisis did not culminate in a breakdown; what occurred instead were a series of conversion experiences or, more accurately, a number of significant "moments" in her "spiritual progress," which began in 1937. If the breakdown in Weil's adolescence provided her with the key to that "mystical kingdom of truth," then the spiritual moments allowed her to enter that kingdom completely.

Weil's conversion did not conform to the "usual" pattern of these experiences. It was not like Paul's epiphany on the road to Damascus, or Augustine's experience in the garden, when each realized in a single dramatic moment that their lives had been transformed. In her "Spiritual Autobiography," Weil related four separate moments in which, by increasing degrees, she felt "the sudden possession . . . by Christ" (W1951b:64).⁹ True to some of her most "rationalist" instincts, she seems to have relied upon not just one, but a series of spiritual revelations to assure her of the truth. The first such moment took place in Italy, where she had gone to recuperate after an injury sustained in Spain. (She had badly burned her leg after inadvertently stepping into some hot cooking oil). After leaving Spain in 1936, "in a wretched condition physically" and suffering from her severe headaches, she went first to Portugal, and arrived in a little fishing village in the evening of the festival day of the patron saint. The fishermen's wives were walking in solemn procession, carrying candles, and singing "ancient hymns of heart-rending sadness" (W1951b:67). The sight of these women stirred her deeply, and the comment she made later revealed her deep identification with suffering (and possibly some unconscious aspects of her gender identity): "the conviction was suddenly born in upon me that Christianity is pre-eminently the religion of slaves, that slaves cannot help belonging to it, and I among others" (W1951b:67). The associations she later established in her mysticism, between suffering and Christianity, and affliction as a kind of slavery, were directly linked to this moment.

Shortly thereafter, in a Romanesque chapel in Assisi, something compelled her to fall to her knees in prayer (W1951b:67–68). This moment seems to have been the prelude for the most profound one, which took place in Solesmes. Weil recounted this moment fully in the "Spiritual Autobiography:"

> In 1938, I spent 10 days at Solesmes, from Palm Sunday to Easter Tuesday, following all the liturgical services. I was suffering from splitting headaches; each sound hurt me like a blow; by an extreme effort of concentration I was able to rise above this wretched flesh, to leave it to suffer by itself, heaped up in a corner; and to find a pure and perfect joy in the unimaginable beauty of the chanting and the words. This experience enabled me by analogy to get a better understanding of the possibility of loving divine love in the midst of affliction. It goes without saying that in the course of these services the thought of the Passion of Christ entered into my being once and for all (W1951b:68).

Here, as in the account of her breakdown, she placed great meaning on concentration or "attention," and upon a rejection of the body (the world) as a way of attaining the divine. The difference between the conversion and the breakdown was that in the former lay Weil's acceptance of the "Passion of Christ," and the legitimation of suffering in Christian terms.

Weil's acceptance of the "Passion of Christ" was further assured when she read George Herbert's poem "Love," upon recommendation by a young English Catholic at Solesmes. Shortly thereafter, she reports, while reciting it in the midst of a particularly painful headache, "Christ himself came down and took possession of me" (W1951b:68–69). "In this sudden possession" she adds, "neither my senses nor my imagination had any part; I only felt in the midst of my suffering the presence of a love, like that which one can read in the smile on a beloved face" (W1951b:69). We might find in her conversion, then, not only a moment of self-releasement, but also a moment of supreme belonging, a "falling into the arms" of Christ.[10]

It would be tempting to interpret the conversion moments as fundamental turning points and, together, as a resolution of sorts in Weil's life. If we accept William James' assertion that "to be converted" means that "religious ideas previously peripheral in one's consciousness now take a central place," then Weil's conversion did cause a dramatic transformation in her life and work (James 1958:162). From 1938 until her death in 1943, her writings were infused with spiritualism, and replete with religious imagery and Christian symbolism. As she noted, "After this I came to feel that Plato was a mystic, that all the *Iliad* is bathed in Christian light, and that Dionysus and Osiris are in a certain sense Christ himself . . . (W1951b:70). But if we are to consider James' more provocative statement that conversion is a "process . . . by which a self hitherto divided and consciously wrong, inferior, and unhappy becomes unified and consciously right, superior, and happy . . . ," then the dramatic nature of Weil's conversion must be qualified (James 1958:162), for there is ample evidence that the "mystical turn" gave her neither optimism nor the joyous monism that so many mystics proclaim. Typically, she did not permit herself the luxury of withdrawal into a world of safety, rest, and comfort. She refused to use religion, faith, or grace from God as a crutch or a buffer, nor was she moved to render an image of a redeemed mankind. Her universe was dark, silent, empty— "the void," in the language of the mystics—and her vision was close to a Gnostic interpretation of a world in which God is absent and humans suffer:

> Relentless necessity, wretchedness, distress, the crushing burden of pov-
> erty and of labour which wears us out, cruelty, torture, violent death,
> constraint, disease—all these constitute divine love. It is God who in love
> withdraws from us so that we can love him (*W*1952a:28).

Whatever else they are, these are not the words of a self "consciously right, superior and happy," and Weil's conversion cannot be summed up in James' terms. Her understanding of the universe is one which incorporates and does not seek to obliterate the reality of suffering and evil. After the conversion, "affliction" became a central theme in Weil's work and her own ever present self-mortification took on new meaning. In the final years of her life her habitual ascesis grew even more intense and manifested itself in the form of voluntary poverty, the rejection of all worldly comforts, and, most notably, a refusal to eat which substantially contributed to her death.[11] This ascesis had both social and mystical significance, both political and spiritual meaning—through it she gained a more immediate understanding of suffering and therefore believed she could identify more authentically with the oppressed. As we shall later see, affliction became the means toward total detachment, which meant the destruction of the "I" was complete and attraction to all worldly seductions stilled.

What is most striking, in psychological terms, about Weil's preoccupation with affliction is the extent to which she found a positive use for both the physical and mental anguish that she suffered so constantly throughout her life. The significance she attached to affliction in her spiritual writings did not alleviate that pain, but it did recognize it and make use of it on a theoretical level, as a universal, not merely a personal experience. Even in her most spiritual writings, however, the preoccupation with "self" persisted, despite its elevation to the language and paradox of the mystical. As Thibon noted, the "I" and its place in the world were vitally important to her always, and there is nothing in her work that suggests that after the conversion moments, the dilemma of worldliness ceased to torment her. Unlike the great Western mystics who found peace through an inner, contemplative, withdrawal—St. John of the Cross or Teresa of Avila—Simone Weil continued to struggle between the human and the divine. She was not unaware of her struggle, as she wrote to Maurice Schumann in 1942: "I feel an ever increasing sense of devastation, both in my intellect and in the center of my heart, at my inability to think with truth at the same time about the affliction of men, the perfection of God, and the link between the two" (W1965:178).

Less than a year later, she was dead. "The deceased did kill and slay herself," the coroner's report read, "while the balance of her mind was disturbed" (P537). What the sterility of this verdict could not capture—indeed, what still remains difficult to understand—is the meaning behind Simone Weil's death. On this matter, perhaps, her thought can be of help. So let us turn now to what she has to teach us, and see if we can come to theoretical terms with both the dilemma of worldliness, and the tension between the human and the divine.

## Political Thought and Personal Identity

The underlying assumption of most authors who have studied Simone Weil's thought is that it radically changed its direction in 1938, following her conversion experiences. As a result, commentators have generally divided her writings into two "stages" or "phases," one political, the other spiritual. For example, Roy Pierce argues that she passed from a "rationalist" phase when she wrote "exclusively on social and political affairs" to a "spiritual" one, when she turned to "religion, spiritualism, and the supernatural" (Pierce 1962:506). Leslie Fiedler calls Weil's early writings "political" but thinks "the culmination of her thought is meta-political" (Fiedler 1951). Simone Fraisse, who recognizes the cross-currents in much of Weil's life, nevertheless characterizes her writings after 1940 as produced "dan un climate spirituel de soumission à la volonté divine" (Fraisse 1975).

On a theoretical level, this "two stage" interpretation of Weil's writings offers an attractive if unremarkable simplicity, insofar as it neatly separates the political from the spiritual, and even limits the "political" to the syndicalist, quasi-Marxist phase of her work. On a psychological level, this two-stage view suggests that Weil achieved some sort of "resolution" in her outlook, or at least a perspective that released her from previous "worldly" concerns. But, on both levels, such an interpretation is at best problematic. As I have attempted to suggest by way of a psychoanalytic approach, the formation of Weil's identity was hardly simple or dualistic, nor by the time she entered adulthood did she have a well-integrated identity in which all tensions were resolved or at least placed in some sort of "balance." Indeed, if attention to her identity teaches us anything at all, it is that the conflict between "I" and "We" (the dilemma of worldliness) was a continuous part of her adult life, and so was the "larger" tension that subsumed it, the tension between worldliness (or involvement in the world), and worldlessness (or withdrawal from it).

With that aim in mind, I want to argue that Weil's thought, like her life, cannot can be adequately interpreted as a simple move from the "political" to the "spiritual." Drawing upon the tensions within her identity, we might best understand her thought not in terms of two discrete "stages" in separable moments in time, but instead as a mélange of themes or "impulses" that surface, recede, and resurface within her thinking, never fully abandoned or completely reconciled. These themes, in turn, coincide with certain aspects of her psychological crisis. The problem of communal identity has its theoretical analogue in the essay "Reflections on the Causes of Liberty and Social Oppression," where she offers a critique of the modern world as a "blind collectivity" that threatens individual autonomy and methodical thought (or "liberty"). The problem of personal identity, or the "need to belong" emerges as a political issue in *The Need for Roots*, where she declares "rootedness in some form of community" the highest need of the human soul and addresses the nature of patriotism. Taken together, these works reveal "the dilemma of worldliness" in its political and theoretical form. Or, to put this another way, Weil's writings address topics of critical political importance—the meaning of individual freedom in the modern collectivity, the nature of community in the nation-state, and the political and social possibilities for an end to the affliction and oppression of the human condition.

Because these issues never ceased to interest her, we cannot rightly say that Weil moved from a "political" to a "spiritual" phase. But it would nevertheless be accurate to acknowledge that these issues plagued her so thoroughly that she sought release from them in a mystical doctrine that counseled exile from this world and attention to the love of God. Thus the pull toward "worldlessness" manifests itself in her thought, as it did in her life. As in her life, however, the lure of of the mystical never fully overcame the political, or stilled her preoccupation with the nature and meaning of liberty and community. Indeed, if anything marks her later writings, it is not the triumph of the mystical over the political, but rather the struggle somehow to reconcile the two. Nowhere is this more evident than in her last long work, *The Need for Roots*, where she seeks a spiritual understanding of patriotism, and fixes the needs of the "soul" to a rootedness in country. The point, then, is not to reduce Weil's thought to "early human" and "late divine," but rather to see how the struggle "between the human and the divine" reveals itself *within* her writings, and over time.

In proceeding on this course, I have chosen three works that I find emblematic, political, expressions of the tensions in Simone Weil's life: "Reflections on the Causes of Liberty and Social Oppression," *The Iliad or the Poem of Force*, and *The Need for Roots*. As we move through them, and look at her other writings as well, we will not only be concerned to capture what is compelling about her political thinking, but also try to understand where it founders or fails, and why. The ultimate purpose here, however, is neither to reduce the thought to a failed enterprise, nor the enterprise to a sad and troubled life, but rather to attend to the lessons Simone Weil has to teach us in her own difficult, remarkable, and demanding way.

## Notes

1. Perhaps the most striking aspect of Erikson's study *Young Man Luther* (1959:14) is his pinpointing of the moment—"the fit in the choir"—when Luther experienced the crisis of identity in its totality. Drawing upon his own clinical observations, he argues that Luther experienced the crisis "in that period of the life cycle when each youth must forge for himself some central perspective and direction, some working unity, out of the effective remnants of his childhood and the hopes of his anticipated adulthood." It may be, however, that Erikson hangs the weight of his argument on a very tenuous hook, for it is unclear whether the "fit in the choir" actually occurred. With Simone Weil we are far more certain. She acknowledges she experienced a "fit of bottomless despair" at the age of fourteen and provides nearly a casebook example of what Erikson elsewhere terms "the normative crisis in adolescence" (Erikson 1968:23).

2. On the whole, Weil's biographers have paid only passing account to the events leading up to her adolescent crisis, and to the crisis itself. Pétrement, for example, mentions it in a short paragraph (P21); Cabaud (1964:22) addresses it a bit more fully and acknowledges that her "confession" "places the moment of her moral and spiritual adolescence." Perhaps without knowing it, he suggests, Simone found at this moment "a definite direction for her whole subsequent development." But he does not pursue this valuable insight explicitly.

3. We might also wonder, of course, whether the "balance" ever existed. Around this same time, in 1930, Simone began to suffer from excruciating headaches (her "affliction") which would plague her for the remainder of her life. Reasonably enough, both Pétrement and Cabaud trace the headaches to sinusitis, brought on by a severe cold she caught after failing to dry off following outdoor athletics. But Pétrement also wonders if "excessive work" might have brought on her physical condition (P69). The psychosomatic nature of her headaches should not be overlooked, since it seems quite possible that a crisis such as Weil's could well issue in extreme physical consequences which, along with the crisis itself, are never fully alleviated.

4. She taught in a series of provincial towns: Le Puy, Roanne, Auxerre, and Bourges, between 1931 and 1936, with a year off in 1934–1935, when she took up work in the factory.

5. At the Ecole Normale, Simone's sympathies for the working class earned her the nickname "the Red Virgin." Near the end of her teaching duties in Le Puy, she wrote in a letter, "When I attended the Ecole Normale from 1928 to 1931, I readily manifested my nonconformist feeling, and perhaps with some exaggeration, as often happens when one is twenty years old. That is why Bougle nicknamed me "the Red Virgin." Unfortunately this nickname has always stuck to me, especially in National Education circles" (P118).

6. It seems unlikely, however, that she actually joined the French Communist Party, although she was generally sympathetic to many of their aims. Pétrement reports that, around 1932, André Weil noticed a letter lying about Simone's room requesting admission to the Party, which began, "Moved by a powerful feeling of solidarity . . ." but apparently, she never sent it (P47). Her friend Boris Souvarine says that in 1932 Simone was a "dissident communist" and had the Party been run in a different manner, she probably would have joined it. But it also seems likely that her persistent hostility to all political parties would have kept her from doing so. Early on, at least, she put her faith in the trade union movement rather than in political parties. She joined the National Teachers' Union (C. G. T.) in 1931, and while in Le Puy apparently spent a great deal of time trying to unify members of the C. G. T. and those of the United General Confederation of Labor (C. G. T. U.) in the Haute-Loire and Loire regions.

7. As we shall see in the following chapter, much of her ambivalence and ambiguity is the result of a carefully thought out critique of orthodox Marxism, and of Marx's theory itself. For a helpful clarification and elaboration of Weil's place within the context of twentieth-century Marxism, see Blum and Seidler (1987).

8. The story of her meeting with Trotsky is by now well-known. Trotsky, whom Weil admired for his vision and lucidity but profoundly disagreed with on various matters of theory and practice, spent an evening at her parents' apartment in December of 1933. In short order, their discussion turned into a heated argument, with Simone reproaching "Papa" for his conduct toward the Kronstadt sailors. At one point Trotsky finally exclaimed, "I see you disagree with me in almost everything. Why do you put me up in your house? Do you belong to the Salvation Army?" (W1974:154). Trotsky might have recalled his own astute observation, made some months earlier in a pamphlet on the Fourth International, where he referred briefly to Simone's criticism of bureaucratism in the Soviet Union and declared: "Despairing over the unfortunate 'experience' of the 'dictatorship of the proletariat,' Simone Weil has found consolation in a new mission: to defend her personality against society. . . . And to think that Simone Weil speaks majestically of our 'illusions'!" (P178).

9. These moments, which I will not relate in detail, are: the experience in the chapel of Santa Maria degli Angeli in Assisi in 1937; the Easter, 1938 experience at Solesmes, where she also learned of the metaphysical poet George Herbert, whose poem "Love" influenced her deeply; in the spring of 1940, while reading the *Bhagavad-Gita*, and in September of 1942, while reciting the "Our Father" in Greek.

10. The psycho-sexual dynamics of Weil's "possession by Christ" cannot go unmentioned. Nor does her own description of a mystical experience leave much question about the transfer she effected between her sexual desires and her religious mysticism. Her account of the experience, found in her *Notebooks* (W1956b:638–39) is riveting, but somewhat embarrassing in its naïveté: she speaks of Christ entering her room and taking her first to a church, then to a

garret. He would speak to her, disappear, and return. They shared bread and wine, "which tasted of the sun and of the soil upon which this city was built." They stretched themselves out upon the floor and slept, and talked some more. Then one day, suddenly, he told her to go. She begged to remain, "clasped his knees," but he threw her out on the stairs. Her heart in shreds, she wandered the streets but she had lost sight of the house where they had been and could not find it again. The account closes with these sad and self-revelatory words: "I know well that he does not love me. How could he love me? And yet deep down within me something, a particle of myself, cannot help thinking with fear and trembling, that perhaps, in spite of all, he loves me."

In the dream are the signs of a demanding and austere mysticism, informed by the absence of God and Christ. It also reveals the isolation and aloneness of the mystic who cannot find love or be assured of her worthiness in either the kingdom of this world, or within that of the divine, but desperately wants them both.

11. But, as André Weil clarifies, on the matter of her self-inflicted starvation, "She did not stop eating: she had gotten into habits where she was eating very little, certainly not enough for preservation of life, partly out of habit, because she was neglectful of her own needs as she had always been. . . . When she was taken to the hospital and they found some TB and naturally prescribed, among other things, overfeeding, she refused it, partly out of principle but partly, I suppose, because she was unable to put up with more food than she had become used to" (W1974:159).

# Part II

## *The Threat to Liberty*

# 3

# A Critique of the Modern World

From December of 1934 until August of 1935, Simone Weil was employed as an unskilled laborer in various French factories in the "Red belt" that surrounds Paris. She spent the first four months in front of the forges of the Alsthom electrical plant, then moved to the Forges de Basse-Indre, working as a packer for a month, and finally, broken and weary, she ended her labors at Renault as a *fraiseuse*, enlarging drill holes. One year later, she wrote a letter to Auguste Detoeuf, the manager of the Alsthom works. Drawing on her own experiences, she expresses what she believes is the "foreign nature" of the working condition:

> The obedience I had to practice can be defined as follows. To begin with it shrinks the time dimension down to a few seconds. . . . My attention had to be constantly restricted to the movement I was performing. . . . Secondly, it is an obedience to which one's entire being is committed. In your own sphere, obedience to an order means directing your activity in a certain way; but for me an order might overwhelm soul and body together because—like some of the others—I was almost constantly at the limit of my strength. . . . In the third place, this discipline relies upon no incentives except the most sordid form of gain, on a paltry scale, and fear (W1965:56).

Weil ends by observing that, "In this situation, the greatness of soul which allows one to despise injustice and humiliation is almost impossible to exercise" (W1965:56).

Although her work experiences had an enormous impact upon her, it would be misleading to suggest that Weil's factory labors shaped or otherwise determined her critique of the modern world and her understanding of oppression. In fact, in 1934 she had completed an essay that set out in more theoretical and analytical terms what her year of work and her factory journal confirmed. The essay addressed, among other things, the implications of modern technology and automation for labor and thinking. More broadly, it attempted to assess the nature of oppression and liberty in the modern world. She called the essay "Reflections

37

Concerning the Causes of Liberty and Social Oppression" (*RLO*) (W1973:37–124).

As its title suggests, the essay revolves around two central organizing concepts, oppression and liberty. Weil argues that oppression is an ineluctable phenomenon, something that is an inescapable part of the human condition (*RLO*70). "It would seem," she concludes, "that man is born a slave and that servitude is his natural condition," but she also insists that there is another aspect to human existence—humans cannot accept servitude, for they are "thinking creature[s]" and their capacity for thought leads them to dream of liberty (*liberté*) (*RLO*83). Although "perfect liberty" is unattainable, the subject of dreams alone, human beings can steer toward the ideal. If they think and act correctly, oppression can be mitigated. Much of the *RLO* is an attempt to suggest how such mitigation is possible, and what sort of thought and action might allow for the realization of liberty.

Weil begins, however, with an analysis of oppression. She is indebted to Marx's materialism, and notes that the "Marxist view," "according to which social existence is determined by the relations between man and nature established by production" is the only appropriate basis for any historical investigation of oppression (*RLO*71). Yet, in the end, Weil's analysis is at a far remove from Marxism. Indeed, part of the unusual quality of *RLO* is that it is written by a thinker and activist who sympathizes with the aims of the working class and respects basic aspects of Marx's thought, but rejects Marxist doctrine and social theory as an explanation of oppression or a program of action.[1] Despite her deep engagement in the French left in general, and the working class movement in particular, Weil's thought in *RLO* is launched from a philosophical position closer to Kant than to Marx, and more inclined toward humanism and respect for the individual than toward any of the varieties of modern antiliberalisms that were emerging in the twentieth century.[2] To see how this is so, and to get some sense of the basic outline of her thought, it might be best to turn first to Weil's critique of Marx. By way of her critique, we can assess her own analysis of oppression and consider its implications for her view of the crisis of the modern world.

## For and Against Marx

Without question, Weil is deeply indebted to Marx's materialist analysis of historical transformation and social change. "Marx's truly great idea," she writes, "is that in human society as well as in nature nothing takes place otherwise than through material transformations" (*RLO*45). Her own analysis of oppression is inspired by this dictum: "To desire is nothing; we have got to know the material conditions which determine our possibilities of action," and the condition that most concerns her is the "method of production" (*RLO*45). Thus, in part at least, the *RLO* can be read as Weil's attempt to apply the materialistic method, "that instrument Marx bequeathed us—an untried instrument," to the study of contemporary forms of social organization and technological development, with a view toward the liberation of the working class (*RLO*46). What is clear from the start, however, is that although she accepts Marx's materialist premise, she does not sign on to his programmatic vision. For her, the analysis of working class emancipation must be divorced from an array of other Marxist beliefs she finds "utopian" and illusory. Foremost among these "utopian beliefs" is, first, Marx's notion that revolutionary change in the ownership of the means of production will, in and of itself, bring an end to oppressive labor and, second, his (never fully developed) assumption that historical progress betokens an unlimited increase in productivity. Embedded in both of these claims is a presumption Weil wants to challenge: that, following the workers' revolution, technology will continue to advance and bring with it the end of oppression. Or, as she puts it, "it is useless to hope that technical progress will, through a progressive and continuous reduction in productive effort, alleviate, to the point of almost causing it to disappear, the double burden imposed on man by nature and society" (*RLO*56).

In developing her critique, Weil notes that Marx considers the development of productive forces to be the catalyst of history, and he conceives of those forces as virtually unlimited, and continuing through time. Most notably, he intimates that "the productive forces will continue to increase alongside the all-round development of the individual," and that under socialism, the creation of needs will also simultaneously create the means to ensure their satisfaction (Marx 1959:119). On Marx's telling, or so Weil writes, "humanity reaches at last a truly paradisal state in which the most abundant production would be at the cost of trifling expenditure of effort and the ancient curse of work would be lifted" (*RLO*43). This "paradisal state" of communism in turn rests on an understanding of the development of productive forces, which Weil finds highly questionable. And she posits a question that recurs throughout her critique: "Why does Marx assert without demonstration and as a self-evident truth, that the productive forces are capable of unlimited development?" (*RLO*44).

In part, Weil answers, this assertion stems from the influence of Hegel and the pattern of the Hegelian dialectic, which tends "indefinitely toward perfection." The progress of Geist, "the movement towards the good through contradictions," which Hegel posited, is transferred by Marx to the material world of productive forces (*RLO*44;Wl973:190). But she offers another explanation for Marx's presumption of automatic and unending production as well, and it brings Marx closer to his own

historical context than he would perhaps have been willing to acknowledge. The one thing that both Marx and the bourgeoisie of the nineteenth century share, she says, is a vision of history as "an unceasing
aspiration towards the best" (RLO44). "The rise of big industry," she
continues, "made of productive forces the divinity of a kind of religion
whose influence Marx came under, despite himself, when formulating
his conception of history"(RLO44). Thus, Marx's "materialistic religion"
guaranteed him an immense influence, not simply because it was
revolutionary, but paradoxically, because it was imbued with the very
spirit of progress that nineteenth-century producers and scientists ex-
pounded. In a fragmentary essay written in 1943, Weil returned to this
idea and noted:

> The nineteenth century believed that in industrial production lay the key
> to human progress. It was the thesis upheld by the economists, the
> conception that enabled industrialists, without the least qualm of con-
> science, to bring about the death through exhaustion of generations of
> children. Marx simply took over this conception and transferred it to the
> revolutionary camp, thus preparing for the emergence of a quite singular
> type of bourgeois revolutionary (W1973:163).

Weil thinks that Marx's theory leads to the same general presumption
as that of nineteenth-century physics; both betoken the eventual emancipation of man. For the scientist, the developments in physics herald
man's emancipation from nature; for Marx, the continual surge of the
productive forces, the motivating power of history, leads to humanity's
emancipation from alienated labor.[3] Weil reminds us, however, that
classical science has been humbled as a result Einstein's theory, and the
grand dreams of mechanics have begun to shatter as well. An analogous
discovery, she argues, simply had not yet been reached regarding
Marxism. She makes this point in the RLO:

> On the plane of pure science, this idea (the abolition of work) has found
> expression in the search for the "perpetual motion machine," that is to say,
> a machine which would go on producing work indefinitely without ever
> consuming any; and the scientists made short work of it by propounding
> the law of the conservation of energy. In the social sphere, divagations [sic]
> are better received. The "higher stage of communism," regarded by Marx
> as the final term of social evolution, is, in effect, a utopia absolutely
> analogous to that of perpetual motion (RLO54).

Given that Marx sees communism as a "higher," more progressive stage
than any that had come before it, he did not even contemplate the
possibility of a breakdown in production, or the dire consequences if
the productive forces are pushed beyond their capacities and throw
society into chaos. Marx optimistically disregarded the possibility that
there might be, in Weil's words, a limit to those "labor-saving factors,"

and a point at which "progress is transformed into regression" (*RLO*50). When she says this, she seems to have in mind a vision of various innovations and technologies becoming more and more expensive and less and less efficient, thereby resulting in the paradoxical condition of a highly automated society that cannot meet its own needs. In fact, she argues, the regression has already begun: "it seems fairly obvious not only that these labor-saving factors contain within themselves a limit beyond which they become factors of expenditure, but furthermore that this limit has been reached and overstepped" (*RLO*53–54).

Marx's shortcoming is not that he utterly fails to recognize this regression, but that he sees it as endemic to capitalist society alone. Accordingly, he constructs a "utopia," the socialist society, based on a dogmatic belief in the unlimited progress of productive forces and the end of oppression. In the name of this utopia, Weil says, revolutions are fought; here is a myth that has the working class thoroughly deceived. "The word revolution," she writes, "is a word for which you kill, for which you die, for which you send the labouring masses to their death, but which does not possess any content" (*RLO*55).

This critique of Marx's "utopian socialism" also leads to Weil's unsympathetic analysis of those states who declare themselves the heirs of Marxism, especially the Soviet Union. Her essay "Prospects: Are We Heading for the Proletarian Revolution?" written in 1933, was, at that time, a prescient condemnation of Stalinism, in the name of the working class (W1973:1–24):

> Descartes used to say that a clock out of order is not an exception to the laws governing clocks, but a different mechanism obeying its own laws; in the same way we should regard the Stalin regime, not as workers' state out of order but as a different social mechanism, whose definition is to be found in the wheels of which it is composed and which functions according to the nature of those wheels (W1973:5).

The "wheels" of the Stalinist regime, Weil writes, are a "centralized administrative system," a professional bureaucracy "freed from responsibility," a police force "freed from control," and a party "only in name" (W1973:4). Rather than the ideal of a society governed by the cooperation between the workers, the Soviet state has fallen, in both political and economic spheres, to "technicians of management" (W1973:11), and in this respect, at least, it resembles the United States, where the bureaucratization and rationalization of capitalism and the alienation of labor have reached their peak. Weil does not mean to suggest that the Soviet Union and the United States are substantially alike, only that in the post-industrial age, a peculiar sort of commonality seems to exist among many otherwise different states: "Whether they style themselves fascist, socialist or communist [they] tend towards the same form of state capitalism" (W1973:19). In this form of capitalism, increasingly sophisticated means of production—the very things Marx thought would release labor from the bonds of necessity—have routinized labor, robbed it of any dignity, reduced workers themselves to little more than cogs in machines, and elevated the material conditions of work over the importance of the workers themselves. As a result of the rise of this "collective industrial machine," in the East as well as the West, the conditions for intellectual and cultural development have been stifled, and the moral well-being of the individual threatened. "We look in vain in Marxist thought," Weil says, for guidance concerning the alleviation of this oppressive condition (W1973:20).

Thus, despite her acknowledged indebtedness to materialist analysis, (or perhaps because of it) Weil is led to rethink both the causes of oppression and the ways it might be alleviated. On both scores, as we might now expect, she is at some distance from Marx.

## Toward a Theory of Social Oppression

Because Weil finds Marx's theory of oppression inadequate on a number of grounds, she argues that we must effect an improvement upon the Marxist approach, not unlike that which Darwin contributed to Lamarck's (RLO58). She is particularly critical of those Marxist determinists who assume that social oppression corresponds to "a function in the struggle against nature" and then take this as the *explanation of* social oppression. "To suppose that such a correspondence constitutes an explanation of the phenomenon [i.e, oppression]", she writes, "is to apply unconsciously to social organisms Lamarck's famous principle, as unintelligible as it is convenient, 'the function creates the organ.' " Thus, instead of confusing function with cause, or the result of something with an explanation for it, we should look to "objective conditions of existence" in order to determine the true nature of oppression (RLO58). Weil's concept of "conditions of existence," drawn from Darwin's evolutionary theory, is thus at the core of her analysis; it is the conceptual starting point for her investigation.

As Weil sees it, the "objective conditions" that characterize human life are determined in three ways—by the natural environment, by the activity of other "organisms," and by the very organization of that environment with regard to capital equipment, armaments, methods of work and warfare, etc. (RLO59–60). Having established these conditions, she proceeds to a more direct consideration of the causes of oppression itself, wherein human beings are denied "direct contact" with the conditions of their existence (RLO62). And she makes explicit the particular focus of her inquiry when she notes, "the causes of social evolution must no longer be sought elsewhere than in the daily efforts of men considered as individuals" (*RLO*59). In an argument that faintly resembles Rousseau's anthropological approach in the *Second Discourse*, Weil holds that the first "objective condition" of oppression is the dividing point between "primitive" life (where "each man is necessarily free with respect to other men and in direct relation to nature"), and "social life" where man has come to be "harried by man." Thus, she writes:

> Certain circumstances, which correspond to stages, no doubt inevitable, in human development give rise to forces which come between ordinary man and his own conditions of existence, between the effort and the fruit of the effort and which are, inherently, the monopoly of a few owing to the fact that they cannot be shared among all. Thenceforward these privileged beings . . . hold in their hands the fate of the very people on whom they depend and equality is destroyed (*RLO*64).

The "forces," which facilitate the rise of privilege are both ideological and material ones, and they include: religious rites, "by which man thinks to win nature over to his side, having become too numerous and complicated to be known by all, finally, become the secret and consequently the monopoly of a few priests"; the manufacture and deployment of arms, which generate the division between warrior and worker and make "the forcible possession of the fruits of other people's labor" possible; and the organization of exchange, when it becomes "the monopoly of a few specialists who, having money under their control, can . . . obtain . . . the products of others' labor and at the same time deprive the producers of the indispensably necessary." Except for money, which has a specific historical origin, none of these factors are culture or time-bound; all are found, Weil says, in all social systems. What differs, "is the way in which they are distributed and combined, the degree of concentration of power and also the more or less . . . mysterious character of each monopoly" (*RLO*64). Thus in any particular analysis, "given conditions" must be carefully examined before, in Weil's words, "the power and responsibilities of individuals" can be determined.

Weil recognizes, however, that privilege alone does not necessarily solidify oppression; societal relations in which some people defer to the authority of others need not be deeply oppressive, nor, she argues, does the division of labor "necessarily turn into oppression" (*RLO*58). Consequently, she offers another "objective condition," based on how we might understand the individual's relationship to "similar rival organisms" within the environment, and it is here that her analysis diverges most decisively from that of Marx.

The causes of oppression, she argues, can only be understood in terms of an inexorable condition, fundamental to human existence—the struggle for power (*RLO*65). Although she never explicitly subscribes to the Hobbesian idea that the "desire for power after power that ceaseth only in death" is deeply rooted in human psychology, like Hobbes, she views the struggle for power as a permanently destabilizing and forever uncertain force in human relations. In part, the struggle for power is the struggle against nature, transmogrified by social life:

> The struggle against nature entails certain inescapable necessities which nothing can turn aside, but these necessities contain within themselves their own limits. . . . It is altogether different as soon as relations between man and man take the place of direct contact between man and nature. The preservation of power is a vital necessity for the powerful, since it is their power which provides sustenance; but they have to preserve it both against their rivals and against their inferiors and these latter cannot do otherwise than try to rid themselves of dangerous masters (*RLO*65).

This Hobbesian characterization of "the relation between man and man" leads Weil to conclude that, in the war of "all against all" no power is ever secure, no victory ever complete. Like Hobbes, Weil considers the unending pursuit of power fundamentally destabilizing: "those who are called the masters, ceaselessly compelled to reinforce their power for fear of seeing it snatched away from them, are for ever seeking a dominion essentially impossible to attain" (*RLO*67).

She explains the interminable nature of the struggle for power in another way also, in terms of ends and means. The "essential evil besetting humanity" is the substitution of means for ends; the methods pursued in the race for power become ends in and of themselves. Because the "end" or "object" of power is never secure, the means toward that end take on a reality of their own. Humans thus become immeshed in the race itself. Losing sight of the ends, they sacrifice both themselves and others to things that are only means to a better way of living (*RLO*69). One of the clearest examples of this reversal of means and ends is found in capitalist accumulation, where the supreme object is the manufacture of more capital or, in other words, the "end" is the "means" of production. But Marx's insight, Weil argues, "extends singularly beyond the framework of the capitalist system" (*RLO*68). She sees it as operative throughout history; men have always been the "plaything of the instruments of domination they themselves have manufactured" (*RLO*69). Citing an ancient example, she writes:

> The real subject of the *Iliad* is the sway exercised by war over the warriors, and, through them, over humanity in general; none of them knows why each sacrifices himself and all his family to a bloody and aimless war and that is why . . . it is the gods who are credited with the mysterious influence which nullifies peace negotiations, continually revives hostilities and brings together again the contending forces urged by a flash of good sense to abandon the struggle (*RLO*28).[4]

Whether humans are caught in warfare or in the acquisition of capital, whether they lived in the past or in the present, is, in a certain sense, incidental. The "form" that the struggle for power takes at any particular moment in history does not alter its constancy; the arguments for or against command and submission do not alter their fundamental reality or, as she so often puts it, its "absurdity."[5] As long as privilege exists, the race for power will continue, regardless of the way in which privilege manifests itself. As long as there is social hierarchy and privilege, those below will struggle for their dignity, those above will seek to maintain their privileges and the established order.

Without doubt, Weil's sympathies lie with the oppressed, "the struggle of those who obey against those who command, when the mode of commanding entails destroying the human dignity of those underneath, is the most legitimate, most motivated, most genuine action that exists" (*RLO*128). But her sympathy does not lead her to call for revolution or to offer optimistic promises of a better future. On this point she breaks with Hobbes as well as Marx, for she believes that the instability that accompanies the struggle for power is so pervasive that the hope for a stable, sovereign order is a misguided one. The "upholders of order" who seek such an end are held in thrall by a "chimera." Weil is careful not to encourage hopes, or to promote any "revolutionary" plan of action. Indeed, her concept of oppression and her portrait of the dreary forces that "unite together or clash" and replace each other "without ever ceasing to grind beneath them the unfortunate race of human beings" seems to leave no room for the possibility of social improvement, the institution of stable authority or the emancipatory promise of political action (*RLO*78).[6] The seductiveness of power and humanity's seemingly relentless and often irrational thirst for it are phenomena to be recognized, and she establishes them as paramount in her analysis of oppression. Here there is no optimistic belief that, once society is transformed, the "riddle of history" will be resolved. Her concluding remarks on oppression, a paraphrase and a darkening of Rousseau's famous dictum, reveal the extent of her pessimism: "It would seem that man is born a slave and that servitude is his natural condition" (*RLO*78).

## "Wretched Haste": *Homo Faber* in the Modern World

Although Weil finds the "servitude of man" an enduring reality of human existence, she is also concerned to note that this oppression—and the struggle for power—manifest themselves differently in various eras of history. In particular, her attention is fixed on the modern age, and on what she says appears to be an advanced and seemingly miraculous "stage of civilization" but is, in reality, simply a new and different version of the power struggle. To understand the oppressive character of post-industrial life, she looks specifically at the organization of the social environment and, more specifically still, at the organization of labor. Because the division of society into "men who command and men who execute" is endemic to the struggle for power, and because the organization of labor is based on just such a division, Weil thinks of labor as something like a lens through which the struggle for power is historically revealed.

> From the time of that primitive hunger up to that of the worker in our large factories, passing by way of the Egyptian workers driven by the lash, the slaves of antiquity, the serfs of the Middle Ages constantly threatened by the seigniorial sword, men have never ceased to be goaded to work by some outside force and on pain of almost immediate death. And as for the sequence of movements in work . . . the constraint is in certain cases incomparably more brutal today than it has ever been (RLO80).

With this observation, the central feature of her substantive analysis of contemporary society begins to emerge: it is the flesh and blood activity of work, as experienced by the individual worker in relation to both "self" and others. But to read Weil as a perceptive and clear-eyed observer of the oppressiveness of working life is both to recognize the significance of her contribution in the RLO and to minimize it. As important as the meaning of modern labor is to her, it is not just the "brutal constraint" of working life that commands her attention. She sees the oppression that characterizes homo faber as symptomatic of a more general disease that afflicts human societies in general. Thus, in a sense, Weil's worker is a symbol of something more universal—the self-alienation of the laborer parallels the world-alienation of all human beings. Before we consider her more general assessment of contemporary social life, however, let us see how she characterizes the world of work and the peculiar oppression of midtwentieth century labor.

The alienation of labor, as Marx conceives of it in his early writings, involves the estrangement of various relations; the laborer is cut off from nature, from fellow beings, from the product of his or her labor, from the very process of laboring, and finally, from his or her own "self" (Marx 1978:75–81). Because Marx posits an ontology rooted in the idea of human species-beingness and sociality, his analysis of alienated labor focuses primarily upon the sociological dimension of oppression and hence on class. Thus, incisive and original though it surely is, Marx's analysis fails to provide any detailed consideration of the estrangement within the individual. The proletariat, not the worker per se is the primary unit of his analysis.[7]

As the passage from her letter to the factory manager Detoeuf indicates, Weil, like Marx, is well aware of the alienation of the individual from his or her fellow workers and the subordination of the worker to the foreman, the foreman to the capitalist. But the nature of class oppression is not her primary concern—both her methodology and her substantive critique in *RLO* rest more securely on understanding the individual as a "self-determining" agent rather than as a social being, or so her observation, "The enlightened good-will of men acting in an individual capacity is the only possible principle of social progress" would imply (*RLO*60).

When it comes to analyzing the estrangement of *homo faber*, Weil is primarily concerned with the denial of the individual capacity for action, and what the denial involves. In developing this critique, she borrows from Marx by focusing on, in his words, the "separation of manual and intellectual labor" within the individual worker. But Weil magnifies and explores this separation far more fully than Marx ever did. The split between the labor of the body and thinking itself is the one she finds most fundamentally alienating. A concrete picture of this form of estrangement appears in both her "journal d'usine," and in "Experience de la vie d'usine" (W1951a:45–126;317–26).[8] In the *RLO*, however, Weil presents the theoretical foundation for condemning it. This foundation has much to do with an ontological premise that reveals her indebtedness to Kant (and Alain) rather than to Marx, for she notes that "thought is certainly man's supreme dignity" (*RLO*105). Thus, it is to "thinking" that she turns in her consideration of the worker's condition.

Weil roots her analysis of labor in what it means to use one's mind to control, survey, and direct one's actions in time, and she concludes that the situation of industrial labor in the twentieth century is one that denies all but the most routinized and stultifying of thought processes, even as it offers highly sophisticated instruments for labor itself. Indeed, the individual "processes" but does not really *think*. In the *RLO* she notes how this condition, to no little extent, results from the development of means of production—"instruments"—that streamline manufacture even as they distort and deaden human experience. The worker is forced to adapt his or her movements to the shape of the instrument, not their instruments to the form of their labors. Thus, in the modern factory,

> one is . . . presented with the strange spectacle of machines in which the method has become so perfectly crystallized in metal that it seems as though it is they which do the thinking, and it is the men who serve them who are reduced to the condition of automata (*RLO* 92).[9]

The humiliation that the worker endures results not only from the method of his or her labors being "crystallized in metal" but from the accompanying distortions of time and mind; modern factory work divorces time from experience, subjects individuals to discontinuities as well as monotonous routines, and denies the fundamental human capacity to control, survey, and direct action with thought. Indeed, Weil contends that in this situation, "action" is impossible, since the work performed simply requires "going through the motions" in an unending, isolated, repetition, day-in-and-day-out—what Hannah Arendt calls *animal laborans* activity.

A number of specific things happen to thinking when workers are reduced to such "automata." First, the worker's very existence, insofar as it depends upon performance on the line or rapid piece work, or the constant tending of highly technical equipment, gets centered upon what, in *La Condition Ouvrière*, Weil calls the "repliement sur le présent"—a turning in upon the present (W1951a:333). There is no moment in which one's mind can relax, wander, and explore. Weil puts it this way in "Expérience de la vie d'usine": "It comes natural to a man . . . to pause on having finished something, if only for an instant, in order to contemplate his handiwork . . . Those lightening moments of thought . . . one has to learn to eliminate utterly in a working day at the factory" (W1951a:338). Confined as they are to one particular moment in time, workers can neither foresee or forestall accident, nor can they attach any significance to their past labors because the past has no distinctive quality; it is identical to the present, and to the future as well.

Secondly, and worse, are the consequences for the worker if he or she should think beyond the present, for there are only "monotonous desert regions of experience," which swallow up the mind and defy exploration (W1951a:333). The future is so bleak and overwhelming, Weil writes, that "thought can only shrink back trembling to its lair" (W1951a:333). All consciousness of continuity in time goes with it.

Third, there is in the condition of these "automata" no incentive for thinking to renew itself—indeed, there is good reason for it to remain closed off, for only then can the hardship, the humiliation, the debasement of the working condition be endured. "Thought withdraws to a fixed point in time in order to avert suffering," Weil says, "and consciousness dims itself as much as the demands of work will allow" (W1951a:339). The worker then sinks into a state of "passive obedience" with all the resigned docility of a beast of burden. And therein lies the final irony; it is not just, as Marx had it, that under such conditions, "the animal becomes human and the human animal," but that the human becomes little more than fodder for a sophisticated machine.

In the *RLO*, Weil refers to such a condition as one in which there is no "correspondence between the motions to be carried out and the passions . . . [where] the body, rendered . . . fluid by habit . . . causes the movements conceived in the mind to pass into the instrument" (*RLO*91). In her essay on factory work, she observes the effect of this daily situation in the immediate and concrete behavior—in the eyes, the movement, the bearing—of the workers themselves. She notes the "emotional tides of workfolk, so mysterious to on-lookers, in reality so easy to seize," and the anxiety, the dejection, the profound weariness, the "looks and attitudes of caged beasts," the pitiful boasts, the few poignant words, the hatred and loathing of the factory itself, that makes comradeship all but impossible to achieve (W1951a:343).

It is not hard to understand why, for Weil, factories are "festering grounds of evil" (W1951a:323). In this regard, we might recall what is at stake both in her own identity crisis and in the *RLO* as well: "Man has nothing essentially individual about him, nothing which is absolutely his own, apart from the faculty of thinking" (*RLO*98). In the factory, where thinking is nothing but an encumbrance for those who "execute," the purview of only those who "command," the very source of human individuality is destroyed, and human beings become as "estranged from and impenetrable to each other" as they are from themselves (*RLO*99). Under such conditions, the struggle for power continues and oppression grows apace. Weil never presents a succinct definition of oppression, but from her analysis of factory work, we can derive a possible one: oppression is any condition under which an individual is denied directly or indirectly by others, the dignity of thinking while acting, of being able to understand and control the efforts of his or her body by the thoughts of his or her mind. Or, to put this in "Weilian" terms, wherever the application and the understanding of a method are divorced from one another, there oppression resides (*RLO*93). Small wonder, then, that when she looks at modern labor she concludes that servitude and oppression mark contemporary civilization as indelibly as they do the past. Because of this, she sees no reason to endorse the Marxist assumption that continued development of the means of production and the automation of working life will help ease the burden of necessity and restore the dignity of labor.

The *RLO* prefigures Weil's factory work; it sets the theoretical bases according to which she later comprehends her own and other workers' experiences. But, as I noted earlier, the essay also stands in its own right as something more than this; in it Weil offers the alienation of the modern worker as a specific instance of something more universal. Loss of control, discontinuity, and a profound inability to think, have invaded the human condition in general and characterize contemporary life. Thus, we must read *RLO* not only as an indictment of *homo faber*'s state, but also as a reflection on the crisis of the modern world. "On the whole," Weil writes, "our present situation more or less resembles that of a party of absolutely ignorant travellers who find themselves in a motor-car launched full speed and driverless across broken country" (*RLO*121). Her recognition of a world in crisis puts Weil in the company of most other philosophers and social and political theorists of the mid-twentieth century but, typically, her analysis of the "present situation" is unique, and in many respects at odds with the prevailing views of her day.

## The Spectre of the Collectivity

If the special oppression of *homo faber* can be understood as a relation between the worker and the machine, then Weil suggests that the more general oppression of humankind can be understood as a relation between the individual and something she calls the "collectivity," (*collectivité*) or the "blind social mechanism." To understand her critique of contemporary existence, we must examine what the collectivity is, how it threatens the individual, and what part it plays in Weil's analysis of oppression.

As is the case with a number of her other central concepts, Weil alludes often to the collectivity, but she never defines it explicitly. In her allusions however, she usually presents the collectivity in opposition to the individual and as a threat to "man's supreme dignity"—thinking itself.

Exactly how and in what form the collectivity impinges upon the individual is where Weil is least precise, or perhaps *too* precise; she introduces the concept in a variety of contexts and has it perform a number of tasks. At times she calls the collectivity something that a human "forms with his fellows" and to which he is then subjected. At other times she characterizes it as a kind of external, blind force which overwhelms all. And in still other references, the collectivity appears to embody something like what post-modernists refer to as "the social construction of normality"—it is a condition that erases the distinction between ruler and ruled, oppressor and oppressed, as it levels all to an "opaque" form of social organization. Weil describes the collectivity as *something* which infinitely surpasses the individual in strength, and as *nothing*, an indiscernible societal power that is difficult to overcome. To the reader the collectivity seems to be both concrete and abstract, natural and artificial, visible and invisible, "in the world," and a conceptual device used to talk about the world. A review of her various treatments of the term, however, allows some meanings to emerge as central.

When Weil writes of the enormous complexity and dynamism of modern social life, she uses "collectivity" in its most concrete form, and associates it with three institutions in particular: giant industry, centralized bureaucracy, and the State itself. We already have some indication, given her assessment of the workers' condition, of how she perceives the factory and the production line. When she associates industry with the collectivity, she means to underscore the extent to which human particularity has disappeared and thought receded in the economic sector:

As big industry is a system of collective production, a great many men are forced, in order that their hands may come into contact with the material of work, to go through a collectivity which swallows them up and pulls them down to a more or less servile task (*RLO*112).

The industrial collectivity is a leviathan, a monster that consumes individuals, reducing them to the indistinguishable mass of bodies necessary to perpetuate and sustain it.

The bureaucratic organization, "that curious machine whose parts are men, whose gears consist of regulations, reports, statistics" also betokens the collectivity (*RLO*110). What Hobbes might have found a fanciful metaphor for an institution that regulates contemporary life, Weil submits as a threat—nothing is more indicative of the dangerous power of the social machine over the individual (*RLO*116). Her observations here prefigure what Arendt was to call "rule by nobody"—the bureaucracy is the collectivity triumphant, a "giant mechanism" that manages, directs, and coordinates life without understanding it. The bureaucracy itself, with its endless chain of unaccountable and seemingly nonresponsible "regulators" is both a creature of modernity and a microcosm of modern society as a whole, where tasks have become specialized and confined, perspectives narrowed, minds severely limited in comprehension. As life becomes increasingly complex and the "scale of things," as Weil says, "is transported into an altogether different order of magnitude," the mind shrinks back (*RLO*109).

Weil also associates the collectivity with the growth of the State, the "bureaucratic organization *par excellence*" (*RLO*115). She argues that the State and its own bureaucratic apparatus are rapidly becoming the centers, the controllers, of social and economic life, and that "every increase in the State's grip on economic life has the effect of orienting industrial life yet a little farther toward the preparation for war" (*RLO*116). These preparations in turn simply reinforce the power of the State and serve to subject other spheres of social organization to its control.[10]

In all of the above examples, "the collectivity" serves as a focal point for Weil's social analysis, and especially to underscore the vastness, the giantism, and the impenetrability of modern life. The latter is a point of view which would become commonplace in social analysis in the writings of Fromm, Marcuse, Ellul, and Arendt, among others, but Weil can in many ways be acknowledged a precursor of it. "We are living in a world in which nothing is made to man's measure," she writes, "everything is in disequilibrium" (*RLO*108). Thus, the collectivity is also a sign of existential helplessness and loss of control—human beings as individuals can no longer even grasp the conditions of their existence, much less act effectively to ameliorate, improve, or change them. The other side of the "social machine" is mental confusion and passivity, the diminishment of human agency.

Since *RLO* is fundamentally concerned with the disappearance of thinking and its impact upon how humans act (or fail to act) in the world, we need to consider Weil's concept of the collectivity in another light as well. Although her concept functions as part of her material sociological analysis, it has another important dimension that brings her closer to an idealist perspective on the contemporary human condition. Weil herself suggests a more idealist position when she writes:

> Now if there is one thing in the world which is completely abstract, wholly mysterious, inaccessible to the senses and to the mind, it is the collectivity; the individual who is a member of it cannot, it would seem reach up or lay hold of it by any artifice, bring his weight to bear on it by the use of any lever; with respect to it he feels himself to be something infinitely small. . . . Why be surprised then, if instead of ideas one encounters little but opinions, instead of action a blind agitation? (*RLO*97).

Perhaps if we reconsider the spatial reference Weil makes in the above observation we can arrive at an alternative sense of collectivity, one that suggests something other than a purely materialist analysis of social organizations. In characterizing the concept, she says that the individual cannot touch or see the collectivity, that it is incomprehensible, impervious to weight, and not locatable in space. Its noncorporeality, in fact, makes the concept seem almost meaningless if it is conceived as a material force or an "external body." The collectivity must be something else, a kind of mental vacuum, perhaps, a concept that signifies the inability of the individual to "come to grips" with the world, a loss of control by the mind, leading to the triumph of "opinion" and "blind agitation" over ideas and action which, for Weil, have everything to do with being "in" the world. The "collectivity," in other words, is itself an abstract concept and *signifies* abstraction, or the absence of a concrete relationship between the mind and the world, between thought and action.

Weil's references in the *RLO* bear out the idea that collectivity is something other than, or in addition to, a material reality. She refers to the collectivity in these ways: "As collective thought cannot exist, as thought, it passes into things (signs, machines)"; "thought only takes shape in a mind that is alone face to face with itself; collectivities do not think"; and, "To the very extent to which what is systematic in contemporary life escapes the control of the mind, its regularity is established by things which constitute the equivalent of what collective thought would be if the collectivity did think" (*RLO*98,110). Because Weil persistently establishes the collectivity as the obverse of thinking, we can consider the concept as standing for a particular sort of mentality or state of mind in which human thought has been entirely subsumed under rationalized processes, incomprehensible scientific jargon, privileged and opaque linguistic orders, and meaningless but reiterated slogans, propaganda, and official doctrines. If we examine the idea of collectivity along these lines, rather than simply as an "external" sociological phenomenon, the true nature of Weil's social analysis expands to include the problem of "thoughtlessness" in the modern world, not just the material conditions that engender it. When Weil writes that the individual who is a member of the collectivity cannot "reach up" or "lay hold of it by any artifice," or "bring his weight to bear by the use of any lever," I think she metaphorically implies that the collectivity is akin to a loss of perspective. That is, the individual who is a part of it cannot "step outside it" or position him or herself in reference to it in any way. The ability to do so would entail a certain critical capacity, a capacity to think *about* or in reference *to* something. Weil speaks of the power of the active mind, the mind that thinks methodically, in a way exactly opposite to the collective mentality, not as trapped or reduced to something infinitely small, but as able to "soar above the social melée," and to achieve a distance and a standpoint through which the world itself becomes, in some way, smaller, or perhaps less overpowering (*RLO*98). The collective mentality, conversely, is the imprisoned mind, unable to achieve a vantage point from whence it can begin to gain a perspective on and act in the world (*RLO*93).

But there is another way to consider perspective that might make Weil's concept of the collectivity even clearer; it has more to do with the idea of "depth," or as modern philosophers put it, with the "ground" of thought, than with gaining distance from or soaring above the world. In fact, the etymological roots of the word "perspective" are better suited to this usage. Those roots are from the Latin *per specere*, "to look through," and "looking through" is precisely what Weil suggests that the collective mentality cannot do. Collectivities are "blind things [which] imitate the effort of thought to the life"; the "play" of collective life is a "blind play"; the individual is completely delivered up to a blind collectivity (*RLO*110,108).

What the collectivity cannot do is "look through" symbols, rules, constructions, signs, abstractions, and slogans and "see" what underlies them or, as Weil puts it, "seize hold of its object" (*RLO*105). She puts this yet another way by saying that the relationship between the "sign" and the "thing signified" becomes obscure, with the sign taking on a life, a logic, a "necessity" of its own (*RLO*93). Necessity is played out through the manipulation or application of these man-made signs, but their meaning, which has to do with their constitutive nature in social reality, or their origin in the activity of real actors and communities, is not accessible.

Weil discusses the contemporary mental opacity that simply *is* the collectivity in a number of ways and in essays other than *RLO*. In most of her discussions, particularly in the *RLO*, she seems to be attempting to articulate what it means to live in a "monolithic truth regime," as postmodernists might say. The "collectivity" is the construction she deploys as a kind of short-hand for this contemporary condition, where thinking is stifled, and rulers and ruled alike are constrained by the same normalizing force. In working this condition out a little more explicitly, she turns to two phenomena—mathematics and politics—which serve as symbolic and practical examples of the meaning and nature of the "collectivity-as-society."

Nowhere, Weil argues, is the hypostatization of symbols and the rigidification of signs—the predominant epistemological features of the collectivity—more evident than in mathematics. In the *RLO* (and in some later essays as well), she contends that modern mathematics is both the domination of symbols over understanding, and a specific instance of a more general phenomenon of the routinized application of methods, without deep comprehension, that characterizes the modern age. Various mathematical sign complexes combine according to "laws governing the things which they signify" but, Weil says, the meaning of the laws themselves is easily lost in the act of manipulating these signs. As mathematics progresses, as it creates signs of signs, the possibilities of being able to trace back to the original meaning diminish even further:

> As at each floor—if one may so express it—one inevitably loses sight of the relationship between sign and thing signified, the combination of signs, although they remain rigorously methodical, very soon become impenetrable to the mind (*RLO*43).

The specific example of this impenetrability, which Weil cites most often, is algebra. In arithmetic or geometry, she says, "all the elements of the solution are given, and man can look for assistance only to his own judgment, alone capable of establishing between those elements the relationship which by itself constitutes the solution sought (*RLO*86). Particularly in geometry, the testing and verification of axioms and postulates is a continuous process; there is a constant dynamic between the "guiding principle" and the application of that principle to a problem; the thinker repeatedly exercises judgment. In algebra, however, judgment may recede as the signs take on an "efficacy which their significance does not account for" (*RLO*94). Through the manipulation and combination of signs like "i" and "π" one might ascertain that it is impossible to square the circle, for example, and yet, the connection between these letters or the quantities they designate, and the problem of squaring a circle is inconceivable. Weil puts it this way:

The process of calculation places the signs in relation to one another on the sheet of paper, without the objects so signified being in relation to the mind; with the result that the actual question of the significance of signs ends by no longer possessing any meaning (*RLO*94).

The connections among signified-sign-mind are broken in algebraic calculation, because the mind does not link the sign with any significance. Instead, it simply "handles" the signs as though there were a significance to them, but the data, as Weil says, are not connected to the solution. The "automatic" nature of algebraic work and its implications for mental activity make algebra similar to the operation of the "automatic" machine. In both cases, method has nothing to do with understanding—its elaboration as well as execution is outside the control of the mind. In both cases, the connection between meaning and application disappears, and when that happens, the consciousness of reality is simply displaced by blind adherence. The ability "to see through things" is difficult, Weil writes, "after a style of too thick a glass which ceases to be transparent" (*RLO*109).

Lest Weil's argument be misconstrued as an attack on mathematics *per se*, or as simply a perverse Weilian observation, it is perhaps helpful to note the similarity she shares on this score with Hannah Arendt. In *The Human Condition*, Arendt, too, fixes upon algebra in her discussion of "world alienation" and the distance between human thought and "sensuously given" reality. Arendt notes that algebra "discloses" a more universal phenomenon—the reduction of "terrestrial sense data" and human relationships themselves, to mathematical symbols (Arendt 1958:265). Like Weil, she sees algebra and modern mathematics as indicative of the diminishing relation between the individual and the world, between sign and signified. Hence, she writes, "the famous *reductio scientiae ad mathematicum* permits replacement of what is sensuously given by a system of mathematical equations where all real relationships are dissolved into logical relations between man-made symbols" (Arendt 1958:264). And, like Weil, Arendt views algebra as antithetical to geometry, the study of terrestrial measures and measurements. Geometry reveals to us that which is the measure of earth itself. When we do geometry we confront our own spatiality. The "real relationships" to which Arendt refers—that is, the relationships human beings have to the earth which we inhabit—are literally before our eyes in the shape of points, lines, angles, surfaces, and solids. In geometry then, to borrow an expression of Weil's, we must "come to grips" with the world; in algebra, we are required to remove ourselves from the world and dwell within the realm of abstractions and increasingly impenetrable signs and symbols. The latter is another mark of the collectivity.[11]

The other context within which the problem of the collectivity can be understood is one upon which Weil concentrates most closely in the *RLO*, as well as in her short essay "The Power of Words" (*W1962*:154–71). Indeed, her comments upon mathematics can be taken primarily as variations upon a deeper theme; for when she says that the collectivity is a "wretched condition" and a "painful state of affairs," she is referring not just to an epistemological issue but to a political problem: human beings who cannot think or act effectively in the world have no control over their lives as political beings. Hence, the collectivity threatens freedom.

In politics, the hypostatization of signs and the rigidification of symbols takes form in the manipulation of language and in the use of words as weapons. The collectivity is open to and feeds on such manipulation. The collectivity, in a sense, is "public opinion," insofar as it is a collection of beings who act and react as one. The collectivity tethers its hopes and its prejudices to words without understanding their significance; it worships symbols without knowing their meaning; it accepts aims, goals, and doctrines without questioning their impact; it believes in abstractions that have no validity and make no sense. "Mental confusion and passivity" of the sort that mark the modern mentality leave free scope to the imagination, Weil argues. As a result, "nothing is easier . . . than to spread any myth whatsoever throughout a whole population. . . . With the popular press and the wireless, you can make a whole people swallow with their breakfast or their supper a series of ready-made and, by the same token, absurd opinions" (*RLO*118–19). From all of this she draws a prescient conclusion: We must not be surprised at the appearance of "totalitarian" regimes unprecedented in history (*RLO*118–19). The collectivity, then, is open to manipulation by those who hold "the power of words."

Weil considers the power of words and its relation to the political crisis of the twentieth century in an essay written, as one historian has put it, in a time when "the voices of disinterested investigation came . . . near to being stifled in a cacophony of abuse" (Hughes 1958:16). The abuse, as Weil sees it, involves a "social and political vocabulary" that has invaded the entire realm of thought. The invasion is one of "mythological monsters": "Finance, Industry, Stock Exchange, Bank" for the working class; "ringleaders, agitators, demagogues" for the bourgeoisie; "anti-capitalists" for the politicians; and for any given nation, a neighbor "inspired by diabolical perversity" (*W1962a*:118). In "The Power of Words," she investigates a number of ways in which the "lethal absurdity" and the cacophony of abuse manifest themselves and seem unending: in the antagonism among nations, in the murderousness of the (so-called) opposition between fascism and communism, in the real but misconceived distinction between dictatorship and democracy, in a civil war between left and right in Spain, where ideals are quickly lost and "replaced by an entity without substance," and finally, in class struggle (W1962b:161–63).

The intellectual decadence of the age, the thoughtless adherence to slogans brought on by what Weil terms the "excessive complication of all theoretical and practical activities," can only insure destruction. Her analysis is reminiscent of her experiences in working class politics and in the Spanish Civil War:

> When empty words are given capital letters, then, on the slightest pretext, men will begin shedding blood for them and piling up ruin in their name, without effectively grasping anything to which they refer, since what they refer to can never have any reality, for the simple reason that they mean nothing (W1962a:156).

Saying this, she does not intend to suggest that these words are intrinsically meaningless or unrelated to the world; in fact, she notes that "all these bloodthirsty abstractions must have some sort of connection with real life; and indeed they have" (W1962a:167). What she is attacking is the stultifying manner in which these words are used, the mindless way they are introduced and paraded through speeches *as if* they have independent, accepted meanings that need not be carefully considered or applied to particular situations at particular times. There is, she acknowledges, a strange security that accompanies being a part of the collective adherence to abstract words. For, regardless of whether an abstraction is employed as a symbol of hatred or worship, the simplistic usage of it reinforces the notion of a fixed and secure world. No choices are required, no circumstances or consequences of action alter things; the word stands, capitalized, as a tribute to its own reality. In this way, "Language is the source of the prejudices and haste which Descartes thought of as the sources of error" (W1978:56). The bad use of language, perpetuated by thoughtlessness, rigidifies perspective, closes off alternative visions, and obstructs openness to change and effective action.

The loss of a sense of concreteness and of the ability to "see through" the slogans and harangues of "spell-binders" has a terrible political cost, as Weil recognizes. Citizens who are incapable of discerning truth from lies, or of exercising what she calls "free thought" and reflection, open the way for their own oppression. Thus, for example, it is not "fascism that annihilates free thought," but rather it is "the lack of free thought which makes it possible to impose by force official doctrines entirely devoid of meaning" and allows fascism to triumph (RLO119).

The only defense against this dehumanizing adherence to the collectivity, Weil tells us, lies in the recovery of thinking "to discredit the meaningless words and to define the use of others by precise analysis"

(W1962a:156). But thinking requires a willingness to forsake the false security of a "fixed" universe for the more tenuous and uncertain journey through the "flux." To think critically is to admit that, as Weil puts it, "Our lives are lived, in actual fact, among changing, varying, realities, subject to the causal play of external necessities, and modifying [sic] themselves according to specific conditions within specific limits" (W1962a:159). What she seems to imply is that a recognition of the boundlessness and uncertainty of human events might check the dangerous (and all-too-human) temptation to find a pattern in or "explain" the world in some fixed and immutable way. We might, therefore, be inclined to act as purposeful but tentative creatures, not ideologues or fanatics. Under such conditions, words become more like imperfect but useful tools that help us come to grips with the world, not *a priori* truths.

She is not optimistic about the recovery of concreteness, clarity, precision, and definition in language, however.[12] In every sphere, she writes, "we have lost the very elements of intelligence: the ideas of limit, measure, degree, proportion, relation, comparison, contingency, interdependence, interrelation of means and ends" (W1962a:156). Political vocabulary in particular is built upon "words and phrases . . . [that] turn out to be hollow" (W1962:163). As long as the collectivity persists— as long as the intellectual climate of the age favors "the growth and multiplication of various entities," the political imagination will fall prey to myths, monsters, and idols.

Weil compares contemporary events to the Hellenic Age, and notes the circumstances under which she writes are not unlike those that confronted Plato, whom she greatly admires. Like Plato, she recognizes the vulnerability of a public realm where dictators and demagogues, not reason or intellect, are in control, and, like Plato, she warns that when thought is diminished and reality obscured, myth and opinion have little opposition. For Plato, of course, the only solution lay in the construction of a hierarchical state governed by men of knowledge and wisdom. For Weil, whose optimism is tempered by the philosophical claims and social events of the modern age, the solution is not quite so clear. Her commitment to the notion of a relentless struggle for power and the seemingly impenetrable "collectivity" seem to leave little room for prescription. Indeed, more than a few critics have read the *RLO* as "all but destroy[ing] hope for social improvement" (Pierce 1966:250). But such assessments are, at best, incomplete. We must remember that numerous, and sometimes contradictory, impulses sweep through her thought, as they did in her life. In this respect, the *RLO* displays a tension within itself, a tension between the "thinking creature, born for liberty" and the creature endlessly striving for power or blinded by the collectivity (*RLO*83). Upon the "creature born for liberty" she proceeds to build some cautious hopes for the modern world.

## Notes

1. For an insightful and far more intensive analysis of Weil's relationship to Marxism that attempts to situate her within the Marxist tradition of the twentieth century, see Blum and Seidler (1987).

2. As we shall see later, however, Weil does not readily fit into the camp of modern liberalisms either. She is indebted to, and somewhere outside of, both Kant and Marx.

3. Weil says little about Marx's corollary to the mode of production, the role *class* plays in social transformations. The determinist perspective she takes on Marx is beyond the scope of this chapter, but as Blum and Seidler (1987) suggest, her criticism must be distinguished from both sides in the debate about whether Marx was a "technological determinist." They argue that Weil rejects both a strict determinist and a "tendency" determinism because she draws no direct causal relationship between "the character of a society" and "productive development" (*RLO*68). She acknowledges, of course, that technology can be a source of oppression, but that its development is not responsive primarily to its own imperatives. Rather, it is the values of those who develop and employ it that are crucial. Hence the role of "power relations" in any given society take on a profound importance for her analysis.

4. This insight emerges again, as a matter for deeper reflection in *The Iliad: A Poem of Force* (1965a). We will address the somewhat different implications of Weil's analysis in that work in Chapter 5.

5. In "Meditation on Obedience and Liberty," she notes: "Some—those on the side which addresses its appeal to the masses—wish to show that such a situation is not only iniquitous, but also impossible, at any rate in the near or distant future. Others—on the side that wants to preserve order and established privileges—wish to show that the yoke is light, or even that it is consented to. On both sides, a veil is thrown over the fundamental absurdity of the social mechanism, instead of looking this apparent absurdity fairly in the face and analyzing it so as to discover in it the secret of the machine" (*W*1973:142–43).

6. It is hard not to read these passages in light of Weil's later experiences in Spain, where she came to the conclusion that all political movements, whether right, left, or center, are inevitably oppressive. Here, however, she is clearly reacting against the overblown expectations of some Marxist political leaders of the French left and perhaps to what Arthur Mitzman has called "the strange mixture of ultra-patriotic and left-extremist demagogy" of Communist propaganda during these years (1933–1937) in France (Mitzman, 1964:365).

7. As Blum and Seidler put it, "Both the notions of 'exploitation' and 'oppression' are present in Marx, but Weil's focus on the latter allows her to give the human damage of a degrading work environment a central role in social analysis not readily allowed by the notion of exploitation" (1987:58).

8. See *La Condition Ouvrière* (1951a:45–46, 317–25 and 326–53), respectively. The factory journal is now available in translation as well. See McFarland and Van Ness (1986).

9. For an alternative, more "orthodox" view, see the one offered by Gramsci in "Americanism and Fordism," where he examines the "dialectic" inherent in American industrial methods and observes: [American industrialists] have understood that "trained gorilla" is just a phrase, that "unfortunately" the worker remains a man and even that during his work he thinks more, or at least has greater opportunities for thinking, once he has overcome the crisis of adaptation without being eliminated; and not only does the worker think, but the fact that he gets no immediate satisfaction from his work and realises that they are trying to reduce him to a trained gorilla, can lead him into a train of thought that is far from conformist" (Gramsci 1971:310). This is precisely the situation Weil wants to question by raising the possibility that factory work and the technological processes that accompany it stifle thinking and dull the mind, rather than give rise to an activist consciousness.

10. Certainly more than just shades of a Marxist analysis color Weil's perspective on the State, but her analysis does not incorporate only a virulent anti-capitalism. In reflecting upon the phenomenon of State power and its domination of all forms of human activity, "above all that of thought," she writes, "Russia presents us with an almost perfect example of such a system; . . . other countries will only be able to approach it . . . but it seems inevitable that all of them will approach it more or less in the course of the coming years . . ." (*RLO*116). Given this prediction, it should be clear that Weil's social analysis is less informed by ideological presuppositions than by the critical position her conception of "the collectivity" allows her to sustain. Despite its opacity, that conception seems to have freed her from ideological constraints and the mere reiteration of unexamined assumptions, a practice all too common on both the left and the right in the 1930s.

11. Weil often used her brother's field for explanatory purposes. But here it seems worth pointing out that André's particular *forte* was algebraic geometry, and that his sister's love of geometry on the one hand, and hatred of algebra on the other, might be understood as another theoretical expression of a personal conflict (namely, her ambivalence toward her brother), as well as an astute analysis of the hypostatization of signs in the modern world.

12. The best study of what happens in politics when "words lose their meaning" remains Thucydides, *The Peloponnesian* War (1951). For a contemporary treatment see White (1984).

# 4

# The Presage of a New Ideal

If CONTRADICTION is to logic what ambivalence is to the psyche, then Weil's logical argument in the *RLO* seems, at first glance, perfectly suited to her. On the one hand, she offers a theory of oppression that appears highly deterministic and structural, in the sense that it understands humans as the objects of particular objective conditions of existence. Oppression, Weil argues, is a ubiquitous aspect of the human experience. It is an implacable condition that, regardless of the pattern of social transformation, remains steadfastly a part of all social conditions—not always and everywhere in the same form or to the same degree, but nevertheless present, beneath or underlying the realm of human activity. Likewise, the struggle for power, which is both the manifestation of oppression and gives way to oppression, is a hidden reality of human life. Weil does not even characterize the struggle in a Hobbesian manner, as the outcome of human psychology; rather she refers to it as a "force"—as both an aspect of "the nature of things" and as ultimately checked by "that justice dealing divinity," Nemesis, which "punishes excess" (*RLO*76). It appears as though both oppression and the struggle for power proceed behind humanity's back and that human beings as agents have absolutely no control over their destinies, no agency at all. To use Weilian terms, in the face of the immutable structure of "the collectivity," the individual is impotent.

On the other hand, however, nothing is more central to Weil's conception of what it means to be human than a view of the individual as an autonomous agent whose actions proceed from the dictates of thought and challenge the collectivity. Far from being the plaything of blind objective forces, she argues on this other hand, human creatures are "born for liberty" (*RLO*83). We can never accept servitude because we have the capacity to think, imagine, and strive for conditions of existence beyond our immediate experience. Thus when she presents her "theoretical picture of a free society," Weil seems far more inclined toward subjectivity than structure, for she establishes the individual as a rational agent, limited by certain objective conditions, but nonetheless capable of transforming the world, lessening oppression, and attaining, if not a perfect society, "the least evil" one possible. Hers is not, on this telling, a romantic or Promethean vision of human potential and possibility, but neither is it (her own words notwithstanding) one of a creature "born a slave" (*RLO*83).

## The Individual as Methodical Thinker

The idea that "thought is certainly man's supreme dignity" (*RLO* 105) and consists of the determination of "ends" and the means toward them, is perhaps the most important ontological conviction that underlies Weil's early work. Without question, this idea guides her substantive concerns in the *RLO* and duly informs her conception of labor and liberty. She values labor, for example, primarily because it is the activity within which individuals most perfectly exercise the kind of thinking she associates with liberty, and she characterizes liberty (one of the concepts she defines explicitly) as "a relationship between thought and action" (*RLO*85). To appreciate her concept of liberty, then, as well as her theory of labor, we need to know how Weil thinks about thinking, and in particular what she means by the "heroic conception" of methodical thought.

No precise definition of methodical thought appears in Weil's essay, but she comes close to one when, in general terms, she says that "man should be able to conceive a chain of intermediaries linking the movements he is capable of to the results he wishes to obtain" (*RLO*88). In another reference, she writes, "the absolutely free man would be he whose every action proceeded from a preliminary judgement concerning the end which he set himself and the sequence of means suitable for attaining this end" (*RLO*85). And, specifically with regard to the worker's condition, Weil maintains that, "the worker should be obliged always to bear in mind the guiding principles behind the work in hand, so as to be able to apply it intelligently to ever new sets of circumstances (*RLO*95). Implicit in each of these statements is not only the notion that methodical thought involves understanding the significance of one's actions, but also that such an understanding comes only when action takes place within a context, when it is guided or directed by mind, when it is based on judgment. Weil's approach is fundamentally a pragmatic or "problem-solving" one in which a certain end or result is anticipated, a particular plan, or principle, or "means" is devised, and action is taken in accordance with that plan. Thus, she says, "a completely free life would be one wherein all real difficulties presented themselves as kinds of problems, wherein all successes were as solutions carried into action" (*RLO*86). However, a "completely free life," based on methodical thought, is impossible—accidents forever arise "to frustrate the most carefully drawn up plans," and those plans are subject to change, given the results of our actions (*RLO*88). The significance of acting in accordance with a method, then, is not that it results in a total mastery of the world, but that it enables us to "structure" the world in a particular way, to test that structure in relation to what we can and cannot do, and to assign a meaning to our action as the result of such testing.

Put in Weil's terms, we "come to grips" with the world when we think methodically. In the process of constantly assessing the relationship between our thought and our actions, between the plans we conceive and the way we go about implementing them, we are forced to return to the concrete world of practice again and again, so that we might apply our plans intelligently, given the objective conditions that confront us. Our action takes on meaning as we think about it within a particular context or order, in relation to other actions which are open to us. As we do so—and this is crucial for Weil—we are not only "in" the present, but anticipate the future and learn from the past. We can control, survey, and direct the flow of time because we have constructed a particular context within which it is possible to do so. What all of this means, in other words, is that by establishing a particular context, or plan, or principle to guide our activity, and by constantly checking and rechecking that context against our action, we order our actions in such a way as to achieve "a clear view of what is possible and impossible, what is easy and what is difficult, of the labors that separate the project from its accomplishments" (*RLO*87). And by doing so, we gain a sense of mastery and an ability to act effectively in an otherwise overwhelming world. For Weil, freedom resides in this relationship between methodical thought and action because we reduce the extent to which we are subject to imagination or superstition or "forces beyond our control." We come to understand, as she says, "that we live in a world in which man has only himself to look to for miracles" (*RLO*89).

Weil is not suggesting, however, that once individuals think methodically and order their actions, they can perform miracles or even overcome necessity. "The human body," she writes, "in no case ceases to depend upon the mighty universe in which it is encased" (*RLO*85). We will always be subject to things beyond our control, to "an absolutely inflexible necessity" (*RLO*85). But we are free, or as she qualifies it, we "steer towards" that ideal, when we understand necessity, and when we circumscribe chance as much as possible:

> If the intelligence has been able clearly to elaborate the abstract plan of action to be carried out, this means that it has managed, not of course to eliminate chance, but to give it as circumscribed and limited a role and, as it were, filter it, by classifying with respect to this particular plan the

undefined mass of possible accidents in a few clearly-defined series (*RLO*88).

An abstract plan of action serves to order the world in such a way that we can think in terms of cause and effect, "if I do this, then this will happen," and that sort of thinking is an immensely valuable guide for action. As Weil says, it enables us to separate the possible from the impossible. "Constraint" becomes an "obstacle" that can be encountered, challenged, and possibly overcome. And all human progress consists in making this sort of transformation.

Perhaps her conception of methodical thinking can be made clearer if we turn to an analogy she employs in the *RLO*, one that integrates the concept of methodical thought with freedom and necessity. She has us consider a sailor who encounters "innumerable eddies formed by wind and water on the high seas" (*RLO*88). The sailor's passion and will, even his intelligence, are incapable of transforming or calming those seas; the ocean prevails despite his desire that it cease raging. But the sailor is not helpless in the face of these forces. We might consider, Weil says, that, "if we place in the midst of these swirling waters a boat whose sails and rudder are fixed in such and such a manner it is possible to draw up a list of actions which they can cause it to undergo" (*RLO*88). The translation here is, perhaps, not quite careful enough— what she means to suggest, I think, is that the sailor who draws up a list of actions (which are, of course, limited) can challenge the swirling waters. The boat, then, is the instrument through which the world is "met" (just as the body is interposed between the mind and the universe) but having the boat alone is not sufficient to conquer force. What is necessary is the control by the mind, the ability to understand as well as apply the craft of sailing. The sailor "defines" the context for action because he keeps in mind the use of craft and strategy, the meaning of setting the sails and rudder, and the significance of the thrust of the wind. His knowledge of these things serves to guide his actions, and by acting in accordance with method, he greatly reduces his chances of being drowned at sea, or dashed on the rocks. What the sailor actually *does*, then, after he circumscribes chance, *appears* necessary; his particular course of action seems to be compulsory. This exact relationship between necessity and autonomy is what Weil refers to as pure freedom or *liberté*.[1]

## Labor and Liberty

Throughout most of the *RLO*, as we have seen, Weil uses the alienation of the modern worker as a way of discussing the world alienation of all human beings, and she maintains that the annihilation of methodical thought characterizes not just the working condition, but the human condition as a totality. But there is a deeper meaning to Weil's emphasis on labor than this; it is not just a metaphorical device. Nowhere is this more obvious than when she declares that the "least evil society" would be one where life [is] devoted to . . . physical labor" (*RLO*107). For Weil, labor is not a metaphor for discussing freedom; when it is liberated, labor is the realization *of* freedom, the condition that makes the human relationship to necessity—human existence as "born for liberty" and "born a slave"—concrete and conscious. Or, to put this otherwise, unalienated labor *is* methodical thought; it *is* the reunification of the understanding and application of "method," concretized in the world. When human beings achieve a mastery of and control over action that, Weil says, begins with "bringing judgment to bear on an objective set of circumstances," then necessity is challenged and in that challenge freedom is realized. And labor is the activity in which that discovery takes place.

To begin with, then, Weil views labor as the "human act *par excellence*," and locates the core of human existence in the relationship "between the nature of work and the condition of the worker" (*RLO*104). Thus, we cannot comprehend Weil's vision of the least evil society unless we understand what she means when she writes, "the most fully human civilization would be that which had manual labor as its pivot, that in which manual labor constituted the supreme value" (*RLO*104). When Weil writes that the fully human civilization must have labor as its pivot, she states explicitly that she is not speaking of labor as "the religion of production which reigned in America during the period of prosperity," or of its equivalent, the Russian Five Year Plan. For her, labor is the activity through which human dignity is realized in the world (*RLO*104–7). Furthermore, "the idea of labor considered as a human value is doubtless the one and only spiritual conquest achieved by the human mind since the miracle of Greece; this was perhaps the only gap in the ideal of human life elaborated by Greece" (*RLO*106). She credits Bacon, Goethe, Rousseau, Shelley, and "above all" Tolstoy, with developing the idea of the dignity of labor, and Marx with giving it theoretical power (*RLO*107).

Undoubtedly, Weil's own view of labor owes a great deal to Marx. She accepts his insight that "man's essential characteristic . . . [is] the fact that he produces the conditions of his own existence and thus himself indirectly produces himself" (*RLO*108). Like Marx, she thinks that labor is the driving force and the highest activity of human life; it is a source of meaning and value, not simply a means toward meaning and value, or a utilitarian endeavor. Thus:

> it is not in relation to what it produces that manual labor must become the highest value, but in relation to the man who performs it; it must not be

made the object of honors and rewards, but must constitute for each human being what he is most essentially in need of if his life is to take on of itself a meaning and value in his own eyes (*RLO*104).

But, although the currents of Marxist analysis run through Weil's concept of labor, they do not run deep. When it comes to determining the exact nature of this essential activity, how and when it is realized, Weil differs substantially from Marx. For example, as her lecture notes indicate, she considers the Middle Ages "a very fine period in which the love of work was the motivating force of production" (*W*1978:136). The guild, she argues, "consisted of comrades working together," and the love of work, mirrored in the great cathedrals, arose from the fact that, "the worker had a clear idea of what his work was and he did not need anyone to do his work for him" (*W*1978:136). Marx, on the other hand, describes the artisan of the Middle Ages as having a "contented slavish relationship to his work" (Marx 1978:446).

Weil can revere the medieval craftsmen because she does not premise the realization of nonalienated labor on the dialectical progression of necessary stages in history, but on the reunification of "knowing" and "doing." At the core of her notion of free labor is not a Marxist emphasis on revolutionary class consciousness, but rather a Kantian respect for the individual and a philosophical concern for the unification of thought and action. We must remember that the ontological foundation of her thought is the capacity for thinking, not species-beingness. Thus, Weil argues that the modern skilled laborer, trained in technical methods, is "perhaps the finest type of conscious worker history has ever seen" (*RLO*122). Such an observation would have been impossible for Marx, for it implies that nonalienated labor is realizable in bourgeois-capitalist society. Given her suspicion of the modern version of Marxist theory and its revolutionary prospects ("the word 'revolution' is a word for which you kill, for which you die, for which you send laboring masses to their death, but which does not possess any content") (*RLO*55), Weil's understanding of the world of emancipated labor is not nearly as revolutionary as Marx's, but neither is it as contingent upon so many social conditions and propitious moments in history. Her skepticism about the efficacy of political and social upheavals, and her reluctance to cheer any doctrine that foretells, or any class that inaugurates, a new era of history leads her to envision change on a far less grandiose level. It also imbues her prescriptions with a very high degree of caution and contingency.

Whether or not Marx finally envisioned a society in which humanity was fully emancipated from labor (Weil seems to think he does) is a debatable issue that has stirred questions of just how "essential" an activity Marx really considered labor to be. The same problem does not arise with regard to Weil's view of the "fully human civilization." For her, such a civilization does not entail the end of labor because, as she dramatically puts it in the essay, "Factory Work," "we have been thrown out of eternity; and we are indeed obliged to journey painfully through time, minute in and minute out. This travail is our lot and the monotony of work is but one of the forms that it assumes" (W1951a:349). The implications are that the "heaven" of a life free from labor is not to be on earth; yet it is doubtful whether Weil would even consider the laborless life to *be* heavenly. She holds a society devoid of work, "a nation of idlers," to be frenzied, perhaps insane:

> We have to bear in mind the weakness of human nature to understand that an existence from which the very notion of work had pretty well disappeared would be delivered over to the play of passions and perhaps to madness; there is no self-mastery without discipline, and there is no other source of discipline, for man than the effort demanded in over-coming external obstacles (*RLO*84).

What Weil is postulating here is the link between labor and human "being" in the world. Labor mediates our realization of liberty and necessity; it is valuable and essential because it transforms the abstract ideal of freedom into concrete reality. If we couple this notion to her emphasis upon an instrumental conception of thinking, then labor is that activity within which humans think instrumentally. Thus, labor literally situates us in the world. Or, in other words, labor can be understood as the existential meeting ground of humanity and nature, where the "abstract ideal" of freedom is played out in the world arena, in reality. Through this activity, the individual can come to know "limits"—what he or she can and cannot do—and that is to realize power as well. Freedom turns, then, not upon the success or failure of the challenge but *in* the challenge, the work itself, in the very act of taking up the tools and instruments with which the world is met. And labor, when it is the fully conscious relationship of thought and action, *is* freedom and dignity.[2]

To make her transition from the abstract ideal of freedom which is expressed in the metaphor of the sailor, to the more concrete terms of conscious, laboring life, Weil offers the following example:

> a fisherman battling against wind and waves in his little boat, although he suffers from cold, fatigue, lack of leisure and even of sleep, danger and a primitive level of existence, has a more enviable lot than the manual worker on a production line, who is nevertheless better off as regards nearly all these matters (*RLO*101).

The fisherman's work is free because he controls his activity in a way the factory worker does not. To put it in Weil's vocabulary, the fisherman understands and executes the method that governs his labor; his efforts are directed by methodical thought and self-imposed discipline. The factory worker, however, has method, movement, and discipline externally imposed upon him. This does not mean that "routine" and "blind improvisation" play no part in the fisherman's labor, for these, Weil says, are never totally absent. We are always subject to that painful journey through time, but we are also given the capacity for thought, "intended to master time" (W1951a:349). And in the fisherman's work, as in all non-alienated labor, the "heroic effort" to master time and circumstance is realized and made possible by the meshing of thought and action. Regardless of the hardship involved, the individual who works in such a way is free—while those who labor without thinking, whether painfully or not, are condemned to servitude. Indeed, to those who prefer the ideal life of the aristocrat or even the empty monotony of factory work over the life of dignified but relentless and uncertain labor, Weil has little to say, except that they are condemning themselves to lives that are less than fully human. The rejection or denial of fully conscious labor results only in a surrender to caprice or mindlessness— we become debased and frenzied—unable to define, order, or think in the world and are therefore enslaved by it and prey to forces otherwise not necessarily beyond our control.

Let us pause here and see where we have arrived. I have argued that Simone Weil's concept of liberty cannot be fully understood until we recognize that she associates liberty with methodical thinking and methodical thinking, in turn, with the activity of labor. For Weil, the achievement of perfect liberty is realized in the understanding and application of a method, when the individual is fully cognizant of the guiding principle behind his other actions and executes a "sequence of events" in accordance with such a principle. The achievement of perfect liberty is not humanly possible, however. The closest we can come to any pure realization of methodical thought in the abstract sense, she says, is in the solution of a problem in arithmetic or geometry. Nevertheless, a concrete condition, analogous to problem-solving, can be approached in human existence, through the activity of labor. Only in labor does methodical thought take form and shape in the world. Labor offers humans the opportunity to realize freedom in the confrontation with necessity and time.

Thus, for Weil, the goal of contemporary social life is neither the routinization and automation of the work process through sophisticated techniques nor the elimination of labor. Both of these aspirations are, in fact, threats to the fully human life—the latter because it would reduce purposive activity to mere caprice, the former because it destroys methodical thought and, consequently, denies human freedom. Weil envisions the only free society or, as she puts it, the "least evil society" as being the one in which labor shines as the human act *par excellence* and in which humans are "obliged to think while acting" and achieve their capacity for methodical thought through labor (*RLO*103). Only then, she thinks, will it be possible for humans to counter oppression in their daily lives and become creatures "born for liberty."

Weil draws a number of concrete, programmatic conclusions from her reflections on methodical thinking and labor, not the least of which is related to her methodological aim of establishing an "ideal limit" or a vision of the completely free life to which real conditions might approximate. Along these lines, she presents a brief utopian sketch of the free society, and it reveals both the strengths and the weaknesses of this aspect of her political thought.

Before we turn to its specifics, it is worth noting that the few critics who have analyzed the "utopian" dimension of Weil's argument in the *RLO* tend to focus on her similarity or indebtedness to Rousseau, particularly with regard to her idea that collective life as a whole "would always be in accordance with the general will" (*RLO*99).[3] But, at best, Weil's indebtedness to Rousseau is minimal, not only because she was far less ambiguous about the primary significance of the thinking individual than he, but also because she was more concerned with the conditions of economic life rather than "principles of political right," or citizenship. Indeed, if any thinkers serve as inspirational sources for Weil's utopia, it is the revolutionary syndicalists, "who place at the core of the social problem the dignity of the producer as such" (*RLO*108), and not Rousseau. Quoting Proudhon in particular, Weil underscores his idea that: "The genius of the humblest artisan is as much superior to the materials with which he works as is the mind of a Newton to the lifeless spheres whose distances, masses and revolutions he calculates" (*RLO*107).

Thus Weil's understanding of the freest possible existence hinges not only on the idea that every individual would think methodically, but also upon a particular notion of the organization of labor—of a sort captured, perhaps, in Proudhon's vision of "mutualism," loose federations of small communities or associations where people live and work in a free and simple manner, without outside interference from external authorities. Accordingly, one of the keystones of Weil's political utopia is the decentralization of all spheres of life, but particularly labor and political power. Not a centralized bureaucracy, but "small working collectivities" would be the core of social organization, not rules and regulations but cooperation would be "the sovereign law" (*RLO*106). Nowhere is her vision of labor as a model for social life in general more evident than when she says:

> it is a fine sight to see a handful of workmen in the building trade, checked
> by some difficulty, ponder the problem each for himself, make various

suggestions for dealing with it, and then apply unanimously the method conceived by one of them, who may or may not have an official authority over the remainder. At such moments, the image of a free community appears in its purity (*RLO*101).

Weil's use of the word "community" to describe the shared activity of the builders is no accident; her assimilation of the idea of political community and free labor is indicative of the extent to which she equates the activity of labor with other spheres of human activity. She does not restrict the consciousness derived from nonalienated labor to that area of life, but in a far more expansive way, uses labor as a model or, as she puts it, a "map," for the reorganization of social and political life. Emancipated, methodical labor serves as guide and goal for the analysis and evaluation of political patterns. So, for example, a civilization of work implies more than the incorporation of unions *into* the state. Rather, it implies a decentralization *of* the state, into small, working collectivities.

In using labor as a model or a map for the organization of political life, Weil is diametrically opposed to a thinker like Arendt, whose analysis of the political realm of action is quite separate from that of labor and work. Weil's analysis, on the contrary, uses work as a point of departure. Consider, for example, some of the conditions she charts in writing of the ideal laboring situation and their more general applicability to political life:

> technical education sufficiently wide-spread, to enable each worker to form a clear idea of all the specialized procedures; co-ordination would have to be arranged in sufficiently simple a manner to enable each one continually to have a precise knowledge of it . . . collectivities would never be sufficiently vast to pass outside the range of a human mind; community of interests would be sufficiently patent to abolish competitive attitudes; and as each individual would be in a position to exercise control over the collective life as a whole, the latter would always be in accordance with the general will (*RLO*99).

Replace the notion of worker with "citizen," the image of fellow workers with "community" and the idea of a cooperative laboring situation with "participatory democracy," and Weil's vision of the least evil society should become apparent. Some debt to Rousseau is certainly recognizable here, not just in her homage to the "general will," but also in her belief that each citizen should think his or her own thoughts, and then come to a collective resolution, a sentiment which Rousseau upholds in the *Social Contract*.[4]

But as I suggested earlier, Weil really cannot be taken as a contemporary version of Rousseau, and for one major reason—her thought in the *RLO* leaves little room for anything like a "healthy" or liberating conception of human collectivities. Admittedly, she refers to the "least evil society" as a "cooperative" one in which human beings recognize their "dependence with regard to one another" (*RLO*99), and she acknowledges that in such a society "men would . . . be bound by collective ties" and engage in "collective action" (*RLO*100–101). But when one looks further for some deeper conception of what this sort of collectivity would encompass, one finds that Weil's conception dissolves into a defense of individual autonomy as methodical thinking and little else. Thus she defines collective life as "a form of material existence wherein only efforts exclusively directed by a clear intelligence would take place" (*RLO*98), and conceives of liberty as the right relation between thought and action within the individual not, as Rousseau would have it, as some form of liberated integration of individual parts into a collective will.

What finally hangs on Weil's failure to bridge the gap between the individual and the collectivity, while she nevertheless endorses a vision of liberty rooted in cooperation and collective action? The answer to this reveals the most serious weakness in her argument in the *RLO*—a weakness that she does not show in some of her other works—her inability to conceive of a "healthy" form of collectivity. But before we turn there, let us consider more closely how the tension between "I and We" manifests itself in Weil's understanding of liberty.

## The Denial of Community

Weil ends the *RLO* with a revealing metaphor—she calls for an "inventory of modern civilization," a "balance sheet," which would list on the one hand, "what belongs of right to man as an individual," and, on the other, "what weapons are in the hands of the collectivity for use against him" (*RLO*123). The task, Weil says, would be to develop the former at the expense of the latter. The metaphor is not entirely arbitrary. In a sense, the *RLO* as a whole is a kind of balance sheet where the pros and cons of civilization are enumerated in terms of the adversarial relationship between the individual and the collectivity. The "site" of that relationship, as I suggested earlier, can be viewed as "inside" or "internal" to the individual, as a struggle between the control of the mind and the attenuation of critical faculties which allows the individual to be absorbed into the collectivity.

There is no question that, in the *RLO*, Weil assigns primacy to the individual mind, to thinking. Quoting Kant in her *Lectures on Philosophy*, she notes: "We cannot represent to ourselves any kind of relationship as existing in the object without having first made the relationship ourselves" (*W*1978:102). The "I," as Weil puts it, is the source of all understanding, and that understanding, she says in the *RLO*, is impossible for the collectivity: "a relationship is never formed except within one mind . . . several human minds cannot become united in one collective mind" (*RLO*82). There are political as well as epistemological implications here, for "collectivity" as Weil uses it, is perjorative in two senses—it signifies both "mindlessness," or all that is opposed to "methodical thought," and the "social," or all that is opposed to the individual. Accordingly, Weil's humanistic determination to preserve the dignity and rationality of the individual as an autonomous creature has serious implications for her view of social and political life.

"Society," with its numbing conformity and its reinforcement of mindlessness, is Weil's adversary. Wherever the collectivity triumphs, the individual is demeaned, and the only hope exists in "leaving the individual here and there a certain freedom of movement amid the trammels cast around him by social organization" (*RLO*121). She is intent upon preserving a sphere of operation for the individual that is as free from the contamination of society-as-the-collectivity. One of the chief problems in the *RLO* arises here, for in her determination to secure that "freedom of movement" for the individual, Weil implies *any* kind of membership in an association is potentially destructive of the individual. There seems to be no alternative; either one is free as an individual or is enslaved by the social. Collective action and communal spirit play no part in Weil's vision of freedom and social progress because she does not have an idea of the "healthy" community as something altogether different from the "sick" collectivity.

To be sure, this adversarial relationship, which Weil establishes between the individual and the collectivity, occasionally breaks down, and she is at her best when she allows herself to recognize the importance of reciprocity and shared activity. She does this, for example, when she offers the image of a free community as one in which workers ponder a problem and arrive at a solution in concert, or when she talks about the realization of the public interest through "small working collectivities," where cooperation would prevail. In these moments, Weil is not only capable of accepting a notion of "togetherness" or "mutuality," or what Rosa Luxemburg called the "school of public life," but of viewing this kind of existence as truly life-enhancing and essential to humans. But, unhappily, these moments do not come often enough. Instead, the spectre of the "blind collectivity" dominates her vision so forcefully that she is unable to conceive of groups, associations, communities, or even public life as fulfilling rather than threatening. It is almost as if she cannot allow for a broader perspective in which the individual is seen as existing *among* others, and in some respects, *for* others, and where a dependence *upon* others becomes a natural and meliorative aspect of human life rather than a debilitating and condemnatory one. Instead,

Weil often sounds as though she perceives the good life as akin to solitary confinement:

> To the extent to which a man's fate is dependent on other men, his own life escapes not only out of his hands, but also out of the control of his intelligence; judgment and resolution no longer have anything to which to apply themselves; instead of contriving and acting, one has to stoop to pleading or threatening; and the soul is plunged into bottomless abysses of desire and fear, for there are no bounds to the satisfactions and sufferings that a man can receive at the hands of other men (*RLO*96).

For Weil, it is primarily the "sufferings" of human beings that are directly related to their existence among others, and can be countered only by rationality and by exercising control over one's own actions. Methodical thought is the offspring of judgment and resolution, the only bulwark against the power of the blind collectivity that sends one into those "bottomless abysses" of fear and desire. The choice, then, is between dignity and abasement, between reasoned control and frenzy, between, as it were, "I" and "We."

Weil's outlook is not unlike the one expressed some years later by her contemporary, Jean-Paul Sartre, who called those who say "We" inhabited souls, in bondage. Indeed, at times she seems to come close to an existentialist position, which holds that one's authenticity, or one's "project," or one's "soul," must be preserved at all costs. Except, for Weil, it is the "mind" that is in danger and, in the end, her sympathies are more closely tied to a form of Cartesian rationalism than to any of the varieties of existentialism. That is, Weil begins with the idea that we are separate, individual persons, each with our own aims and ends, and with a capacity to realize ourselves as free agents. Although she does not formulate what some contemporary theorists call the "unencumbered self" (she is too unlike traditional liberals for that), she nevertheless offers a conception of liberty as the condition under which the (solitary) individual surveys, assesses, and undertakes a chosen plan toward a given end. What is missing in her conception is any sense of community or context, as well as some sense of the "liberated self" as formed and influenced by an inescapable and diverse world of others.

Up to a point, of course, Weil's vision of liberty serves a necessary and important purpose, for it stands to remind us of some of the most deeply held convictions of the Western tradition, including the most fundamental idea that the individual is the source of any understanding of human beingness, the repository of reason, knowledge, and unique dignity. Weil's argument also serves to remind us of the dangers that emerge from mindless collectivism where both suspicion and solidarity hold sway. Her discussion of the "collectivity" is valuable because she will not let us rest easy in ideological bondage or in passivity with others; she understands all too well the malevolence and destructiveness that so often come attached to group membership. Doubtless enough, those who commend their minds to the direction of others forsake what modest control they have over their lives to forces beyond their supervision. These forces, these "social relationships," as Weil calls them, then "cause madness to weigh down on mankind in the manner of an external fatality" (*RLO*96). There is, no doubt, more than a little prophetic wisdom in this observation written in 1934.

Nevertheless, Weil's primary inadequacies in the *RLO* stem from her reluctance to admit that humanity's madness, of which she is so acutely aware, might be checked not just by shoring up strength and control by the "I," but by building and maintaining a responsible and meaningful "We" as well. Her tendency is to forsake any idea of public action or even human togetherness because she (rightly) fears the thoughtlessness of the collectivity. Consequently, the *RLO* gives us a vision of the least evil society as a noncommunal, noncommunicative world in which methodical heroes recognize and meet necessity independently, while always cognizant of the "blind social mechanism" that threatens to transform each individual into parts of its collective machinery.

To get a deeper sense of what is politically problematical about Weil's vision of the least evil society, perhaps we might hold her argument more directly up against that of Arendt. Although *The Human Condition* is by no means secure from criticism (Weil, in fact, can help us see problems with Arendt's conceptions of labor and work), it nevertheless provides a perspective that serves as both a counter to and a critique of Weil's, especially with regard to two issues in particular: the primacy of politics, and the nature of political thinking. Let us first, briefly, consider the general outline of Arendt's argument and then reassess Weil's in its light.

Perhaps more than any other theorist in the twentieth century, Arendt seeks to reconceptualize freedom in terms of politics, participatory citizenship, and a "common public space" into which "freemen" insert themselves by word and deed (Arendt 1958:148). On an abstract level, Arendt associates freedom with the realization of the specifically human condition of "plurality"—the paradoxical commonality we share with others by virtue of our individual differences as revealed through speech and deed. On a more concrete level, she links freedom to politics; in the political realm our plurality becomes apparent in the world. She characterizes freedom in the following way:

> freedom clearly was preceded by liberation: in order to be free, man must have liberated himself from the necessities of life. But the status of freedom did not follow automatically upon the act of liberation. Freedom needed, in addition to mere liberation, the company of other men who were in the same state, and it needed a common public space to meet them—a

politically organized world . . . into which each of the free men could insert himself by word deed (Arendt 1968:148).

The release from social oppression or the end of economic exploitation—"mere liberation" as Arendt puts it—are not in and of themselves sufficient conditions for freedom. There must also be a "space of appearances" where individuals act collectively, as political beings, to determine the arrangement of their common world.

Arendt also associates a particular sort of thinking—a state of mind—with action and politics. Drawing upon Kant, she transforms his conception of aesthetic judgment into a political faculty, and calls it, variously, "representative thinking," "judging insight," or simply "the enlarged mentality" (1968:241,220–24). The distinctive feature of representative thinking—and the one Arendt uses to distinguish the "enlarged mentality" from other attitudes of mind—is its intersubjectivity.[5] Representative thinking is the faculty appropriate to action because it presupposes the idea of a shared world of human interrelationships, of our "sameness in utter diversity" (Arendt 1968:57). It is a perspective that is eminently human and political, insofar as it is guided by a respect for persons as agents—as "speakers of words and doers of deeds." This distinctive political faculty thus proceeds from the notion that politics involves "thinking in the place of everyone else" in a manner that is open, communicative, and aware of individual differences and shared concerns. Embracing the idea of "sheer human togetherness," representative thinking, as revealed through politics, allows freedom to become embodied as a worldly reality. In this sense, representative thinking is the antidote to what Arendt identifies as the "tranquilized" behavior of *animal laborans* (whose activity is submerged in the biological life process) and the sheer instrumentalism of *homo faber* (whose activity transforms the given, material world).

If Arendt's argument is important and correct (as I think it is, at least with respect to politics) then we can immediately see that a major problem with Weil's conception of liberty is that it is not attentive enough to the sort of politics and intersubjectivity Arendt wants to promote. At best, Weil merely intimates that cooperative, decentralized, work can serve as a model for citizenship; at worst, she drastically reduces liberty to the realization of methodical thinking through labor. Her characterizations of the "absolutely free man" and the "completely free life" confirm this—they are informed by one particular human activity, labor, and are thus singularly devoid of any political references to democracy, citizenship, participation, or self-government.

To put this another way, by turning her gaze solely upon labor as the human act *par excellence*, Weil drastically reduces the full scope of the human, of a world in which speech and deeds—"politics" in Arendt's sense—are as important as work. She does not, or cannot, acknowledge that in the least evil society human beings make themselves and meet the world otherwise than simply through manual labor. Arendt's argument, that one reveals one's "self" most fully in the engagement with peers in a public "space of appearances," plays no part in Weil's conception. Indeed, Weil often seems to relegate human action as well as liberty to the hardship of physical labor or the fabrication of durable goods, so long as they are undertaken by individuals thinking methodically, in small cooperative associations. Thus, despite her awareness of the emancipatory potential in labor, Weil seems open to much the same charge that Arendt levels against Marx—by subsuming all human activities under the core concept of labor as the "human act *par excellence*," she mistakes the liberation of *homo faber* for the freedom of *homo politicus*. Thus Weil came close to reducing the concept of *liberté* to a particular relationship between thought and action in the economic realm, a state of theoretical affairs Arendt finds thoroughly unsatisfactory, and one her concept of action was intended to correct.

The weakness of Weil's concept of liberty and her inability to allow for politics as participatory citizenship have much to do with the critique of contemporary social life she offers in the *RLO*. Instead of interaction, she witnesses the triumph of force; instead of community, she observes the blind collectivity; instead of language used to create a sense of mutuality, she sees language used to deceive, to proselytize and to inhibit the life of the mind. That is enough to make her turn to the individual as the last bastion of freedom, and, more seriously, to envision a fully human civilization in which exchange, communication, and speech are replaced by methodical thought and solitary activity. This is not to say that Weil herself conceives of her least evil society as a collection of isolated, laboring creatures—she often declares it, as I noted earlier, to be one in which friendship would prevail. But what is the basis of this friendship? One suspects that she views such sentiments as springing more from the fact that everyone labors or has essentially the "same" activity, rather than from a bond created by constant speech and "shared" activity. There is no sense, to borrow Arendt's phrase, of "a web of human relationships" in Weil's least evil society.

Even if Weil had made the connection between liberated work and politics explicit, however, a more serious problem would remain with her conception of liberty. What is striking, and problematical, about the argument is that it ties liberty so tightly to what social theorists call "instrumental rationality," to the cognition of an "end" and the means or procedure necessary to reach it. As in her example of the workers in the building trade, Weil finds liberty in the cooperative association of discrete "methodical thinkers" whose interconnection is marked by a common capacity to set ends and determine the means toward them. What is missing in this vision is any notion of Arendt's "representative thinking," or of a conception of action as a good in and of itself.

Thus Weil's "free men" seem to think and act rationally, and with an "end" before them, but not mutually, *about and with* others, for the sake of such activity itself. As a result, her notions of liberty and thinking are radically incomplete. In Weil's telling, thinking takes on the features of a utilitarian calculus in which a "definite aim" is sought and where a method and its application are understood in terms of ends and means. It seems that, for her, thinking is always aimed "toward" something, or involves the idea of some sort of goal and its attainment. Arendt categorizes this kind of thinking as "cognition": "a process with a beginning and end, whose usefulness can be tested and which if it produces no results has failed" (Arendt 1958:171). And when Weil writes about thinking in the *RLO* she almost always uses the concept in this way. This is perhaps a surprising turn for a thinker who is so basically nonutilitarian in other respects, particularly in her critique of the "utility" calculations of modern thinkers and in her understanding of labor, which she views as a rewarding and revelatory activity *in and of itself*. Why is this instrumental view of thinking so predominant in the *RLO*?

Weil's instrumentalism hinges, in part I think, on what she believes is the primary challenge to humanity in the modern world. The world is, first and foremost, increasing in vastness and complexity and our task, first and foremost, is to keep it within our grasp and to prevent the horizontal expansion of bureaucratic, industrial, military, and political institutions from overpowering us. She is not so concerned with thinking in its creative, imaginative, artistic, or even intersubjective senses, because for her the immediate problem has to do with preventing unlimited extravagance and growth in technical, social, and political enterprises. The determination of optimum dimensions is, for her at least, a "technical" problem, a "practical consideration" that requires a plan of action and an end goal. Given the way in which Weil has set up the challenge to humans, it seems that control can be re-established only through those mental activities that spring from reason rather than passion, and are spurred by definite aims, not by wonder, inspiration, contemplation, imagination, or shared discourse. Hence, she elevates the faculties of "examining, comparing, weighing, deciding, and combining," and focuses on craftsmanship in her examples of methodical thought (*RLO*88–89). Weil's resemblance to Plato is striking in this respect. Like Plato in the craft analogies of the *Republic*, she limits the art of thinking to the correct application of means to an end, without considering a much different problem related to thinking—the ambiguities of ends themselves, particularly in areas such as morality, ethics, and politics, where "ends" are not readily apparent or, perhaps, do not "exist" in the same way at all. Ironically, it seems that in her attempt to eliminate the "automated," mechanical behavior of humans, which she finds so odious and oppressive, Weil argues for a rather mechanistic concept of thinking that is means-and-end oriented and directed by the "free," calculating, individual.

What Arendt gets us to see is that instrumental, "means-end" thinking and rational individualism of the sort Weil appreciates are not to be taken as the hallmarks of collective action. Rather, the hallmark is an integrative type of thinking by virtue of which individuals see things "in the perspective of all who happen to be present" (Arendt 1968:221). This gives Arendt's conception of freedom both a normative and a consensual dimension that Weil's concept of liberty lacks. Even more importantly, however, Arendt's emphasis on "representative thinking" allows her to escape both the Scylla of atomistic individualism and the Charybdis of blind collectivism by positing a notion of human commonality that rests on autonomous individuals thinking reciprocally "with other people's standpoints present" in their minds (Arendt 1968:241–42).

Weil's passage was not so fortunate. Her concept of liberty as methodical thinking founders on the rocks of individualism. Why is she so unable to imagine a mode of thinking that was, in Arendt's sense, "representative"? Arendt herself might have answered that the fatal flaw in Weil's perspective is her commitment to a mode of thinking appropriate only to the individualism of *homo faber*. But since Weil understood *homo faber*'s activity as potentially cooperative, that cannot be quite right. Instead, I think the answer hinges on a spectre that so completely dominates the *RLO* that it precludes her from conceiving of any form of collective thinking at all, much less a valuable one. That spectre is the "collectivity." Because the idea of collective thought or action holds such negative connotations for her (as her very choice of the word "collectivity" suggests), Weil cannot imagine any alternative to collective mindlessness except a highly individualistic mentality, fixed within the interior reaches of a mind "face to face" with itself and a difficulty to be solved. Nowhere is the crippling effect of this conception of thinking more evident than when Weil writes:

> The number 2 thought of by one man cannot be added to the number 2 thought of by another man so as to make up the number 4; similarly the idea that one of the co-operators has of the particular work he is carrying out cannot be combined with the idea that each of the others has of his respective task . . . the expressions "collective soul" and "collective thought" . . . are altogether devoid of meaning (*RLO*82).

The spectre of the "collectivity" leaves Weil no room, then, to conceive of thinking in a richer context, as a "human capacity" that transcends narrow subjectivity and is, in Arendt's words, "world open and communicative" (*RLO*168). Rather than acknowledging the liberating nature of "sharing standpoints," Weil can only equate liberty with the individual's capacity to hold a schema within his or her own mind, without interference from others. Hence, in that suggestive example of the builders, she makes the outcome of their activity the application of a method "conceived by anyone of them" not a method that is collectively determined or the result of combined ideas. Once in the *RLO*, Weil does venture to say that "collaboration" might be the remedy for tasks that cannot be understood or accomplished alone, but then she hastily retracts that idea when she decides the collaboration, "is never absolutely free from rivalry; it gives rise to infinite complications" (*RLO*72). Hence, the only recourse is back to those "essentially individual" faculties of examining, comparing, weighing, and deciding—to those faculties that Weil would have us believe can best be realized in solitude, apart from the "trammels" cast by social organization. In this sense, her conception of thinking is closed to the world and noncommunicative.

By offering this comparison of Weil and Arendt, I do not mean to suggest that the adversary relationship Weil establishes between the individual and the collectivity is theoretically unimportant or politically abstruse. On the contrary, her warnings about the oppressiveness of the "social mechanism," her respect for the individual, and her concern for the dignity of the rational, independent, thinker need to be taken seriously, particularly in an age where political theory seems increasingly inclined toward imagining the world as an all-encompassing regime of power. What I do want to suggest, however, is that Weil does not take full advantage of her own keen awareness of the dangers of the collectivity as a "regime of power." Her Kantian equipment is sufficient for restoring the concept of the individual and the dignity of thought, but not for another task that requires more than just a condemnation of the blind collectivity that "cannot think" and is a result of the estrangement of humans from themselves. What is also required is a condemnation of the blind collectivity that destroys citizenship, community, and mutual deliberation over public, political issues. Had she offered this sort of condemnation, Weil might have succeeded in giving us some sense of what it means to be not just a thinking being that can "soar above the social mêlée," (*RLO*98) but also a citizen who can, with others, enter and change the social mêlée through collective action. What is missing in the *RLO*, however, is precisely this affirmation of collective, human action. As usual, Weil is not totally unaware of the limitation inherent in her elevation of the "thinking individual;" she acknowledges the incompleteness of her argument when she writes:

It is true that mind by no means constitutes a force by itself. Archimedes was killed, so it is said, by a drunken soldier; and if he had been made to turn a millstone under the lash of a slave-overseer he would have turned it in exactly the same manner as the most dull-witted man. To the extent to which the mind soars above the social mêlée, it can judge but it cannot transform (*RLO*98).

It is debatable (given both Kant's and Arendt's treatment of judgment) whether Weil's methodical thinker is even capable of that—but regardless of whether or not instrumental rationality encompasses the faculty of judging, it is quite clear that Weil's conception leaves little room for transforming the world. If one is to understand politics as being, at least in part, about conflict, collectively challenging existing conditions, and struggling, in particular, against oppression, then Weil's fear of the "collectivity" renders her argument politically impotent. Because she is unable to sanction collective political action, she can offer only the methodical thinker to counter social oppression and recover freedom. But surely any concept of liberty without at least some trace of communitarian citizenship is of questionable value in the face of the crisis of the modern world and in the face of the "collectivity" about which Weil rightly warns us.

Thus, in her attempt to suggest a way in which oppression might be mitigated and the struggle for power controlled, Weil follows the path of those theorists who allow participatory politics to "disappear" and who avoid the problem of conflict and the achievement of community rather than confront it.[6] Instead of giving us a picture of a "least evil society" in which struggle and conflict prevail within "limits," Weil does two things in the *RLO*: she either abandons the issue completely by turning to the individual and concentrating upon the strength of the mind, or she annuls the issue when she gives us a conception of the "fully human civilization" based on small laboring collectivities. In the first case, the problem of collective action and the possibility of social change by people who think and act together is eliminated by her wholesale condemnation of the "collectivity." In the second case, by superimposing the (Proudhonist) idea of small, cooperative, workplaces onto the political world, she automatically exorcises those things which, in part at least, make politics what it is—power, competition, conflict, the clash of different views and interests, passion, and volatility. She salvages such qualities as cooperation, reason, brotherhood, and friendship, but her vision seems to be an overly sanguine, not to mention an unrealistic, picture of human life. As she herself admits, her fully human civilization is "still farther removed from the actual conditions of human existence than is the fiction of a Golden Age" (*RLO*100).

What Weil ultimately does, then, is to offer an illusory conception of human relationships as kinds of cooperative, friendly communions among fellow citizens. Here in particular, she might have learned something from Arendt, who certainly valued the qualities of brotherhood, friendship, and love, but nevertheless viewed them as fundamentally antipolitical. To call for a civilization in which "nothing is so beautiful or so sweet as friendship," as Weil does, is to be both noble and, at the same time, to miss the point, for it serves to negate or deny the realm of the public in favor of virtues that are fundamentally private in nature (*RLO*100). But in the end, it is precisely the public which Weil must deny; her rejection of the collectivity necessitates this. Perhaps, had she been able to accept some "healthy" or well-integrated notion of collective action, she might have, in turn, been able to conceive of politics not simply as the struggle for power, but as something valuable to the human experience—as a tribute to the human capacity to act and collectively determine the conditions of existence, within limits. Had she done so, she might have been far more determined in her "magnum opus" to redeem not just the thinking ability and personal dignity of each human being as "I," but to restore the public spiritedness and citizenship that elevates and augments all by virtue of their membership in some greater "We."

## Notes

1. "If one were to understand by liberty the mere absence of all necessity, the word would be emptied of all concrete meaning; but it would not then represent for us that which, when we are deprived of it, takes away from the value of life" (*RLO*85). Hannah Arendt expresses a similar idea when she writes: "Man cannot be free if he does not know that he is subject to necessity, because his freedom is always won in his never wholly successful attempts to liberate himself from necessity" (Arendt 1958:121).

2. Some further clarifications concerning Weil's conception of labor are in order here. First, when she calls labor the "spiritual core" of life, Weil is not referring to a "reward" in the religious sense, but rather to an awareness that comes from labor and makes life here on earth more meaningful. As such, labor is its own reward; the activity itself and not some distant goal or disconnected "end" is what makes it the human act *par excellence*.

Second, Weil's conception is also at odds in with one version of a "humanist" viewpoint—that labor is the confirmation of man against nature, the way in which humans exercise their power and dominion over the earth. For her, humanity never "dominates" nature or overrules necessity; the "victory" is not one in which we become the "measure" of all things. Rather, our accomplishment lies in our ability to control our *own* actions, and to challenge external obstacles with methodical thought. In this way labor requires self-mastery and discipline, and in its most perfect form, labor does not "dominate" nature, but meets or mediates it. She favorably quotes Bacon's dictum, "We cannot command Nature except by obeying her," and says it ought to form "the Bible of our times" (*RLO*107).

Third, Weil is also careful not to idealize labor to the extreme that some theorists do when they argue that labor is pure pleasure or as fully satisfying as leisure-time activity. She is perfectly conscious of the fact that work even when it is free, is arduous, dangerous, and fatiguing. When Weil writes of labor as liberating, she does not mean "fun." Overcoming the "pressure exerted by necessity" is neither a game nor a pleasure, nor, indeed, something which all people want to do. To reduce labor to any of these is to misunderstand its meaning of human life. Weil's less than utopian view of labor is evident in her conclusion to "Factory Work," where she says the aim of fully conscious labor is "Not to render men docile, nor even to make them happy, but quite simply not to force them to abase themselves" (W1951a:353).

3. See, in particular, Pierce (1962) and Ashcraft (unpublished manuscript).

4. Rousseau says in the *Social Contract*: "if the general will is to be clearly expressed, it is imperative that there should be no sectional association in the state, and that every citizen should make up his own mind for himself" (Rousseau 1968:73). Weil resembles Rousseau in both her dislike for "sectional associations" and in her emphasis on the capacity of the individual to "make up his own mind for himself," but not, I think, in her "utopian" vision.

5. For a more detailed discussion of Arendt's conception of representative thinking, see Beiner (1983).

6. The theorists I have in mind here include not only the usual suspects—Plato and Hobbes—but more recent thinkers as well, particularly Nietzsche and Foucault. While recognizing the very real differences among them, we might nevertheless find in all a reluctance (whether born from revulsion, fear, suspicion, or epistemological critique) to envision or engage in debate about the nature of truly self-governing democratic communities and the achievement of freedom as participatory politics.

# Part III

## *Force and Exile*

# 5

# Reading the World

SIMONE WEIL PUBLISHED her most famous essay, *L'Iliade ou le poème de la force*, in 1940–41, under the pseudonym Emile Novis, and in *Cahiers du Sud*, a literary magazine hostile to the Vichy regime.[1] The appearance of this work is often taken as signifying a dramatic break in Weil's thought. One scholar sees a "renaissance" in her writing after 1939; another notes that a "different orientation" toward religion and the supernatural appears in the writings that follow her conversion experiences after 1938. With few exceptions, Weil's commentators share a tendency to view the *RLO* as the apex of her "political" thought, and *The Poem of Force* (*TPF*) (and much of what follows it) as exemplary of a spiritual or "other-worldly" strain that was to distinguish her thinking until her death in 1943.[2] In keeping with this tendency, Simone Pétrement argues that the subject of *TPF* "is not directly political or social, and does not have a close connection with the actual situation in which [Simone] wrote it" (during wartime and in self-imposed exile from Occupied France). Rather, Pétrement notes, Weil's main concern was "to understand *The Iliad* and to construct "a powerful and original psychology" based upon the concept of force (*P*361).

There is no doubt that *TPF* (1956a) occupies a special place in Weil's writings; it is remarkably different from the *RLO* in both its presentation and its tone. And, although it is not (contrary to what one commentator has indicated) the only essay Weil ever devoted entirely to a literary work, *TPF* is her most extended effort in the interpretation of a self-contained text.[3] Nevertheless, to read *TPF* as a turning point in Weil's thought or, more precisely, as a literary rather than a political work, written "outside" the course of immediate events, is to miss both the full significance of the text and the continuity that exists between her political sensibilities and the distinctive modes of her thinking after 1938. It is almost impossible to imagine, for example, that Weil intended *TPF* solely as a kind of detached reflection upon Homer's great epic. Her essay is wonderfully reflective, but it is also much more.

*The Poem of Force* was written during the long summer of 1940,

85

following the fall of France and the occupation of Paris. Thus, when Weil notes that, "the whole of the *Iliad* lies under the shadow of the greatest calamity the human race can experience—the destruction of a city," it seems she has her own city in mind, not just Troy, and her fellow citizens before her eyes, not just Homer's audience (*TPF*31). In other words, her meditation on the *Iliad* is not only an act of literary analysis, it is also a regret "that men are capable of being so transformed," and a lament upon the awful and immediate reality of war in her own time (*TPF*32). In this latter respect, *TPF* continues rather than diverges from Weil's earlier work, for in it recurs a theme that marks most of her previous writings. The theme is the idea of force, *la force* which suffuses the world and holds all living creatures in its grip. We have already noted that in the *RLO* Weil conceives of a mechanistic universe driven by a struggle for power that enslaves all of humanity. The struggle for power is a "force of nature" that can never be wholly defeated but, at best, only limited by the exercise of individual methodical thought against the "collectivity." In *TPF* the "struggle for power" is conceived more explicitly, as war, and the *Iliad*—"the only true epic the Occident possesses"—is invoked as the most perfect mirror of war as force.

Weil begins by declaring: "The true hero, the true subject, the center of the *Iliad* is force. Force employed by man, force that enslaves man, force before which man's flesh shrinks away" (*TPF*1). Immediately, she draws our attention toward the same invisible, pervasive element that governs her analysis of oppression in the *RLO*. Thus, far from marking a decisive shift in direction, *TPF* pursues a line of thought Weil had already begun in the *RLO*, but did not develop. The beginnings of this line of thought are evident in the *RLO*, when she comments upon "the race for power" and writes, "it is the reflection of this frenzy that lends an epic grandeur to works such as *Comédie Humaine*, Shakespeare's *Histories*, the *chansons de geste*, or the *Iliad*" (1973:68). In particular, however, she focuses on the *Iliad*, and notes that its primary theme is the "sway exercised by war." Thus, she concludes, "in this ancient and wonderful poem there already appears the essential evil besetting humanity, the substitution of means for ends" (*RLO*68). The substitution of means for ends, and the phenomenon of war taking on an life of its own, continues to guide Weil's reflections in *TPF*.[4] She chooses France's defeat and her own exile as the occasion to examine the universality of force more closely. And the *Iliad* is the text which, for her, brings this political context most vividly to life.

## The Dominion of Force

What, precisely, does Weil mean by "force"? We might characterize her understanding of this idea much as we did the "collectivity"—force is both some "thing" and nothing, a "sinister mesh of circumstances" that overwhelms human agents, and an indiscernible power. Weil makes it both concrete and abstract, physical and spiritual, natural and social, visible and invisible. In *TPF* she writes, "To define force—it is that *x* that turns anybody who is subjected to it into a *thing*. Exercised to the limit, it turns man into a thing in the most literal sense: it makes a corpse out of him" (*TPF*3). Force, it seems, is best understood by looking to it consequences—its ability to turn a human being into a thing—rather than to its origin, or to its cause, or to something like its "internal nature."[5] But, as one critic has argued, Weil's concept of force tends to take on "a global range of meanings" in her work, until it becomes "a metaphysical spectre that benumbs thought" (Ferber, in White 1981:83). I think we can make more of her notion that this however. To do so, let us consider what might be called a "first" and a "second" reading of force in *TPF*.

In the first reading, Weil presents force as a power that one individual or a group holds over another. But it is not just any sort of power; it is one that dehumanizes. Force "turns a man into a stone . . . a thing that has no soul" (*TPF*4–5). In its most summary form, force literally kills. From the *Iliad*, she draws upon the death of Lycaon, son of Priam, at the hand of Achilles: "he grasps the fact that the weapon which is pointing at him will not be diverted; and now, still breathing, he is simply matter; still thinking he can think no longer" (*TPF*5). But force is not only the two-edged sword "sunk home to its full length." It also kills metaphorically, by turning a human being into a thing "while he is still alive" (*TPF*4). Weil notes that the idea of a person's being a thing seems like a "logical contradiction;" yet what is impossible in logic can be true in life. For human things, the "days hold no pastimes, no free spaces, no room in them for any impulse of their own" (*TPF*8). This dehumanization without death, this "compromise between a man and a corpse" comes in the *Iliad* with the wartime triumph of the conqueror over the conquered. And Weil introduces the metaphor of slavery in order to underscore the abject condition of the defeated: "To lose more than the slave does is impossible, for he loses his whole inner life. A fragment of it he may get back if he sees the possibility of changing his fate, but this is his only hope. Such is the empire of force, as extensive as the empire of nature" (*TPF*10).

Thus force involves the diminishment of some human beings by others, and the suffering of some at the hands of others. Weil's reflections here—on thinghood, on the loss of "inner life," on the fragmentary and wasted nature of the existence of the slave/vanquished in whom "memory itself barely lingers on"—recall the graphic imagery of factory work she presents in *La Condition ouvrière*. The worker's condition stamps upon him or her "the mark of the slave:" "things play the role of men, men the role of things" (*TPF*337). Like those who are defeated or enslaved by war, the worker lives a life that "death congeals before abolishing," and is prey to caprice and impersonal brutality. We would be mistaken, of course, to draw from this the conclusion that Weil is somehow erasing all distinction between the extremities of factory work and the horror of war. Yet if we read *TPF* with her earlier essays in mind, it is difficult not to see her preoccupation with the dehumanizing aspects of earthly life. War is one example, but factory work is another, and equally lamentable, for it too reveals the force "that does not kill, i.e., that does not kill just yet" (*TPF*4). In the end, both examples serve to remind us of her almost Manicheaean awareness of force as the struggle for power that pits "those who command" against "those who execute."

Despite the importance of this conception of force, however, it provides only a partial account of what Weil means when she refers to its "empire." One of the most powerful moments in the essay occurs when she shifts from a discussion of force as the "possession" of one human being over another, to a second reading of force as no one's possession at all. Suddenly, we are asked to conceive of the *Iliad*'s world of victor/vanquished in a different way:

> The human race is not divided up, in the *Iliad*, into conquered persons, slaves, suppliants on the one hand, and conquerors and chiefs on the other. In this poem there is not a single man who does not at one time or another have to bow his neck to force (*TPF*11).

The reality of war, then, is larger than the dualism of conqueror/conquered suggests. For in war, all humans are transformed into things, although perhaps in different ways. As Weil puts it, "Force is as pitiless to the man who possesses it, or thinks he does, as to its victims; the second it crushes, the first it intoxicates" (*TPF*11). The point is that in this condition, there is no fixity, no stable identity; the intoxicated and the crushed are one and the same. And this is not only because, as in the *Iliad*, the progress of war is a "continual game of seesaw" where the victor one day is vanquished the next. More importantly, war reduces everyone to a common denominator, to thinghood. It petrifies human sensitivity, compassion, generosity, and respect. Souls "castrate themselves of aspiration," "words of reason drop into the void" (*TPF*22,20). Within this deeper context of thinghood, victory and defeat become almost incidental, for the sheer momentum of the events themselves take precedence over all else, and draw human beings on all sides, "brothers in the same distress" in their wake (*TPF*19). Thus, Weil observes that

> war effaces all conceptions of purpose or goal, including even its own "war aims." It effaces the very notion of war's being brought to an end. To be

outside a situation so violent as this is to find it inconceivable; to be inside it is to be unable to conceive its end (*TPF*22).

This subjection to a set of shared circumstances obliterates all that is humane—the "far-away, precarious, touching world of peace, of the family, the world in which each man counts more than anything else to those about him." In this world "far from hot baths" force reigns supreme, the true hero, and all "human heroes" quake before it (*TPF*12).

Yet no one recognizes this. Part of the "terrible necessity" of war, then, is that it blinds men to the fact that "they belong to the same species" (*TPF*13) and to the reality of force in the second sense, as a shared condition to which all are subjected. War actually plays to force in the first sense—as that power that the strong hold over the weak. Weil suggests that men would rather be deceived by the polarity of "strong versus weak," and therefore they approach force as a "possession." Homer's epic is, in part, a vision of the extent to which this first reading controls the actions of victor and vanquished alike:

> We see men in arms behaving harshly and madly. We see their sword bury itself in the breast of a disarmed enemy who is in the very act of pleading at their knees. . . . We see Achilles cut the throats of twelve Trojan boys on the funeral pyre of Patroclus as naturally as we cut flowers for a grave (*TPF*14).

What these men who operate on the first reading—particularly the victors—fail to comprehend is precisely the reality the second reading reveals. They do not see that force as a "possession" is a limited thing, not a permanent state. Moreover they "have no suspicion of the fact that the consequences of their deeds will at length come home to them" (*TPF*14). It is this retributive power (in *RLO* she calls it Nemesis) "which operates automatically to penalize the abuse of force" that Weil finds at the soul of the *Iliad*, and indeed, at the center of all Greek thought. This "justice dealing divinity" serves to remind those who exercise force that their powers are, in the end, not boundless but limited and subject to chance: "they too will bow their neck in their turn."

What is missing among us, then, (and the reason why Nemesis must play her part) is any shared recognition of a "culture rooted in a common humanity" that would grant human agents a sense of limit and mutuality, and render the world more humane.[6] Weil suggests, however, that a willingness to recognize "the truth of force" (i.e., what the second reading reveals) is not entirely closed to human beings. She characterizes this willingness as a special attitude, "reflection," and writes: "where there is no room for reflection, there is none either for justice or prudence" (*TPF*14). Reflection, the ability to see one's self and one's fellows as all subject to the same irremediable necessity, changes the way one acts. In the sense that Weil uses it in *TPF*, reflection is a miracle, the antidote to the "petrifactive" quality of force. But, as she also notes, "such miracles are rare and of brief duration" (*TPF*27). That Homer lends to his narrative a few "luminous moments" in which the heroes reveal a fleeting reflection only serves to reinforce the overwhelming nature of force's vast kingdom and the rarity of the second reading of force as "the same for all."

Part of Homer's genius, then, is his ability to show how the world of war is itself the protagonist of the epic. The so-called heroes are merely subject to its oscillating power to transform souls either "to the level of inert matter which is pure passivity, or the level of blind force, which is pure momentum" (*TPF*26).

From this discussion of force, we can perhaps gain some sense of Weil's perspective on literature, or at least on the *Iliad*. Most obviously, for her, Homer is more than a poet who vividly captures the reality of an age. She leaves to others, for example, a reading of the epic as constitutive of a shame-culture in which Greek heroes compete for glory in agonal contests. She views literature in general as the embodiment of values (both moral and immoral) that extend over time, and the *Iliad* in particular as the only true epic the Occident possesses, "the purest and loveliest of mirrors" of a universal truth.[7] Without question, philosophical and conceptual entanglements underlie Weil's universalist approach to literature; contemporary literary critics would undoubtedly find her approach terribly *passé*. But I do not wish to pursue her literary theories here. My interest is a rather more political and moral one, and it concerns Weil's specific moral assessment of the "Homeric vision" and its significance for Western society. In "The Great Beast," she gives some hint of her assessment when she writes: "the West has never recovered that incomparably humane accent which makes the *Iliad* and the Greek tragedies unequalled" (*W*1962b:133). And (more cryptically) in her notebooks, she observes: "Acceptance and bitterness. Condition in which beauty emerges. *Iliad*. But why is this so?" (*W*1956b:285). The answer to that question Weil herself provides in *TPF*: the beauty of the epic can be found within the poet himself, in what she calls Homer's "extraordinary sense of equity." This equity serves as the basis for moral engagement in the world, and it is the mark of one who, like Homer, "has measured the dominion of force, and knows how not to respect it" (*TPF*34).

## Recovering What is Humane

If, for Weil, the "empire of force" is the universal truth of the *Iliad*, then Homer's sense of balance, his great impartiality that transcends parochial concerns, is its universal value. In the epic, as she insightfully notes, "One is barely aware that the poet is a Greek and not a Trojan" (*TPF*32). What she finds extraordinary is Homer's capacity for what James Boyd White calls "imaginative disengagement"; the poet achieves a vision that is not possible for either the conqueror or the conquered. To put this in the terms established above, Homer's gift is his ability to reject a social reality in which force is perceived in terms of "strong versus weak" and conceive of a deeper reality in which both Greek and Trojan are recognized as equally human and equally vulnerable before force. Thus, even as Homer gives us particular accounts of contending warriors—of both Hector and Achilles, for example—and has each one come alive in his own moment of agonal struggle, he also moves us outside the struggle, to a prospect where we can see what neither Achilles nor Homer themselves see: their common condition, their "belonging to the same species." As Weil so aptly puts it, "victors and vanquished are brought equally near us; under the same head, both are seen as counterparts of the poet and the listener as well" (*TPF*30).

To make "counterparts" of these oppositions requires, on the poet's part, a deeper conceptualization of humanness than a view that is caught up in a self-interested preoccupation with one's own circumstances. Homer's genius, according to Weil, is his awareness of the death-bearing range of force for all men, not just for those who are immediately at the point of the sword. Accordingly, his gift to the reader is to allow her to experience precisely the sort of "humanized" sympathy denied the actors in the poem, and yet to have her remain aware that the actors themselves are caught in a "first reading"; they do not see the common condition that unites them. Put another way, Homer provides a deeper level of awareness that includes and explains the incompleteness of the first, surface reading. Thus the epic gives us both the experience of immediate events and a perspective that allows us to distinguish the outline of events, and war itself, without delusion. In the latter sense, as Weil says, we "perceive conquered and conquerors simultaneously" and come to understand how "both [are] blinded" (*TPF*33).

What Weil appreciates in Homer, of course, is not merely a literary technique, the mastery of "levels" of reading that move from appearance to a deeper sense of reality. Above all else, the poet's genius is a moral, not a technical one. The second reading wherein victor and vanquished are brought equally near us is not simply a different way of seeing, but a *humane* vision, a right "way-of-being" in the world. In Weil's telling, then, Homer is more than a poet—he is also "the man who does not wear the armor of the lie" (*TPF*36). Likewise, the *Iliad* is a lesson in morality. We must ask, then, what does this morality entail? What does it mean to reject the "armor of the lie?"

*The Poem of Force* does not dwell at length or in an analytical fashion on the nature of the Homeric vision. Weil is generally content to invoke, through her own translations, passages from the epic itself, and to allow them to stand as examples of the poet's "extraordinary equity." She would have us take the meeting between Priam and Achilles as a moment in which Homer brings mortal enemies together and erases their hostility, a "moment of grace":

> But when thirst and hunger have been appeased,
> Then Dardanian Priam fell to admiring Achilles.
> How tall he was, and handsome; he had the face of a god;
> And in his turn Dardanian Priam was admired by Achilles,
> Who watched his handsome face and listened to his words. And when
> they were satisfied with the contemplation of each other . . . (TPF29).

There are a few passages, however, immensely intriguing in part because they are so brief, in which Weil suggests more directly what the Homeric vision means: "Nothing precious is scorned, whether or not death is its destiny; everyone's unhappiness is laid bare without dissimulation or disdain, no man is set above or below the condition common to all men; whatever is destroyed is regretted" (TPF30). The prevailing characteristic of Homeric vision, then, is the equal treatment of all. Or, as White has noted, in the Iliad, "A death is a death, Trojan or Achaean . . . the same language describes the same events" (White 1984:40). The sameness of language—what White calls the "formulaic" tone of the epic—is not, for Weil, notable only as a matter of style. The ability to avoid dissimulation or disdain, to set no one above the condition "common to all," is a special sort of moral capacity. It is a way of comprehending that Iris Murdoch has, in a different context, described as the awareness "that there is more than this" (Hauerwas and MacIntyre 1983:88). In the Iliad, where everyone's unhappiness is equally laid bare, Homer reveals his own recognition "that there is more than this."

As Weil points out, the morality of the epic lies in its impartiality. The poet shows the reader what it means to see through (borrowing again from Murdoch) "the tissue of self-aggrandizing and consoling wishes and dreams which prevents one from seeing what there is outside one" (Hauerwas and MacIntyre 1983:13). This is precisely the point behind Weil's remark that one can hardly tell that Homer is Achaean and not Trojan; there is no hint of bombastic pride or competitive tribal loyalty in the poet's presentation. Indeed, Weil notes, whenever the agonies of war are placed before us, "the enemy's misfortunes are possibly more sharply felt":

> So he fell there, put to sleep in the sleep of bronze
> Unhappy man, far from his wife, defending his own people (TPF30).

The poet even caresses the monuments of the Trojan city, making them an object of "poignant nostalgia" for the fleeing Hector, and thereby for the reader as well:

Close by there stood the great stone tanks
Handsomely built, where silk-gleaming garments
Were washed clean by Troy's lovely daughters and housewives
In the old days of peace, long ago, when the Greeks had not come
Past these did they run their race, pursued and pursuer (*TPF*31).

Because she appreciates Homer's imaginative disengagement, Weil gets us to appreciate, in turn, how remarkable it is that the Trojans live on in Western consciousness as exemplary fallen heroes—noble in defeat. And Troy itself remains a richly symbolic city, remembered for its years of brave resistance against all odds. What is remarkable, however, is not so much the memories themselves—tales of noble heroes and great cities endure in human cultures—but the fact that these heroes and this city are the legacy of a poet who was not Trojan at all. More remarkable still, the poet was an "enemy," a man whose native allegiances might have led him to magnify the greatness of Achilles and dismiss Hector, but for the "there is more than this," which raised in him a consciousness of our "belonging to the same species."

We must be careful here, however, not to conclude that the equal treatment Weil praises in Homer is something like a "levelling disinterestedness" or a "detached neutrality" that denies emotion and stands ouside the world. To the contrary, she finds the *Iliad* absolutely unique in its depth of emotion—in the poet's bitterness "that proceeds from tenderness and that spreads over the whole human race, impartial as sunlight" (*TPF*30). Complementing this bitter tenderness are "justice and love" which "bathe the work in their light without ever becoming noticeable themselves, except as a kind of accent" (*TPF*30). In essence, what distinguishes the epic is not an above-the-battle aloofness, but a passionate involvment that renders the poet's equity even more miraculous. The bitterness, the regret, the justice and love that accent the epic, bear testimony to a moral outlook that neither detachment nor neutrality achieve. The impartiality the *Iliad* reflects—at least as Weil would have it—is born of something quite other than a mere "refusal to take sides," or a commitment to neutrality, or a willingness to "referee." More exactly, the condition common to all that Homer perceives emerges from a tenderness that extends *to* all, and from a love of humanity intensified by the poet's bitter awareness of human mortality and the dominion of force. Reflecting similarly upon the epic, John Cowper Powys observes Homer's love of human things as both all-encompassing and attentive to minute detail:

the "secret" of Homer is indeed the isolation of, and the poetic deepening of our consciousness of, those recurrent situations, necessities, significant human gestures, in the span of any ordinary life that . . . have been repeated since the beginning. What the Homeric way of thought delivers us from is the accursed habit of taking the essentials of life for granted which cheapens, debases, and vulgarises all (Taplin 1986:39).

And George Steiner has written, "[the Homeric world] is the affirmation that life is, of itself, a thing of beauty, that the works and days of men are worth recording, and that no catastrophe—not even the burning of Troy . . . is ultimate" (Taplin 1986:42). Weil, I think, is not convinced of the latter point; her vision of force is to desolate to allow for too temperate a view of human catastrophes. But, with Powys and Steiner, she would have us consider the poet's interweaving of "celestial moments" of human experience amidst the "monotonous desolation" of combat. Homer's regret that men are "capable of being so transfcrmed" is made possible by what he knows they can also be; hence we find, as Weil relates, that "there is hardly any form of pure love known to humanity, of which the *Iliad* does not treat" (*TPF*27). Drawing upon Powys' insight that the *Iliad* is a "poetic deepening of our consciousness," we might add that, for Weil, the epic offers us an example of what it means to be fully human and humane; it is, itself, an act of justice, and embodiment of truth, and a rejection of force.

Weil's reading of the *Iliad* is likely to meet with resistance from those who would view Homer's epic as a narrative of mighty deeds, aggression, glory, and revenge. Of course, she acknowledges that these "Homeric values" inhabit the poem, but to remain fixed on them is to be blind to the poet's true gift. That is, if we read the epic only as a tribute to the "masculine warrior hero" or as a saga of swords, shields, and chariots, we are not reading deeply enough. The purpose of *TPF* is to have us shift our sights, with Homer, and see not the warrior as hero but the true hero, force, and not the glory of agonal contest, but its terrible annihilation of human beings and human things. Most of all, Weil implies, to read the *Iliad* only as a cultural artifact of pre-Socratic Greece is to deny oneself the moral vision, the "poetic deepening of consciousness" the epic would have us experience. Simone Pétrement is correct—what Weil attempts in her meditation upon the *Iliad* is the construction of a powerful and original psychology. But this psychology (Pétrement's views notwithstanding) has a political purpose as well. At the least, we cannot forget when and where it was written. *The Poem of Force* is a lesson in political morality for a nation newly vanquished, and for a world at war. Its great achievement is that, like the *Iliad* itself, it transcends the temptation to play to force, even though it acknowledges its pervasiveness. It also refuses to villify the enemy or kindle the fires of false hope and revenge, even as it captures the evil of war with its spiritual and physical destruction of millions of human beings. What it does, through Homer, is attempt to instill, or give voice to, a special sort of political disposition. To put this disposition generally: only in the refusal of the will to force and in an awareness of the equal humanity of all, lie a peoples' hope for preserving and protecting those human treasures which, as Weil says elsewhere, "warm and nourish the soul and without which, short of sainthood, a *human* life is not possible" (W1952b:133). This is the truth—the deeper reading—she would have the French and indeed, all of Europe, achieve even amidst the empire of force. She ends her reflections equivocally; yet she calls us back to the fundamental and unmatched truths of Homer's *Iliad*:

> perhaps [the peoples of Europe] will yet rediscover the epic genius, when they learn that there is no refuge from fate, learn not to admire force, not to hate the enemy, nor to scorn the unfortunate. How soon this will happen is another question (*TPF*37).

I began this chapter by suggesting that *TPF* does not, as some commentators would have it, signify a radical shift in Simone Weil's thinking or a rejection of her earlier ideas. Insofar as certain themes of previous interest to her reappear in her "postconversion" writings, we cannot readily conclude that a decisive break in her thinking occurred around 1938. We especially run the risk of misunderstanding if we accept an "early political" versus "late spiritual" orientation in her thought. Nevertheless, I think it is possible to speak of a "renaissance" in Weil's thinking, and to locate it within the period she wrote *TPF*. Taken literally, the renaissance marks the rebirth or reprise of an idea that had always been a part of her outlook, but one she had not intellectually pursued, or perhaps even consciously articulated for herself in her more materialist essays.[8] At the center of this idea is the faculty that was, as we have seen, so decisive in alleviating her adolescent breakdown: attention.

Put simply, for Weil the theorist, attention is the *sine qua non* of human goodness, the ability to read through appearances and penetrate first impressions and thereby achieve a deeper insight on things and events in the world. Although she does not call it this in *TPF*, attention is what Homer achieves and the *Iliad* embodies; it is what Weil goes on to explore in a variety of essays and her notebooks as the essence of moral agency. As we shall see, attention is quite distinct from methodical thinking, the faculty that she linked to liberty in *RLO*. In fact, one of the most striking aspects of this renaissance in Weil's writing has to do with her changed perspective on what it means to "be" in the world, and on the nature of human dignity. In her post-conversion writings, she seems to abandon the instrumentalist perspective of the *RLO* for a more expressly moral conception of personhood and human agency. And if in the *RLO* her ultimate concern is for the achievement of liberty as a certain kind of individual rationality in labor, then in *TPF* and beyond she seems drawn to a different sort of liberation, one tied to the character of moral judgment and the recognition of others.

Weil's preoccupation with attention is usually associated with the "spiritual turn" in her thought and, accordingly, with a move away from the political. But, as I will argue in what follows, attention assumes various dimensions or levels of applicability in her writings, not all of which are "otherworldly," or, as some critics would have it, "antipolitical." We might proceed, then, by way of introduction, to sketch an outline of this faculty or "power" Weil thinks all humans possess, and see if we can determine what she means when she calls attention "a method for the exercise of intelligence, which consists of looking" (W1952a:109).

## The Faculty of Attention

Ironically, perhaps, but not inappropriately, we can find in Simone Weil's work the same spirit she attributes to the *Iliad*—a "monotonous desolation" seems to weigh upon it, except for a few "luminous moments" that make her vision possible for the soul to bear. The "luminosity" of the *RLO*, for instance, takes form in her conception of liberty as the counter to the oppression of the blind collectivity, and in her notion of methodical thinking as a way of escape from the domain of "unrelenting necessity." In her later work, where necessity continues to preoccupy her, there is also a luminous quality to the faculty of attention, which Weil presents as an antidote to force. Attention reveals humans to be neither the mere objects of natural forces, nor wholly bound by necessity; we may be subjected to the mechanical universe, but we are also capable of pressing against it, of being other than what force would make of us. Much of Weil's writing during these years can be understood as a pedagogical attempt to bring attention to light in an increasingly bleak world dominated by force. She makes this point in her *Notebooks*, where she writes: "There are two ways of changing for other people the way in which they read sensations, their relationship to the universe: force (that kind of which the extreme form is war) and education. They are two actions exercised over the imagination" (W1956b:24). What she would educate us in, by exercising our imaginations, is the faculty of attention; what she would thereby have us challenge is the pervasive empire of force.

We might begin a more detailed consideration of attention by looking to what J.L. Austin calls the "trailing clouds of etymology" all concepts leave behind them. The root of the French *attention* is the Latin *ad tendere*, meaning literally, "to stretch toward," or, less literally, "to give heed or consider," as when we "pay attention" to a person, an event, or a thing. In both of the latter senses, there is the idea of mental "preparedness" or concentration, as well as an act of observation that moves well beyond one's immediate self. Our English cognate includes a further dimension, that of "caring for," as when one gives "attention" to the ills or difficulties of another. Hence we might say that attention might involve both an attitude of mental preparedness toward others and a concern for others. There is also, of course, the imperative form we associate with the military command "Attention!" which expects a "preparedness," but only of a physical kind, in the military sense. In the latter, there is none of the comprehension or mental engagement we associate with "paying attention" or "giving attention" to a person or problem or thing. In fact, in the military sense "attention" means that one must stand rigidly erect, stare ahead, and not think or engage with others at all.

There is yet another dimension to attention however, one that the English word does not capture as precisely as does the French cognate *attendre*. *Attendre* means, literally, "to wait for," but also "to expect," and, more passionately, "to long for." In varying degrees, each of these usages captures a passive state, or at least a condition of suspended readiness. The quiescent quality to which the verb *attendre* gives rise is perhaps the most vital aspect of Weil's conception of attention; but traces of the other etymological features—mental preparedness, release from the self, an orientation of "care," a suspension of thought processes (or at least of "calculating" thought processes), an expectation—can be found in her conception as well. Given all of these etymological clues, we might say that, for Weil, attention is a quality of openness to the world, a quiescent readiness toward the "out there," without any solid expectation of what one will find. To be attentive is not to "pursue," but "to wait." In her *Notebooks*, she remarks:

> The heat of the chase. We must not want to find: as in the case of excessive devotion, we become dependent on the object of our efforts. . . . It is only effort without desire (not attached to any object) which infallibly contains a reward. . . . By pulling at the bunch, we make all the grapes fall to the ground (W1952a:106).

At best, however, etymology can take us only part way toward understanding what Weil means by attention. Even if we supplement our etymological inquiry with passages from her *Notebooks*, we are likely to remain puzzled about the state of being attention is meant to capture. As intriguing as they are, Weil's remarks in the *Notebooks* are at most allusive, sometimes cryptic and confusing—if we are not to "pull" at the grapes, then what should our attention make of them? Fortunately, she does not leave us entirely in the dark on these matters. In an essay entitled "Reflections on the Right Use of School Studies with a View Toward the Love of God," (SS1951b:105–15) written in Marseilles in 1942, Weil addresses the notion of attention more systematically, and pursues the link between attention and education. "Although people seem to be unaware of it today," she writes, "the development of the faculty of attention forms the real object and almost the sole interest of studies" (SS 105). On this remark she builds her commentary.

The essay on school studies is addressed to the young who, while still uncorrupted in thought, might learn to do more than "contract their brows, hold their breath, stiffen their muscles" and think that this means they are paying attention (SS109). (Clearly, then, the *military* "Attention!" is not what she has in mind.) The "great treasure" of academic work lies not in this exercise of sheer physicality that makes us "set our teeth," but rather, Weil argues, in the experience of contemplating, "attentively and slowly" with an intelligence that "grows and bears fruit in joy" (SS110). She acknowledges that there is an intrinsic interest and a value to any given sort of study, but she also says that love of a subject matter is secondary. What truly counts is the faculty all studies, when pursued in the right way, develop and bring to light, and not simply the subject-matter as such. This rather unusual pedagogical view leads Weil to say some rather unorthodox things: "Students must . . . work without any wish to gain good marks, or to pass examinations, to win school successes" (SS108).[9] Focusing more particularly, she notes: "There is a way of giving our attention to the data of a problem in geometry without trying to find the solution, or to the words of a Latin or Greek text without trying to arrive at the meaning" (SS113). On this account, attention apparently has little to do with reaching an answer or achieving any conventional kind of academic success. And it surely does not seem to involve the sort of methodical thinking Weil earlier elevated as the means toward a particular end. If the exercise in geometry leads to no solution it is not necessarily a failure; if one has paid attention, a different but even more valuable sort of progress accompanies one's study. Or, to put this otherwise, light may suffuse the soul, even as we struggle unsuccessfully with a problem or a text. Thus, "the useless efforts made by the Curé d'Ars, for long and painful years, in his attempt to learn Latin bore fruit in the marvelous discernment that enabled him to see the very soul of his penitents" (SS108). For Weil, what is important is the idea that the Curé's power of attention emanated from his studies. He did not seek to become attentive and then employ his studies to that end. Attention, she suggests, emerges almost in spite of ourselves—it is a power that thrives on our own unselfconsciousness about its presence, and directs us outward.

So what, then, does attention require? Weil answer this question explicitly:

Attention consists of suspending our thought, leaving it detached, empty, and ready to be penetrated by the object; it means holding in our minds, within reach of this thought, but on a lower level and not in contact with it, the diverse knowledge we have acquired which we are forced to make use of. Our thought should be in relation to all particular and already formulated thoughts, as a man on a mountain who, as he looks forward, sees also below him, without actually looking at them, a great many forests and plains. Above all our thought should be empty, waiting, not seeking anything (*SS*111–12).

From this passage, it appears that the primary attribute of attention is something like a contemplative awareness that is quite distinct from such diverse mental processes as cognition, calculation, judgment, and introspection, but also from the reasoned emotion of compassion, imagination, empathy, and concern. In this formulation, at least, Weil seems most intent upon emphasizing the quiescent readiness attention captures, rather than a "caring for others," mental concentration, or knowledge *per se*. Neither reason nor emotion seem to play dominant roles here; it is as though attention is rather more like a form of "willing" or perhaps a "willingness not to will" but rather to receive. She emphasizes a meditative stillness and an expectation that is directed toward nothing, but open to "the all." Openness seems primary. When one is attentive, Weil observes in her philosophy lectures, "one's consciousness is open to illumination" (*W*1978:92). She also draws an analogy between attention and artistic creation: "An artist creates a state of silence for himself and so the soul's forces are marshalled together but he is not responsible for the inspiration itself" (*W*1978:205–6). Like the artist through his art, school children through their studies might learn to open themselves to a silence of the soul and wait, and so become familiar with a special sort of looking. "Whoever goes through years of study without developing this attention within himself," Weil writes, "has lost a great treasure" (*SS*114).

She leaves no doubt, however, about the difficulty involved in developing this power. Attention requires an enormous effort, and it has its own attributes. Both a quiet suspension and an alertness are required; one cannot be tired and also "wait." Attention also demands an unselfconsciousness about itself as a given state: "when one gives all one's attention to something one is not aware that one is doing it." And she quotes Descartes: "It is one thing to be conscious, quite another to be conscious that one is" (*W*1978:95). Perhaps one reason why Weil finds school studies so important is that they make the unselfconscious state so necessary to attention easier to achieve. They are a little like "training wheels" that the novice (or "apprentice") can use as he or she works toward full attentive power. Weil implies as much when she says that school exercises develop a "lower" kind of attention, but nevertheless are "extremely effective" (SS105). With sufficient practice, it seems, one can become attentive without the mediation of studies. All of this demands great effort, however; attention is not a "natural" state. "Something in our soul has a far more violent repugnance for true attention," Weil observes, "than the flesh has for bodily fatigue" (SS111).

I have now suggested that attention has a number of predominant features: it is contemplative without being self-conscious, a waiting rather than a searching for, a quiescent openness to illumination, a certain kind of silence, a will-not-to-will. In all of these respects, attention recalls the *vita contemplativa* revered by so many ancients and moderns alike—Plato's *thaumazein*, Augustine's "soul set free," the "openness to the all" exalted by St. John of the Cross, Bergson's "l'âme ouverte," Heidegger's "releasement" or *Gelassenheit*. Without doubt, this defense of attention is a blow struck for a particular kind of moral agency in the political as well as the personal realm. One scholar, noting the prevailing winds of existentialism and neo-Marxism in the European intellectual atmosphere of the early 1940s, has called Weil's writing on these matters" a magnificent vindication of the contemplative spirit" (Frenaud 1953). But we are also entitled to ask: what does this "spirit"— this state of suspended thought—bring? What is its reward? If in the *RLO* methodical thinking was the source of liberty, then what does Weil's newly vindicated faculty of attention promise?

Given the strikingly opposed characters of the calculating, purposive, instrumental mentality Weil defends in the *RLO* and the contemplative quiescence she turns to in her later work, we might expect that the reward of attention would be exceedingly different from those of methodical thinking as well. The fisherman who thinks methodically and struggles against high seas in his little boat surely has little in common with the "man on the mountain" whose attentive gaze receives the landscape that encloses him. The fisherman realizes his freedom in challenging and overcoming necessity; the mountaineer's purpose is not to challenge anything at all, but simply "to wait." Despite these distinctive differences, however, Weil's fisherman and mountaineer do share something in common; or perhaps it is more accurate to say that despite her turn from methodical thinking to attention, Weil continues to address an existential problem that preoccupied her in the *RLO*. The problem concerns how human beings might "come to grips" with reality and render that which is "impenetrably obscure" transparent and open to the understanding.

As we have seen, in the *RLO*, these impenetrable obscurities took form in the collectivity, in automatic techniques, technological processes, mechanized labor, and the logical relation of hardened symbols and significations. Methodical thinking was the faculty that allowed these impenetrables to be brought under the control of the mind and made the subject of purposive human action. In her later writings, Weil's preoccupation with freeing the mind from the weight of rigidified signs, symbols, images, and abstractions persists. She muses in her *Notebooks*, "It is not so much that things make us believe that they are real, for in a sense they are real. But they make us believe they are real otherwise than as they actually are" (W1956b:59). Only now a different sort of faculty promises release from false appearances, and a different perception of the problem informs her analysis. No longer does she enlist the language of oppression and liberty, or rely upon a materialist analysis of technology to explain the opaque and seemingly enigmatic condition of contemporary life. Indeed, after 1938, Weil seems far less concerned with causal explanations of the contemporary condition than with what it means to be both trapped within and unable to pierce through the illusions, the deceptions, and the unexamined assumptions of our prevailing beliefs. Or, as she puts it in metaphor: "Others. To see each human being (an image of oneself) as a prison in which a prisoner dwells, surrounded by the whole universe" (W1952a:121).

In her later work, Weil addresses the problem of how we might escape from the "prisons" in which we dwell. In a hermeneutical language that stresses the notion of "reading" (*lecture*), she describes the world as "layers" of meaning. Escape from our self-contained prisons requires the capacity to "read through" the meanings we impose on the world, toward a clearer, more comprehensive vision. This better, deeper, reading of the world is what attention brings—to see things "as they actually are" is its reward. Thus attention is a preparatory state for *lecture*, for "reading reality."

As we might expect, Weil does not treat the relationship between attention and *lecture* in any systematic fashion. But in a number of essays and in her notebooks she alludes to the connection between the two, and we can draw some insights from what she says. In her "Essai sur la notion de lecture" (W1946a), she argues that the world itself is not unlike a text that bears within it certain "significations." And just as we are "seized" by the meanings we read (say, in a letter or a book), so in every instant of our lives we are seized by the meanings we read in appearances. The world, in other words, is a "tissue of meanings"— "The sky, the sea, the sun, the stars, other human beings, everything that surrounds us is nothing more than something we read" (W1946a:15). Some of these readings we fix upon, Weil notes, and others we reduce to phantoms. A passage in her *Notebooks* puts this idea in another way:

> *Reading.* All we are ever given (in a sense) is sensations, and whatever we may do about it we can never, never, think anything else (in a sense) but

sensations. But we can never actually think sensations, we read through them, as through a medium. What do we read? Not just anything at all, according to inclination. Nor, of course, something which does not depend in any way whatever on ourselves.
The world is a text containing several meanings, and we pass from one meaning to another by an effort—an effort in which the body always participates, just as when we are learning the alphabet of a foreign language this alphabet has got to enter into our hand by dint of forming the characters.
Apart from that, any change in the manner of thinking is illusory (W1956b:23).[10]

Weil's concept of *lecture*, as should be obvious from the above, challenges the notions that sensory experience is fixed and neutral and that there is a "given" world subject to various interpretations. Rather, she wants to suggest that the world is a medium for our interpretations or "readings," and that the search for what philosophers of science call an "observation-language" is a misguided task, one that ignores, among other things, the historical character of our epistemological and scientific presuppositions.[11] This is not the issue she develops most fully however. What she seems to be more concerned with, in both her notebooks and her essays, is what she refers to above as the "effort" it requires to pass from one meaning to another in our reading of the world-as-text. The effort entails a "method," but it is not a ratiocinative one like "method-ical thinking." She indicates this when she writes: "A method is necessary for the understanding of images, symbols, etc. One should not try to interpret them, but contemplate them until their significance flashes upon one . . . finally what is illusory is dissipated, and what is real appears" (W1956b:334). What is at stake in passing through layers of meaning, then, is adopting a certain way of being (both physical and mental) that will open one up to experiencing "the immediately given" in a different way. Weil describes that way of being as a stillness that allows for the light to dawn. With this, she brings us back to attention; for when we are attentive we pierce through layers of meaning and thereby attain even deeper, clearer insights or "a change of level" on the world. Accordingly, Weil argues, we (like Homer) can challenge the dominion of force. Attention serves as an antidote to force because it allows us to pass through the brute readings impressed upon us by our unexamined perceptions and by the pull of "the collectivity." She comments: "Reading—except where there is a certain quality of atten-tion—obeys the law of gravity. . . . With a higher quality of attention our reading discovers gravity itself and various systems of possible balance" (W1952a:122).
If attention's reward is a "fuller comprehension," then in what form or forms does this comprehension emerge? In other words, what sorts

of activities or practices does Weil think attention enhances? What does it bring into "possible balance"? From what we have seen, it appears that attention does not necessarily enhance our studies (if by that we mean a comprehension of subject matter, expertise, or good grades). Nor does it (unlike methodical thought) seem to emancipate labor, enable us to coordinate means and ends, or add in any discernible manner to our store of practical knowledge. Despite these qualifications, however, Weil does not suggest that we view attention in isolation from particular relations or practices. If it makes us hospitable to "reading through appearances," then it must be connected to particular things that we read. In *SS* she acknowledges this to be the case, and suggests that attention is the "substance" of at least two human orientations: an orientation toward God, on the one hand, and toward "neighbor" on the other. These two orientations, the theological and the moral, form the central core of her writings between 1940 and 1942.

## Notes

1. The essay, written after the occupation of Paris, was initially intended for the *Nouvelle Revue Française*, but government censors would not allow it to appear there.

2. See, among others, Rees (1959), Pierce (1966), and Oates (1977). Hellman (1982:17) supports the argument of Dujardin (1975) and notes: "A scholarly study of her 'ideology and politics' concluded that the most coherent period of her life, politically speaking, was brief: from the end of 1928 . . . and her beginning factory work in December 1934 and her period of political militancy was only from 1931–1934. Thus in an important way Simone Weil had "outgrown" politics at 25." Even more assuredly, Oates asserts: "When Weil turns away from politics and the classics . . . stimulated by a conversion experience that seems to have begun in 1937 when she was 28, [she] begins to write about spiritual matters [and] floats off into a void of sheer vaporous rhetoric" (1977:34). Even in the narrow sense of politics as public "activism" neither of these views seem persuasive to me, much less in the broader sense of "politics" as that which concerns, among other things, matters of citizenship, community, justice, rights, and moral agency. Weil continues to reflect upon all of these issues, and others, in her writings after 1937. The inability of most critics to acknowledge her continuing politicalness may have something to do with our contemporary reluctance to see any compatibility between the spiritual and the political. Thus, it seems, wherever one appears predominant, the other must not exist. As I will argue more fully in Chapter 8, one of the great contributions of Weil's thought is her attempt to render these two perspectives—the spiritual and the political—compatible in the modern age.

3. Her other essays on literary texts include: "Antigone," (1957b:18–23); "Prometheus," (1957b:60–73); and "Symposium" (1957b:106–32).

4. Also, see her article "Ne Recommençons pas la guerre de Troie," (W1960) published in April, 1937. There Weil uses the Trojan War and Homer's Greece as the starting point for her reflections on the threat of war in Europe. This

essay should give pause to those who find her future meditations on the *Iliad* "spiritual" or "literary" but not in any way political.

5. A slightly different rendition of force occurs in the *RLO*, however. There she says: "What needs to be understood above all is not the manner in which use is made of some particular force, but its very nature, which determines whether it is oppressive or not" (W1973:63).

6. The phrase "culture rooted in a common humanity" comes from James Boyd White, who offers a treatment of the *Iliad* in *When Words Lose Their Meaning* (1984) that is sympathetic to Weil's own sentiments in *TPF*.

7. See also Weil's essays "The Responsibility of Writers" (Panichas 1977:186–89) and "Morality and Literature" (Panichas 1977:290–95) for a more general and extended treatment of the meaning and value of literary texts.

8. In her lectures on philosophy, presented at the girls' lycée in Roanne between 1933–34, Weil addresses both methodical reasoning and attention, but it is the former, which she associates with "ordering our actions" and overcoming necessity, that she pursues in the *RLO*. The latter, which Weil describes as "what above all distinguishes man from animals" (1978:205) is not even mentioned in the *RLO*, but only returned to later, after 1938. Hence my suggestion that there is something like a "renaissance" in her thought, a return to an earlier "impulse" that had not previously been thoroughly explored.

9. Weil was apparently true to this principle in her own teaching at the girls' lycées; her courses did not seem to stress the accumulation of facts and information that passes for learning—and as a result her students rarely did very well on the French state examinations.

10. In an attenuated but still relevant sense Weil's reflections are clearly akin to a number of arguments found in contemporary philosophy of science, particularly in the writings of Thomas Kuhn (1962) and Norwood Russell Hanson (1958). Hanson argues that the problem for science is not how to understand "brute sensations" (or "sense-data," as Russell would have it) but rather, given that all scientific sensations are interpreted, how to understand our interpretations. The problem, as Hanson neatly puts it, is that "there is more to seeing than meets the eyeball" (1958:7). And as Kuhn notes, "What a man sees depends both upon what he looks at and also upon what his previous visual-conceptual experience has taught him to see" (1962:113). We might conceive of Weil's conception of *lecture* as the practice through which the individual becomes aware of his or her own "visual-conceptual experience" and of the world itself as a tissue of such experiences, rather than as a fixed set of objects that are simply interpreted differently by different persons. Drawing even further upon Kuhn's language of paradigm change, we might understand Weil's concept of attention as a mental state hospitable to a paradigmatic shift in vision; it allows for the same sort of "lightning flash" or "scales falling from the eyes" that Kuhn notes scientists often experience and cannot fully articulate in the language of perceptual observation or scientific discovery. Since my primary concern in Chapter 6 is to show how Weil applies the "shift of vision" attention for and *lecture* induces to questions of theology and moral agency, I cannot engage these issues more elaborately here. Nevertheless, it would be interesting to explore further the way in which attention and *lecture* inform Weil's analysis of contemporary science in "Classical Science and After" (1968:3–43), which predates and in many ways resembles Kuhn's.

11. She articulates this idea most clearly in her essay "Classical Science and After," (1968:3–43), but without any direct references to her hermeneutics of *lecture*.

# 6

# Between the Human and the Divine

ONE OF THE MOST difficult struggles of Simone Weil's later life, following her conversion experiences in Solesmes, was the clarification of her position in relation to the Roman Catholic Church. Her hesitations concerning baptism were fueled by her reluctance to accept membership in an organized chuch with a history, as she puts it, of "the most appalling cruelties" and a missionary zeal "accompanied by guns and battleships" (1953:31–33). Even more deeply, however, Weil's reluctance to join the Church was symptomatic of her abiding ambivalence about all manner of human collectivities, worldly engagements, and ideologies. The occasion of her struggle with Catholicism, particularly between 1940 and 1942, simply reintroduced the same sort of tension she experienced in the mid-1930s regarding her political engagement in the trade-union movement and, even more dramatically, in the Spanish Civil War. Only now she found herself torn between a religious, mystical impulse toward exile from all organizations, and the world itself, and a relentless urge to continue to "rub shoulders with politics" and earthly things. As Daniel Berrigan has noted:

[Weil] seemed to have had, . . . in the midst of her wish to transcend herself and to adore God this other sense of plunging into history and into mankind. Her whole spirit was distended grievously, between these two realities, the reality of God and the reality of human suffering and human death; and she took part in both, embracing both (Berrigan and Coles 1970:141).

Weil herself was not unaware of the "distended" nature of her spirit. In a series of letters written in 1942 to her friend Father Perrin, the Catholic priest, she expresses some deeply conflicting views. Exploring the possibilities of joining the Church, she notes her hesitations about separating herself from "the immense and unfortunate multitude of unbelievers" and adds: "I have the essential need, and I think I can say the vocation, to move among men of every class and complexion, mixing with them and sharing their life and outlook" (W1951b:48). But a short time later in another letter she amends her views on mixing "with the paste of common humanity" and tells Perrin, "I do not want to be adopted into a circle, to live among people who say "we" and to be part of an "us," to find I am "at home" in any human *milieu* whatever it may be. . . . I feel that it is necessary and ordained that I should be alone, a stranger and exile in relation to every human circle without exception" (W1951b:54). Recalling her previous sentiments, she acknowledges the latter view might seem "to contradict" the former, then she adds: "I do not know if I have succeeded making you understand these almost inexpressible things" (W1951b:55).

In essence, the rest of Weil's life's work can perhaps be understood as an attempt to express "the inexpressible" and to give meaning to the persistent "pull" between the human and the divine, or worldliness and exile, that envelopes her. From 1940 until her death, her writings can be viewed as a series of dramatic oscillations between a mystical renunciation of the world, evident in her writings on the love of God, affliction, decreation, and death, and a political commitment to it, revealed in her essays on affliction and the love of neighbor, human personality, justice, and earthly "roots." Before we turn to these writings in detail, however, I think it is important to illuminate more fully the nature of the tension between the human and the divine in Weil's thought. What I want to reiterate is a claim that has, from the start, framed my perspective on her work and challenged the conventional view of her writings as "early political" and "late spiritual." In brief, the claim is this: I think we can most fruitfully interpret Weil's work as constantly beset by a tension between the political and the spiritual and also characterized by an almost palpable sense of urgency to reconcile the two. Let us now consider the theoretical bases of this tension in more explicit detail.

## For Plato

If one looks closely at the existing scholarly treatments of Weil, it is almost immediately apparent that her commentators fall into two discrete groups, informed by the "conventional view" mentioned above. There are those (many) who study her spiritual, Christian ideas—or what Gertrude Blumenthal has called her "way of the Cross" (1952:225).[1] There are also those (few) who address the political ideas she formulates, primarily in the *RLO* and in her various critiques of orthodox Marxism.[2] At first glance, this division of labor seems reasonable, for as I noted in Chapter 5, Weil's treatment of central problems and concepts shifts decisively in tone and approach between 1934 and 1938. As Blum quite correctly observes, in reference to Weil's materialism:

> [in this later turn to Christianity] a notion of materialism understood as the conception of . . . society in terms of force is combined with an entire absence of any systematic notion . . . that once we understand the real structural causes of oppression we can work toward changing them (Blum and Seidler 1987:125).

One does not have to read very far in the later writings to see that not only is there an absence of any sort of materialist social analysis in Weil's thinking, but there is also a marked hostility to "society" and the "social order" in general. In her notebooks, for example, she writes: "The social order is irreducibly that of the prince of this world. Our only duty with regard to the social is to try to limit the evil of it" (W1952a:145). Even more decisively, she argues: "Man is a social animal and the social element represents evil. . . . The world is uninhabitable. That is why we have to flee to the next. But the door is shut. What a lot of knocking is required before it opens! . . . to be able to enter in . . . one has to cease to be a social being" (W1956b:466).

This decidedly pessimistic view of society is further bolstered in Weil's later writing by her adaptation of Plato's conception of the "Great Beast" to a Christian perspective: "The essential idea in Plato—which is also that of Christianity . . .—is that man cannot escape being wholly enslaved to the beast, even down to the innermost recesses of his soul, except insofar as he is freed by the supernatural operation of grace" (W1973:165). Two things should command our attention here, and serve to emphasize the distance Weil has travelled from her "magnum opus" on oppression and liberty.

First, it seems, she has traded Marx for Plato. No longer convinced of the usefulness of (even a revised) Marxian materialism as a way of analyzing oppression and moving toward liberty, she contends that the Great Beast—force, gravity, necessity, the collectivity, "the Devil disguised"—rules this world. Furthermore, humans are "weak enough to worship" it (W1973:165). Indeed, Weil is now willing to subsume all of Marx into this single Platonic insight: "*The Great Beast of Plato.* The whole of Marxism, insofar as it is true, is contained in the page of Plato on the Great Beast; and its refutation is there too" (W1952a:147). In two lines, she reinterprets her project in *RLO* in terms of a Platonic and Christian vision rooted in a notion of evil in the world.

The shift from Marx to Plato notwithstanding, we might initially be inclined to find some familiar sentiments in this Hellenic-Christian version of Weil's social critique. What else is the Great Beast but "the collectivity" of the *RLO* in a different guise and perhaps more morally constituted language? And how different is her notion of "limiting the evil" of the social order from her observation in her "magnum opus" that we can never entirely escape, but we can perhaps lessen, the servitude that is our "natural condition?" Her further notation, "Society is the cave. The way out is solitude" (W1952a:145) might even call up the idea of the methodical thinker who struggles against the twin dangers of necessity and chance in an effort to gain liberty.

As a closer look at the context of Weil's critique reveals, however, these similarities do not capture the full meaning of her mystical thinking. And here a second point should command our attention. To escape our enslavement to the Great Beast, she writes, we must turn to "supernatural" grace or, to follow her earlier metaphor, to the "door" that is tightly shut. Not only has Plato displaced Marx, but "grace" has displaced methodical thinking, and "movement toward the next world" has displaced liberty in this one. These displacements are interrelated. Weil argues that like Plato, Marx sought justice, truth, and moral value, but he looked toward the wrong place when he expected to see a "non-poisoned society" emerge in *this* world. Since society is irremediably tainted by force and can never "eliminate its own toxins," no mind that fixes upon it can achieve truth and justice (W1973:156–57). Hence, she notes:

> The true road exists. Plato and many others have followed it. But it is open only to those who, recognizing themselves to be incapable of finding it, give up looking for it, and yet do not cease to desire it to the exclusion of everything else. To these it is given to feed on a good which, being situated outside this world, is not subject to any social influence whatever. It is the transcendental bread mentioned in the original text of the Lord's Prayer (W1973:157).

The gift that Plato (and, for Weil, almost all of the ancient Greeks except Aristotle) offers is the key to a spiritual transcendence of the earthly realm, to being situated "outside" the world.[3] This Pre-Socratic and Platonic predisposition leads Weil to say some very odd things, as, for example in her notebooks: "Civilization of the Greeks. No adoration of force. The temporal was only a bridge" (W1952a:134). No one who has read Thucydides (as of course Weil had) could take this very seriously. But Weil's deeper insight, drawn largely from her careful meditations upon Plato's dialogues, concerns something else—the orientation toward truth, beauty, the divine, and the contemplative spirit, which the Greeks revered and Christianity pursued.[4]

In keeping with her respect for the idea of the temporal as only a "bridge," Weil observes that the "perfectly pure and luminous core" in Plato's work is his recognition of might as an "absolutely sovereign thing," and at the same time absolutely "detestable" (W1957b:116). The grandeur of Plato's thinking lies in his realization that the divine alone escapes contact with might, but that "men who have transported and hidden a part of their souls" in the divine may also partly escape it (W1957b: 116). The key to this transport of the soul is contemplation of beauty and the Good:

> Plato says that he who contemplates beauty itself has almost reached the goal, which indicates that there is still something else. In the myth of the cave, the object of contemplation immediately before the sun, is the moon . . . The sun being the good, it is natural to suppose that the moon is the beautiful. In saying that he who as attained to beauty has almost arrived, Plato suggests that the supreme beauty is the Son of God (W1957b:145–46).

In a series of essays on the *Symposium, Republic, Timaeus,* and the Pythagorian doctrine, Weil stresses the "truth" of the Platonic doctrine in terms of the rejection of earthly illusion and a Christian love of God. To escape from the errors imposed by the Great Beast, she argues, one must choose to carry one's heart beyond space and beyond the world, to God (W1957b:134). This is the meaning of the parable of the Cave and of the other powerful images of the sun and the line that Plato presents in the *Republic.* For Weil, then, the dialogues themselves are to be understood as vindications of the contemplative spirit, and Plato himself as the paradigmatic example of a soul directed toward God. Her failure to read any of the Platonic dialogues—especially the *Republic*—in a more explicitly political light, is merely one more indication of the extent to which Weil takes flight from the "social order" in these writings. The "political Plato" who wrestles with the relationship between the soul and the state, the virtuousness of the citizen, the harmony of the social order, and the degeneration of earthly polities does not feature at all in her analyses. Indeed, in what will become a predominant (and shifting) metaphor in her thought, Weil suggests we understand Plato as "rooted" not in this world, in the political, but rather in the heavenly. Accordingly we might understand the "sovereignty of the soul," which Plato expressed in the *Timaeus* as:

> that part which we say dwells in the summit of our body and lifts us from earth toward our celestial affinity, like a plant whose roots are not in the earth, but in the heavens . . . for it is to the heavens . . . that the divine part attaches the . . . root of us. (Plato 1959:90a–b).

The tragedy of the modern world, as Weil sees it, is that these "divine roots," or in her other metaphor, the "bridges" to the divine—so much a part of Greek philosophy, science, and drama—are nearly lost. "The bridges of the Greeks," she muses:

> We have inherited them but we do not know how to use them. We have thought they were intended to have houses built upon them. We have erected skyscrapers on them to which we ceaselessly add storeys [sic]. We

no longer know that they are bridges, things made so that we may pass along them, as by passing along them we go towards God (W1952a:132–33).

Although this comment appears only as an allusion in her notebooks, in other writings during this period we can gain a more explicit idea of what Weil means by the "skyscrapers" we have erected on the bridges of the Greeks. These structures are the manifestation of the Great Beast—the symbolic, scientific, political, social, philosophical, and ideological creations of a civilization that lives in "the cave." "We are offered nothing but lies," Weil says, "we think we perceive ourselves but all we see is our shadow. . . . All we see is the shadow of the artificial" (W1968:108). What is artificial is humanity's (modern) presumption of its own sovereignty, not the "sovereignty of the soul" but the sovereignty of the self to know and control the universe. In philosophy, this presumption is betrayed in the elevation of "man" as the source and measure of all things, and in the removal, as Arendt has put it, "of the Archimedean point into man himself" (Arendt 1958:281). In classical (Newtonian) science, the presumption is found in the aspiration toward "powers analogous to those which a man can effectively acquire over himself" and to the construction of, in Weil's words, "a closed, limited, and precisely defined universe" (W1968:21,31–32). In religion, the presumption reveals itself in a blind adherence to dogma and hardened symbols that reduce the mysterious dimension of spirituality to a mélange of apocalyptic visions and eschatological slogans. In political life, the presumption to sovereignty emerges in ideological positions and alignments that foster fanaticism, and threaten to become lethal to those who challenge the "truth."

All of these modern presumptions, be they intellectual, scientific, moral, or political, share something in common—they are closed to what Weil terms "the mystery of existence" and to the recognition of human limitations, the "necessity" that the universe imposes upon us. The attitude the Greeks called *thaumazein*, "speechless wonder," has entirely disappeared in our relationship both to this world and to another world of eternal truth. We are so busy constructing "skyscrapers" on the bridges of the Greeks, we have banished the *vita contemplativa* to history books on the ancients. "We have kept those bridges," as Weil avers, but only "as something to look at" (W1968:90).

In her essay, "Some Thoughts on the Love of God," (W1968:148–52) Weil pursues the Platonic metaphor of roots drawn from the *Timaeus*. Freeing the soul from the grip of social prestige, force, and our own illusions of power, she argues, requires us to dispose ourselves toward grace and thus to nourish the "supernatural" roots that will attach us to the heavens and not to the earth. Her indictment of the contemporary world must be read, then, in spiritual terms—or, more exactly, as commentary upon the loss of the contemplative element that opens us to "supernatural morality" and frees us from the natural morality of "the herd" (W1968:99). Not surprisingly, she takes as a credo a notion that distances her from any human *milieu* and turns instead to the growing of "heavenly roots": "The city gives us the feeling of being at home. We must take the feeling of being at home into exile. We must be rooted in the absence of a place" (W1952a:34). As we shall see, Weil's longing for rootedness "in the absence of a place" leads her to an intensely personal theology, driven by a desire for selflessness, or what she more darkly terms *dépouillement* the "stripping away of the 'I.'" If there is any doubt about the distance she travels from her earlier writings on individual liberty, her doctrine of *dépouillement* should quell it. So, too, should her assertion in "The Pythagorean Doctrine," that liberty itself is "to desire to obey God. All other liberty is false" (W1957b:186).

Given the antipolitical force of these sentiments, which (as we shall see in more detail momentarily) pervade Weil's writings on Christianity and the love of God, it is no wonder that so many critics and commentators have, metaphorically speaking, made "Marx" or "Plato" the focus of their analyses of her work. That is, they have settled themselves either within the so-called materialist or within the spiritualist phase of Weil's thought. Yet a closer look at her writings during the so-called spiritual phase belies the idea that now she fixes her attention upon the heavens alone and never again looks back toward the city. If after 1938 she loses her materialist analysis, she nevertheless retains a concern for the human and the political, even amidst her denunciations of "the prince of this world" and an increasingly neo-Platonic preoccupation with the divine. We must, therefore, understand her despair over living in an age "when we have lost everything" as something that distances her from the human world but also keeps her attached to it. For the things that are in jeopardy in modern society are exactly what she thinks make a *human* life possible and must be preserved. Thus, even as she mourns the loss of the *vita contemplativa*, and recommends *dépouillement*, she also asks: "What is it a sacrilege to destroy? Not that which is base, for that is of no importance. Not that which is high, for, even should we want to, we cannot touch that. The *metaxu*. The *metaxu* form the region of good and evil" (W1952a:133). The *metaxu* are the "relative and mixed blessings" of home, country, tradition, and culture "which warm and nourish the soul" (W1952a:133). In short, they are those human things that mediate our existence "in-between" the Great Beast and God.

Of all the *metaxu*, Weil is most concerned with country. Part of the deep ambivalence in her writing at this time can be found in her longing for rootedness both in the "absence of a place" and in a real, concrete, human *milieu*. Following the latter impulse, she enters this in her notebooks: "We must not have any love other than charity. A nation cannot be an object of charity. But a country can be one—as an environment bearing traditions which are eternal. Every country can be that" (W1952a:149). Here, at least, Weil seems intent upon remaining attentive to those *earthly* things that challenge the rule of the Great Beast, even as she calls for an exile from the earthly *as* the Great Beast in almost the same breath.

In Chapters 7 and 8, we shall consider how, in 1943, Weil's concern for the *metaxu*—especially for "country"—leads her to write *The Need for Roots*, a text inspired by her devotion to France and by an understanding of "roots" as belonging to a place, not the absence of one. However, although *The Need for Roots* may be the most vivid example of her commitment to the human and the political, it is not the only one. There are equally visible indications of her continuing worldly sensibilities in her writings between 1940 and 1942. I have already suggested that these sensibilities can be gleaned from *TPF*, where she mourns the destruction of an earthly city as the greatest calamity the human race can experience. But Weil's concern for the *metaxu* is also evident when she writes of attention as the love of neighbor, and as a certain kind of justice the political order must revere. There is a line of argument in her writings of this period that connects "attention as justice" to the social order where the soul, in her words, can find warmth and nourishment. And this line of argument stands in stark contrast to the one where attention is associated with the renunciation of the social order and a "waiting for God."

To work through this ambivalence about attention that distinguishes Weil's work after 1938, let us turn first, and in more detail, to her theological ideas, where attention is coupled with *dépouillement* and hatred of the Great Beast. Then we will consider the alternative notion of attention as justice, and the implications it holds for preservation of the *metaxu*. What I wish to argue is that Weil's struggle between the human and the divine is not resolved in her writings between 1940 and 1942, but rather revealed in the form of two overlapping, but nevertheless opposing perspectives. The first perspective counsels withdrawal from the world; the second presumes engagement in it.

## Attention as the Love of God

Simone Weil's personal theology is perhaps the most difficult and demanding aspect of her entire *oeuvre*. To grasp its meaning, one cannot rely on rational or strictly analytical modes of analysis, for these merely undermine the "suprarational" attitude that an appreciation of the mystical requires. As Fritz Staal observes, "Mystical experiences, like any other experiences, may be valid or invalid . . . but it makes no sense to say that they are rational or irrational" (1975:23). Much the same might be said of mystical ideas, which frequently employ the language of paradox and contradiction, symbol and mystery. There is, in other words, no easy access here, no singular set of meanings or symbolic truth to which Weil's mysticism gives rise; nor is there any one doctrine or belief system to be established (her religious eclecticism alone makes such a thing unlikely). Indeed, Weil's mysticism is perhaps best conceived of as a way toward insight, rather than an "insight" in and of itself. Following her own analogy, we might approach her mystical writings as we would a Gregorian chant or a prelude by Bach: with a view neither to affirm nor deny, but simply to attend, and to contemplate.

Even as we "contemplate," however, we might also approach Weil's mysticism with our larger context in mind, and situate it within an overall analysis of her writings. Because her theology has been subject to more discussion and critique than all of her other work combined, I will leave the difficult debate concerning its "orthodoxy" or "heresy" to those far more knowledgable in matters mystical and theological. My aims in this discussion are more modest in intent: to present a broad and necessarily sketchy outline of the predominant features of her mystical ideas, and to explore their place within the wider schema of her work. Let us turn first, then, to what Gabriel Marcel has described as an expression of belief "piercing to the heart,"—to Weil's demanding mysticism.

The core of Weil's theology lies in her unwavering determination to make sense of the fundamental misery and evil of human existence. She thinks of this condition in terms of gravity (*pesanteur*), a spiritual force analogous to the natural one, only *pesanteur* pulls the soul toward what is base. "The law of gravity which is sovereign on earth, over all material motion," Weil argues in "Some Thoughts on the Love of God," "is the image of the carnal attachment which governs the tendencies of the soul" (W1968:151). In Weil's mystical writings, gravity is akin to *la force* she emphasizes in *TPF*; it is also a transmutation of the oppression she despises in the *RLO*, and opposes to liberty. But this new Manichaeanism is inspired by the opposition between gravity and God's grace. Gravity draws us away from God, toward the carnal and the base, and the Great Beast compels us to idolatry. This idolatry in turn diminishes our awareness of who we are in relation to God.

Weil likens this sort of attitude to a failure of attention: "Idolatry is due to the fact that, while athirst for absolute good, one is not in possession of supernatural attention; and one has not the patience to let it grow" (W1956b:505). To "let it grow," that is, toward God, by nourishing those supernatural roots that defy the earth-boundedness of gravity's pull, and "fix the soul's gaze" with longing for that which is "the beyond" (W1956b: 527).

So there is a possibility of deliverance from *peasanteur*, despite its overwhelmingly downward pull? Weil wishes to affirm this, but with a caution, because the force of the Great Beast is so overpowering; "it chains us to the earth," and places us in the service of "the false God," from whom we can escape only by dint of the most enormous effort. The effort Weil demands, as we now should expect, is attention. "Absolutely pure attention" is attention directed toward God in prayer. And it is through prayer that we can attain to grace. In "Some Thoughts on the Love of God," Weil makes clear that attention is not a predisposition to "believe" in God—that, she says, is not a decision we can make. "All we can do is decide not to give our love to false gods," and "fix" our attention toward the true and only God, "bringing it back when it has wandered, and fixing it sometimes with all the intensity of which one is capable" (W1968: 148,155). The point is not to search, or attach one's love to this world, but to remain without attachment, "spiritually motionless," realizing that "to search is to impede rather than to facilitate God's operation" (W1968:159). In this endeavor, the Lord's Prayer provides a starting place:

> The words of the Lord's Prayer are perfectly pure. Anyone who repeats the Lord's Prayer with no other intention than to bring to bear upon the words themselves the fullest attention of which he is capable is absolutely certain of being delivered in this way from a part, however small, of the evil he harbors within him (W1968:149).[5]

Thus by fixing our gaze upon something pure and "waiting for God," we train ourselves to receive his grace, his "elevating force."[6] Or, as Weil delightfully puts it, God "gives us wings."

Weil's concept of attention is a crucial part of her theology, in part because it sets her apart from those who employ such ideas as "leaps," "searches," "introspections," "declarations of faith," and so on, in the discussion of God and grace. She rejects the shrill commercialism of the evangelical, the comfortable faith of contemporary Protestantism, ritualistic practices that give the appearance, but not the reality, of attention, and the intellectualized belief of some existentialists, among others.[7] More generally, then, Weil's conception of attention can be taken as her commentary upon what it means to be in the right "attitude" toward God. Since some notion of attitude or "authenticity" is fundamental to almost all religious quests for the divine, we should not be surprised to find her addressing this problem carefully. What is "piercing," however, especially for those who take Weil's religious writings seriously, is the attitude toward "self" that she demands accompany attention to God. Paul, Luther, Calvin, Pascal, Kierkegaard—even Augustine's vision—

pale in comparison to what she requires of the soul oriented away from this world and toward grace. In short, what she calls for is the destruction of the "I": "May God grant me to become nothing" (W1952a:30).[8]

To understand the impulse behind Weil's renunciation of self, we might return momentarily to the essay on school studies. For there, in the midst of her account of attention as love of God, she reveals a psychological feature of attentiveness that returns with a vengeance in her more explicitly mystical writings. Indeed, the essay on school studies itself displays a momentary but nonetheless abrupt change in tone that augurs the mystical attitude to come. The psychological attitude she associates with attention is humility. Noting that the "virtue of humility" accompanies a true attention to the faults and errors in one's studies, she then continues:

> From this point of view it is perhaps even more useful to contemplate our stupidity than our sin. Consciousness of sin gives us the feeling that we are evil, and a kind of pride sometimes finds a place in it. When we force ourselves to fix the gaze . . . upon a school exercise in which we have failed through sheer stupidity, a sense of our mediocrity is born in upon us with irresistible evidence. No knowledge is more to be desired (SS109).

It is telling that in her essay Weil rejects the temptation to fix upon one's sinfulness and instead calls the student's realization of his or her mediocrity and stupidity "the right foundation" and "as good a road to sanctity as any other." The self is too much enthralled when it delves into its own sinfulness, Weil fears, and it is too tempting to turn one's sin into a fixation that reinforces rather than erases the "I." It is also telling that she takes a traditional Christian virtue and pushes it further toward *dépouillement*. Humility is not merely the modesty blessed in the Beatitudes; in the Weilian world it is a visceral sense of one's own inferiority and total insignificance.[9] The road to sanctity is, first, paved with the comprehension of our own mediocrity, and then with a recognition that grace demands the full excising, the total destruction, of the mediocre "I."[10]

What does this renunciation of self entail? Weil gives the following response:

> Renunciation demands that we should pass through anguish equivalent to that which would be caused in reality by the loss of all loved beings and all possessions, including our faculties and attainments in the order of intelligence and character, our opinions, beliefs concerning what is good, what is stable, etc . . . like Job (W1952a:31–32).

Renunciation is total loss—what Weil also calls "accepting a void in ourselves" (W1952a:10). We must achieve the same state *within* ourselves as Job experienced—complete and utter anguish, emptiness, and loss. The idea is not a new one—in the language of the mystics, the "void" or the "dark night" usually refers to the experience of total renunciation and emptiness. In Weil's thought, as in the practice of such mystics as Teresa d'Avila and St. John of the Cross (both of whom she admired immensely), the void is a way toward God. But, again this is not a definite promise: "whoever endures a moment of the void either receives the supernatural bread or falls. It is a terrible risk, but one that must be run" (W1952a:11).

Some of Weil's most searing observations, in both her notebooks and her essays, follow from this dictate to renounce the "I" and experience the void. A sampling of her remarks should set the tone:

> To empty ourselves of the world. To take the form of a slave. To reduce ourselves to the point we occupy in space and time—that is to say, to nothing (W1952a: 12).

> May I disappear in order that those things that I see may become perfect in their beauty from the very fact that they are no longer things that I see (W1952a:37). This irreducible 'I' which is the irreducible basis of my suffering—I have to make this 'I' universal (W1952a:129).

> All the things that I see, hear, breathe, touch, eat, all the beings that I meet—I deprive all these of contact with God and I deprive God of contact with them to the extent to which something in me says "I" (W1956b:379).

At the foundation of this last expression is Weil's belief that our very existence is an affront to God. God has created us, but it is up to us to strip ourselves of our false divinity ("I") so that no barriers exist between God and that which he has created. She articulates this very difficult idea in a variety of paradoxical and by no means easily accessible ways; but two central points stand out most clearly. One has to do with how she perceives of God in the universe. The other involves the meaning or significance of affliction (*malheur*).

First, Weil argues that God gives us being in order that we may give it back to him. Part of the humility we learn through attention is the refusal to exist outside God. Thus, when we pursue *dépouillement* we remove the barrier between God and his love or, as Weil also puts it, "between God and God." Sometimes she refers to *dépouillement* as an act of "reciprocity"—we make of ourselves matter to be consumed by God, even as He makes Himself matter and is consumed by us. At other times, she presents the destruction of the "I" as an act that allows for contact between God and the universe by removing "the screen." "If only I knew how to disappear," she writes, "there would be a perfect union of love between God and the earth I tread, the sea I hear. . . . If I go, then the creator and the creature will exchange their secrets" (W1952a:36–37). And still elsewhere, she draws upon the language of crucifixion to reinforce the idea that we must destroy our "selves": "In our being God is torn asunder. We are God's crucifixion. My existence crucifies God" (W1957b:564). By stripping ourselves of the power to say "I", we engage in something like an act of atonement. And Weil's God wants this to be: "Our existence," she writes, "is made up only of His waiting for our acceptance not to exist. He is perpetually begging from us that existence which he gives. He gives it to us in order to beg it from us" (W1952a:28).

But there is yet one other way we can consider the act of *dépouillement* as a "giving back" of our selves to God. Weil argues that this decreation is significant because it is an imitation of God's own act of decreation— his renunciation of the world. Her God is not an ever watchful deity who is omnipresent, bestowing grace. When she speaks of God's decreation, she moves in the other direction and suggests that God created and then, in spirit, withdrew "at an infinite distance" from the world. Thus, He must be conceived of as both creator of and absent from the universe. Or, in her language of paradox: "God can only be present in creation under the form of absence (W1952a:99). Responding directly to a more orthodox view, she contends:

> It is God who in love withdraws from us so that we can love him. For if we were exposed to the direct radiance of his love, without the protection of space, of time, and of matter, we should be evaporated like water in the sun; there would not be enough "I" in us to make it possible to surrender the "I" for love's sake (W1952a:28).

According to Weil's theological calculus, then, God's love not only requires us to cease to be, it is also withdrawn from us as we are—we must endure "the void" and the ineffable silence of God. "We have to be on a desert," she says. "For he whom we love is absent" (W1952a:99). Weil sometimes refers to the situation in which God places us as a "trap"—"God gave me being in order that I should give it back to him. It is like one of those traps whereby the characters are tested in fairy stories and tales on initiation" (W1952:35). Upon her telling, we pass God's test once we embark upon the renunciation of the "I."

The second central feature of Weil's conception of *dépouillement* is affliction (*malheur*), which she says does not "create" but rather "reveals" human misery. In an already demanding and difficult theology, Weil's ideas on affliction are undoubtedly the most demanding and difficult of all.

The moving essay, "The Love of God and Affliction" (*LGA*) (W1968:170–98), written immediately before Weil left for the United States in 1942, never again to return to France, is the central expression of her views on affliction. Her initial characterization of it seems to betray both her own fragile physical state and the devastating impact of war and its uprooting consequences:

There is not real affliction unless the event which has gripped and uprooted a life attacks it, directly or indirectly, in all its parts, social, psychological, and physical. The social factor is essential. There is not really affliction where there is not social degradation or the fear of it in some form or another (*LGA*171).

Weil describes affliction as something quite apart from "simple" suffering (*souffrance*). It recalls, on yet another level of applicability, the situation of the "vanquished" in *TPF* who face "the force that kills but does not kill just yet." Affliction is neither momentary, like a physical blow, nor only a physical condition. Nor is it a "thinking" condition, but rather one where thought has fled, "as an animal flies from death" (*LGA*171). Above all, affliction is a total state, a complete "uprooting" of life, a "more or less attenuated equivalent of death," "quasi-hell on earth" (*LGA*171; W1952a:25). It is an attack on all parts of a human being: the social, the psychological, the physical, the spiritual. Weil describes it as a kind of "horror" that "submerges the whole soul." In what is probably her most graphic account of *malheur*, she makes us realize exactly how horrible it is:

> In affliction, the vital instinct survives all the attachments which have been torn away and blindly fastens to everything which can provide it with support, like a plant fastens its tendrils. Gratitude (except in a base form) and justice are not conceivable in this state. . . . Affliction, from this point of view, is hideous as life in its nakedness always is, like an amputated stump, like the swarming of insects. Life without form (W1952a:24–25).

What role does this condition of "life in its nakedness" play in Weil's theology?

If we remember her use of the Platonic metaphor of rootedness as a spiritual awareness of the divine, we might understand affliction as the tearing of those roots; it is spiritual disintegration, the absence of God made visceral. For Weil, however, affliction is, or can be, a source of revelation, insofar as it rends all attachments from us and makes us detached, or turns us toward false attachments so that we may see the wretchedness of attachment itself. Put more simply, affliction makes possible (though it does not guarantee) the "recognition of human wretchedness" which is the first step toward the renunciation of the "I." Indeed, Weil suggests in this entry from her notebooks, affliction may even assist attention:

> The irreducible character of suffering which makes it impossible for us not to have a horror of it at the moment when we are undergoing it is destined to bring the will to a standstill, just as absurdity brings the intelligence to a standstill . . . so that man, having come to the end of his human facilities, may stretch out his arms, stop, look up and wait (W1952a:102).

She also suggests that one in whom the "I" has already been destroyed could fall to affliction, and then affliction moves the human being to a "plane of perfection." And this is the state of being that "produces the absence of God." The plane of perfection is a contingent condition at best, however. In *LGA* Weil notes that an afflicted person, caught in the experience of God's absence, may cease loving in the void (*LGA*172). In that case, God's absence becomes final. Only if the soul goes on "at least wanting to love" is the plane of perfection attainable, and one day open to God's revelation of the beauty of the world.[11]

The theological details of Weil's argument should not derail us from what seems to be her paramount concern. She confronts the problem of affliction so that we might give meaning to God's love in an evil world. It is not enough to declare His love *in absentia* (although this declaration underscores the "absurdity" she claims for human existence). We must also explore, and attempt to make sense of, what Weil calls "the great enigma" of human life—affliction itself. Hence, she observes:

> It is not surprising that the innocent are killed, tortured, driven from their country, made destitute or reduced to slavery, put in concentration camps or prison cells, since there are criminals to perform such actions. It is not surprising either that disease is the cause of long sufferings, which paralyse [sic] life and make it into death, since nature is at the mercy of the blind play of mechanical necessities. But it *is* surprising that God should have given affliction the power to seize the very souls of the innocent and to possess them as a sovereign master (*LGA*171–72).

Confronting one of the oldest of theological dilemmas—how to reconcile suffering in the world with the idea of a loving God, Weil takes the dilemma a step further and asks how is it that God can reduce the innocent to living in a "quasi-hell" on earth? To develop fully her highly idiosyncratic response would require a far more intensive pursuit of her conception of human nature, the causes of evil, redemptive suffering, and supernatural love than we can engage here. But it is nonetheless important to emphasize that her response is grounded in a recognition of affliction as an indelible, but not damning part of human existence. Her "cosmic pessimism" (to borrow a phrase from Tillich) holds that, in the wretchedness of life and the suffering of the innocent lie the way toward beauty, contemplation, and the love of God. The model she offers here is Job but, more centrally, Jesus, whose cry of crucifixion and anguish, "My God, my God, why has thou forsaken me?" is proof "that Christianity is something divine" (*W*1952a:79). Weil perceives the supernatural part of Christ's mission—"the sweat of blood, the unsatis- fied longing for human consolation, the supplication that he might be spared, the sense of being abandoned by God" (*W*1952a:79)—as the great, paradigmatic example of the quasi-hell of affliction, and also of its promise of God.[12]

The reason why Weil is so absorbed with the Crucifixion and the Passion of Christ, rather than the Resurrection or the Ascension should now be clear. It seems that her theology rests not only on the reality of gravity's "down drag," and God's grace, but also and most decisively, on the idea of redemptive suffering—on the belief that through affliction we come to know the love of God. "Redemptive suffering," she writes, "is that which strips suffering naked and brings it in its purity right into existence. That saves existence . . . God is present in extreme evil through redemptive suffering through the cross" (LGA1952:82). One cannot fail to suspect what Weil herself makes explicit with regard to redemptive suffering, namely that its ultimate form is death: "To love truth means to endure the void and, as a result, to accept death. Truth is on the side of death" (W1952:11).[13]

## The AntiPolitics of Spirituality

The dangers—theological, psychological, as well as political—of a position such as this are extreme. Little wonder that Weil's writings on these difficult matters have aroused storms of controversy. It is tempting, on the theological plane, to agree with Gabriel Marcel's observation that Weil's doctrine can only arouse a hatred for God in anyone who has not achieved mystical insight (1949:16). "If the love of God is cruelty, torture, violent death, etc.," Marcel declares, "may we be preserved from any such form of loving!" And Hans Meyerhoff offers this possibility: "surely, it is not inappropriate to ask whether this woman, consumed by the purging fires of salvation, did not also mishear the voices of demons for the silence of God" (1957:19).

On the psychological plane, we might wonder if a doctrine that strives to give *meaning* to affliction does not run the risk of fetishizing it, and thus of turning believers into masochistic seekers of *malheur*, or at least into embodiments of self-contempt. Or, in Nietzsche's terms, is it not possible that the humility Weil calls for is simply an inversion of the afflicted's own frustrated will to power and *ressentiment*? If so, then the Weilian project is, perhaps, nothing less than the legitimation of a "sick" psychology.

Most terrible, of all, however, a doctrine like Weil's might be read as providing, within itself, possible rationalizations of evil *for the evil doer*. If the affliction of the innocent in all its horror is a way toward God, then crimes committed against the innocent might take on a perverse but powerful rationale of their own. For Weil to conceive of such a theology when she does—as millions of people are being sent to their deaths in the concentration camps of Europe—may now seem the cruelest of cruel ironies, or at least as the most life-threatening confirmation of God's grace ever to be articulated.[14]

I think it is fair to say that she tried to obviate some, although not all, of these dangers. On the matter of fetishizing affliction, she noted that there is a tendency for it to "make the soul its accomplice" and for the person to become "complicit" in perpetuating his own state, thereby failing to seek deliverance (*LGA*174). "It is as though affliction had established itself in him as a parasite and was directing him for its own purposes outright," she avers (*LGA*174). And she also writes: "It is wrong to desire affliction; it is against nature and it is a perversion" (*LGA*184). Along these same lines, she warns that one cannot "choose the cross," by which I think she means that genuine affliction "takes us" as it were, we cannot "take it up" as a cause or a consciously developed state of being. To do so would imply that some state of thought (or at least premeditation) accompanies this condition, but Weil is very careful to point out that affliction is absence of thinking, not a rationalized activity, or a way of "proceeding" toward grace.

She also reiterates, often, that affliction is not awe-inspiring, glorious, admirable, or noble; nor is it a form of martyrdom. Neither is it an example of courage nor a willingness to die for a cause. Drawing a sharp distinction between Jesus and those martyrs who go to their deaths in defiance of persecution, Weil writes:

> Those who are persecuted for their faith and are aware of it are not afflicted, in spite of their suffering. They only fall into affliction if suffering or fear fills the soul to the point of making it forget the cause of the persecution. The martyrs who came into the arena singing as they faced the wild beasts were not afflicted, Christ was afflicted. He did not die like a martyr. He died like a common criminal, in the same class as thieves, only a little more ridiculous. For affliction is ridiculous (*LGA*176).

Affliction bears within it the crucial element of chance, and Weil also suggests that it has more than a trace of absurdity about it—it is ridiculous. Few of the orthodox would follow her, no doubt, on the matter of Christ's "ridiculous" death, but we might understand Weil's depiction as an attempt to quash the "romance" of affliction as well as its nobility. The "I" who faces it as an opportunity to "imitate the passion of my God" is not, in Weilian terms, afflicted.[15] Neither are those who cultivate extreme forms of self-contempt, or glorify *malheur* for the sake of salvation. Like attention, affliction must be understood as an unselfconscious—indeed, unwilled—state, not as any kind of "striving for" or "dying for." But unlike attention, it is neither an "effort" nor a state of being assumed by the moral agent. Affliction is simply imposed.[16]

Despite all of this, a problem nags. Weil's is a doctrine which, at once, condemns affliction and gives it purpose and meaning. Sometimes the former predominates, driven as she is to identify with the suffering of innocent beings, and to condemn "human crime," which she says is the cause of most affliction (LGA176). More often, however, her condemnation of human crime is superceded by what we might call her near obsession with the nature and supernatural purpose of affliction itself. This mysticism offers no hope for altering the earthly conditions—the human crime—that brings affliction into existence, only a way of stripping oneself of the "givenness" of such conditions. For the mystical way is not to change the world, but to withdraw from it. In this respect, we have to understand Weil's mysticism as utterly antipolitical.

To make this clearer, we need only compare Weil's treatment of liberty and labor in her mystical essays with that in the RLO. In the former, Weil thinks of liberty in relation to "obedience to necessity," and "necessity," in turn, in relation to God. Hence, she argues that "necessity" is the obedience of matter to God; likewise, "liberty" is the obedience of humans to God (LGA186). "What is more beautiful," she asks, "then the effect of gravity on sea waves as they flow in ever-changing folds, or the almost eternal folds of the mountains?"(LGA178). Human beings, she goes on, must strive to emulate the "docility of matter" in their obedience to God. To be free, then, is to desire to obey God. Weil takes this point further by pressing a fundamental tenet of her mysticism—"passing to God's side," and thereby being able to see necessity differently, requires us to "renounce thinking in the first person" (LGA186). Although she acknowledges (in a passage reminiscent of her critique of the collectivity) that the "first person plural" is infinitely further removed from purity than the "first person singular," she nevertheless goes on to call for the renunciation of the latter as well—as a condition of freeing the soul toward God. In these writings, then, both "I" and "We" are dispatched, and in the wake of this renunciation emerges a "consent to necessity" that Weil equates with liberty and obedience to the divine. This seems a far remove indeed from the notion of liberty as methodical thinking and methodical thinking itself as the "meeting" of necessity she presents in the RLO. But what is even more evident in the shift between these works is the replacement of the thinking subject, the rational, "methodical individual," with the decreated being who accepts the "docility of matter" as his or her model.

Perhaps the antipolitical nature of these claims can be rendered even more concrete if we consider how the mystical Weil conceives of labor. There are some echoes of her earlier notion of labor as the human act *par excellence* in her mystical doctrine, and she occasionally acknowledges something like her previous conception of labor as the means through which the forces of nature and human creativity are brought into equilibrium. But now she seems primarily intent upon understanding labor—particularly labor as "toil"—as the preeminent form our "consent" to necessity might take. She does not advocate this form of labor, of course, but as with affliction, she attempts to make sense of it, glean some purpose from it. Thus, the most monotonous and routinized form of labor—what Arendt refers to as *animal laborans* activity—appears to Weil as the human equivalent of nature's submission to necessity. To toil is essentially to allow one's strength and one's very life to pass away every moment into matter—obediently to die daily.[17] Therein lies the spirituality of labor.

For Arendt, this form of human activity is the very opposite of freedom, divorced, as it is, from speech, action, and the plurality of citizens in a public realm. Labor as toil is a grinding, solitary, process-laden enterprise, that offers only an imitation of the endless and unchanging cycles of natural movements. "Laboring always moves in the same circle," Arendt observes, "which is prescribed by the biological process of the living organism and the end of its 'toil and trouble' comes only with the death of this organism" (Arendt 1958:98). Part of Arendt's critique of the human condition involves the notion that *animal laborans* has become the predominant form of human thought and activity in the twentieth century, and she associates this event with the alienation of the modern age. In short, to be "enslaved by necessity," to pursue only the activity of *animal laborans*, is to forfeit a fully human life.

For (the mystical) Weil, the "enslavement to necesssity" that toil brings with it is the very treasure of labor itself. That such toil "culminates in death" is not a reason for mourning, but a truth about the fragility and the wretchedness of human existence. It is also, potentially, the source of our salvation, insofar as such endless toil with its daily death brings us closer to the condition of docility and subservience to necessity. This is what I think Weil is referring to in *SS* when she tells the student that peasants and workmen "possess a nearness to God of incomparable savor," found in their poverty, endless suffering, and social alienation. The cyclicality of their labors condemns them to an earthly travail, to futility, and a less than fully human life. But at the same time it brings them closer to God. She puts this idea in another way in her notes:

The spirituality of work. Work makes us experience in the most exhausting manner the phenomenon of finalty rebounding like a ball. . . . It is when man sees himself as a squirrel turning round and round in a circular cage that, if he does not lie to himself, he is close to salvation (W1952a:158).[18]

With these words, Weil bleeds from labor whatever creativity or autonomy it contained in *RLO*. Rather than a vision sympathetic to Marx's conception of "conscious life-activity" or to her own earlier view of the "human act *par excellence*," she now conceives of labor as "spiritual" in *and because of* its deadly routinization and monotonous repetition. To put this in the terms I introduced in Chapter 4, the mystical Weil reduces *homo faber* to *animal laborans*, and the human condition itself to something like a state causally determined by physical forces and laws of nature. More precisely, she holds that as a species we move closer toward God if we replicate the docility of matter, namely, in toil. "Action" in Arendt's sense, as political engagement, is out. Weil has dramatically altered her vision: no longer is labor the means according to which the fisherman in his little boat challenges necessity creatively, methodically. Now labor is the experience through which we become one with the folds of the universe, deny ourselves, and consent to God. Like the squirrel in the cage, we must move in a worldless realm of cyclicality, creatures going round and round in an infinity of space and time, ever the closer to God because of our obedience to necessity.

If we couple this conception of *animal laborans* to Weil's argument for *dépouillement*, we get some sense of just how bereft of political possibility—of action (individual or collective), social transformation, emancipation, even the mere betterment of everyday life—her mysticism is. Not only does it render existence on earth a form of daily death, where the most meaningful action is that closest to the rhythms of the natural world; it also repudiates the earthly world as the realm of the Great Beast. She directs our gaze, our "attentiveness," outward. We must be rooted "in the absence of a place," not in an earthly city or a political collectivity. Thus, her mysticism grants no value or meaning to either individual autonomy or collective, public action. In this perspective, "I" and "We" are equally unfit as identities; all that matters is God's love, His grace, and His absence.

Whatever the contribution and value of her theology, (and Weil has been called "this century's most original religious thinker inspired by Christianity") we cannot help but conclude that it has little to do with the political world (Vetö 1965:285). We must not forget, of course, that much of her theology is inspired by an intensely political consciousness—by her deep concern for those who are afflicted and oppressed, by her horror of the terrible ruination of war, by her despair over the uprootedness and exile of so many millions of people in the twentieth century. As one commentator has noted, "More than any other period in human history, the contemporary world appeared to [Weil] as a world delivered into the power of hostile, blind, anonymous mechanisms, grinding human beings into fragments in a hell of wars, destruction, destitution, and moral injury" (Blumenthal 1952:227). Accordingly, the political significance of her mysticism could be assessed as an attempt to give some meaning, some luminosity (bare and cold as that luminosity might be) to the unavoidable and inalterable reality of *mal-*

*heur.* But, at most, her mysticism follows in the path of many other mystics, and encourages a genuine passivity in this world—an attitude of motionlessness. For those with political sensibilities of an earthly sort, the rewards of such motionlessness are dubious, not in the least because the attitude Weil promotes is likely to render some human beings pawns of others, and subject to the very oppression she denounces in the *RLO*. We must also acknowledge what Marcel (1949:14) calls the "genuine hatred for existence" that fuels this mystic like a great fire. Her hatred forges what is, from an earthly perspective, an antipolitics so refractory to autonomy and to action that it must ultimately be rejected if we are to locate any ground for the pursuit of human dignity and freedom in this world rather than the next.

## Attention as Love of Neighbor

As it is always with Simone Weil, however, a tension persists here. Depite the fact that the "dark night" of her mystical journey takes powerful and profound hold in her writings between 1940 and 1942, she sounds a contrary theme during this time as well, one that is very much of this world. But few commentators have noticed, and fewer still have analyzed—the political ideas that continue to emerge, both implicitly and explicitly, alongside her renunciation of the world. One of the truly remarkable features of Weil's writing during this time is the degree to which it escapes being totally overwhelmed by "the void," and weighed down by the deep cosmic pessimism. Indeed, it would probably be no exaggeration to say that the great wonder of Weil's later work is not her mysticism, but rather the extent to which she resists its pull and remains attentive to issues of human morality and politics. She took to heart, it seems, and struggled to obey, Augustine's instruction: "No man must be so committed to contemplation as, in his contemplation to give not thought to his neighbors needs nor so absorbed in action as to dispense with the contemplation of God." We might approach Weil's concept of attention with this in mind, for she develops it both in relation to the contemplation of God, and in relation to the love of neighbor. It is the latter that concerns us now.

In the essay on school studies, Weil suggests that attention has much to do with the love of God in prayer. But she also suggests another practice or activity that has attention as its substance, the "love of neighbor." Attention, then, is also an attitude toward others or, to return to the idea of *lecture*, a right way of "reading" others. "The soul empties itself of all its contents," she observes, "in order to receive into itself the being it is looking at, just as he is, in all his truth" (*SS*115).

In *LGA* Weil considers this capacity to "look at others in the right way," especially those "others" who are afflicted. "What we are commanded to love first of all is affliction," she writes, "the affliction of man, the affliction of God" (LGA192). In this two-fold commandment to "love God," and "love your neighbor," there is a two-fold dimension to affliction—it is not only a way toward the divine, but also a state to which others, i.e., those who are not afflicted, must respond. In other words, affliction is an "earthly" condition as well as an orientation away from the world, and the unafflicted must be prepared "to face affliction with steady attention when it is close to him" (LGA188). What this sort of attentiveness morally entails, and how it informs our "recognition of persons" are central aspects of Weil's later work.[19]

The first thing Weil tells us about our capacity to attend to "our fellows in misfortune" is that it is an uncommon human trait, and those who think they possess it are usually mistaken. "The capacity to give one's attention to a sufferer is a very rare and difficult thing, it is almost a miracle; it is a miracle" (SS114). More often than not human beings are closer to the "impenitent thief" than to the miracle—we are inclined to seek consolation in "contempt and hatred" for those persons who are afflicted. We resolutely refuse to see ourselves in them (LGA183). Weil goes even further to suggest that many of us who are ultimately reduced to affliction ourselves have been accomplices—through "cowardice, inertia, indifference, or culpable ignorance"—in plunging others into a state at least as horrible as our own (LGA184). In the face of terrible crimes against others, and living within "atrocious" institutions and customs, we might have expressed our condemnation but: "We neglected to do so, or even approved [these crimes], or at least we concurred in the expression of approval around us (LGA184). Weil charges us, at the very least, with being involved "in the guilt of criminal indifference" toward others, at most with being criminal ourselves.[20]

Yet she also sets enormously difficult standards, not all of them consistent. In the essay on affliction, she declares the "knowledge of affliction is the key of Christianity," and those whom Christ recognizes as his benefactors are those whose compassion rests upon this knowledge. But she also says this knowledge is "by nature impossible" both for those who have experienced affliction and for those who have not. These contradictory statements are not satisfactorily resolved in LGA but Weil ultimately seems to hold that knowledge of affliction, coupled with attention, is possible for those who have "seen the face of affliction or are . . . prepared to;" thus she leaves room for both the afflicted and the unafflicted to be the "benefactors of Christ" (LGA189–90). Primarily, however, she is concerned with how the unafflicted approach those who are beset by malheur, rather than how the afflicted themselves come to understand their condition. In the essay on school studies, she refers to the former as persons who can experience the love of neighbor by saying with all due attentiveness, "what are you going through?"

(*SS*115). And it is the meaning of this question, and its connection to attention, that she proceeds to develop elsewhere.

When Weil turns to the attitude or way of being "love of neighbor" encompasses, she declares that "warmth of heart, impulsiveness, pity, are not enough" (*SS*114). She does not fully pursue this claim in *SS* but in *LGA* she takes the question "What are you going through?" farther, and establishes some important moral distinctions betwen true and false attention to the afflicted. Her discussion is echoed in Iris Murdoch's later observation, "it is very difficult to concentrate attention upon suffering and sin, in others or in oneself, without falsifying the picture in some way while making it bearable" (Hauerwas and MacIntyre 1983:88). Weil would have us consider what it means to make affliction bearable rather than attend to it. Accordingly, she offers the example of those who give of themselves:

> . . . capriciously, irregularly, or else too regularly, or from habit imposed by training, or in conformity with social convention, or from vanity or emotional pity, or for the sake of a good conscience—in a word, from self-regarding motives. They are arrogant or patronizing or tactlessly sympathetic, or they let the afflicted man feel that they regard him simply as a specimen of a certain type of affliction. In any case, their gift is an injury. And they have their reward on earth, because their left hand is not unaware of what their right hand gave" (*LGA*189).

From this biting criticism, we can draw a number of lessons. First, not just any attitude or moral outlook will count as attention to the afflicted. The intentions behind one's "giving" are, for Weil, as important as the gift itself. She is not inclined to judge an act of benevolence or care on the merit of the material given. To the contrary, what she implies is that the gift itself and the giving of it—or what inspires the giving—are inseparable. The motivation of the giver enhances or detracts from the gift, and the motivation determines whether the gift is a treasure or an injury. Weil is blunt about the specific motivations that tarnish and diminish attention—the reflex-response of habit, the acquiescence or conformity to social custom, the desire for praise or approbation from others, fawning pity, the salving of conscience—none of these ask "What are you going through?" in a deeply authentic way.[21]

Why these motivations are inadequate, indeed poverty-striken, is best comprehended in terms of a second lesson Weil offers: true attentiveness requires a concern for persons in their concrete specificity, not as general categories. She makes this clear in *SS* where she writes:

> The love of neighbor in all its fullness simply means being able to say to him: "What are you going through?" It is a recognition that the sufferer exists, not only as a unit in a collection, or a specimen from the social category labelled "unfortunate" but as a man, exactly like us, who was one

day stamped with a special mark by affliction. For this reason it is enough, but it is indispensable, to know how to look at him in a certain way (SS115).

Weil would have us understand how the language of generalized grouping—"the poor," "the unemployed," "the needy," "the homeless,"—reduces and obscures the specific suffering of real persons, thereby making it easier for us to deal with them or "to falsify the picture," as Murdoch says. When the afflicted become "units in a collection," suffering is transformed into a distant and more bearable thing, and that is not what attention is about.

Weil's critique of "specimen thinking" is more than just a simple reminder that we must recognize real persons, however. Weil also implies that the tendency to categorize also renders the afflicted "doubly stripped," as it were, of personality. Affliction itself, she reminds us, is a destruction of the "I," a "lapse into anonimity" (LGA190). When one treats the afflicted as a category or a stereotype, what little is left of them as persons is totally erased—what distinctive identity the sufferer could have retained, at least in the view of others, is now completely submerged in the category. Thus a "specimen thinking" on the part of would-be Samaritans only further pulverizes that man who "quivers like a butterfly pinned alive to a tray" (LGA182). Weil concludes that an act of giving prompted by specimen thinking is not, in one respect at least, all that different from outright maltreatment of the afflicted. Both reduce the person to anonimity:

> The afflicted are stripped of their humanity by misfortune. In affliction, that misfortune itself becomes a man's whole existence and in every other respect he loses all significance, in everybody's eyes including his own. There is something in him that would like to exist, but it is continually pushed back into nothingness, like a drowning man whose head is pushed under water. He may be a pauper, a refugee, a negro, an invalid, an ex-convict, or anything of the kind; . . . in any case whether he is an object of ill usage or of charity he will be treated as a cipher, as one item among many others in the statistics of a certain type of affliction. So both good treatment and bad treatment will have the same effect of compelling him to remain anonymous. They are two forms of the same offence (LGA190).

The question, then, is how might we avoid either of these offences—what does a true attention to affliction require? We have already seen that the sort of attention Weil has in mind presupposes what Kant called a respect for persons, and characterized as treating human beings as ends, not means. Or as Weil herself indicates in her lectures on philosophy: "the real demand of justice is to think of each human being as an end (Kant)" (W1978:213). Much of Weil's moral thought and particularly her discussion of affliction, is guided by this maxim. The actions she praises are those in which the afflicted are treated as ends, not as "objects," or means. Likewise, attention is a way of looking that fixes upon the person as a subject, not as "an inert or passive thing." Drawing upon the Biblical parable, she emphasizes that the Good Samaritan's recognition of "the little piece of flesh, naked, inert, and bleeding beside a ditch" was born of a supernatural love of neighbor and an attentiveness that "reads" that heap beside the ditch as a human being, a person in need of care.[22] Throughout her various accounts of "love of neighbor" run the Kantian threads of respect for persons as ends, and the autonomy of the moral agent.

Yet Weil's discussion of attention toward the afflicted also reveals that she is at some distance from Kantian precepts. To put this simply, part of the Kantian ethic is premised upon the notion that our treatment of others entails a rational requirement to abstract from personal involvement and move toward the viewpoint of the impartial judge. That is to say, we must respect others as rational creatures and, in judging others, we must aspire to the "rational" and "objective" viewpoint of the detached observer. Weil diverges from this perspective by suggesting that attention toward others is not an act of impartial disengagement at all, but rather an act through which the unafflicted "project their being" into the afflicted. Relatedly, she insists that attention to the afflicted is not rooted in our recognition of any one attribute, like the rational dignity of a man, but instead is consumed by the whole person, the "neighbor" in his or her completeness. Let us consider these Weilian views more closely, again with reference to Kant.

One of the guiding metaphors of Kant's discussion of the self and the other is the notion of distance; it is distance that lends a rational perspective, freed from entanglements in personal prejudice and self-involvement, to the moral agent. When one achieves distance and moves "outside" one's own experience, a morally superior, impartial, and detached vision of others, as equally worthy of respect as oneself, is made possible. By this process of distancing, Kant suggests, one arrives at the "point of view of a member of an intelligible world." Insofar as she considers "self-regarding motives" destructive of true attention, Weil too thinks a moral attitude toward others is one that must check the self-inclinations that lead us to view the afflicted "behind a veil of illusion or falsehood" (*LGA*190). But at the same time, she rejects the idea that attention involves a distancing or the achievement of some Archimedian point from which the impartial "I" can then engage. The "benefactor of Christ, when he meets an afflicted man," she writes, "does not feel any distance between himself and the other. He projects all his own being into him" (*LGA*190).[23]

Elaborating upon this idea, she notes: "To project one's being into an afflicted person is to assume for a moment his affliction; it is to choose voluntarily something whose very essence consists in being imposed by constraint upon the unwilling" (LGA191). She offers an example: "It follows that the impulse to give [the afflicted] food is as instinctive and immediate as it is for oneself to eat when one is hungry" (LGA190). And she says of the benefactor: "Such a man would not think of saying that he takes care of the afflicted for the Lord's sake; it would be as absurd to him as it would be to say that he eats for the Lord's sake. One eats because one can't help it" (LGA190).

What is intriguing about these formulations is the degree to which Weil emphasizes instinctive impulse and the merging with the other. The attitude toward the afflicted, born of attention, thus sounds something like an unavoidable contact with necessity, an irresistible giving-over of identity to the suffering of the other, so as to make one's self the other's. And, in fact, she argues that those who project their own being into the afflicted "give them for a moment—what affliction has deprived them of—an existence of their own" (LGA190). If we understand this conception of moral agency as "becoming the other," then it is clear why Weil's benefactor cannot say, "I take care of the afflicted." For this claim presumes a separation, a detachment. But in Weil's example, there is no detachment—as the "benefactor of Christ" I have given my being to another, to his or her whole person. There is little question that Weil means this almost literally; to be attentive to our neighbor requires some form of dépouillement. Attention to the afflicted is, then, both a creative and a renouncing act. Creative, because it involves an effort of the imagination, a giving to someone whom others (and even the afflicted one) do not "see." Attention to the afflicted is also a renunciation because it involves the movement of "self" into the other. Thus, like Kant, Weil wants to associate moral agency with a kind of detachment from self, only Kant would move the self "outside" both itself and the other, while Weil would have it move inside the other while erasing the self.

We need to ask more precisely, however, what this "projection of being" Weil argues for really involves. I think we can conceive of it, given what she writes, in two ways—one more extreme, and less accessible than the other. The two ways also complement the two forms attention takes in her work—as dépouillement and as justice.

The first way we might think of this "projection of being" takes us back to Weil's theology. Quite clearly in LGA she associates love of neighbor with the destruction of the "I." The benefactor of the afflicted is, in essence, a conduit between Christ and the one who suffers. As she puts it, "What these men who give to the afflicted whom they succor, when they project their own being into them, is not really their own being, because they no longer possess one; it is Christ himself (LGA1968:191). He who gives from true compassion, then, and not self-regarding motives, gives Christ himself—"for who could be Christ's benefactor except Christ himself?" (*LGA*191). This version of the recognition of others, informed by the Weilian notion of *dépouillement*, and possession by Christ, brings to the forefront of Christianity the reality of suffering and the question of the Christian's obligation in the face of this human reality. Weil thinks that for too long Christians have evaded the responsiblity to attend to affliction: "All the talk about original sin, God's will, Providence and its mysterious plans . . . and future recompenses of every kind in this world and the next, all this," she writes, "serves only to conceal the reality of affliction or else fails to meet the case" (*LGA*195). She finds an "intellectual malaise" and a derailment in Christianity—both doctrinally and symbologically—in the direction of eschatological preoccupations and visions of heavenly grace.[24] What is lacking is a theological case for the recognition of others, a doctrine that will bring the Good Samaritan to life amidst the reality of human affliction.

To those believers who are transfixed by the promise of God's love and Christ's Resurrection and do not attend to the meaning of the Passion and the Crucifixion, Weil is saying something important and jarring. (Even if her theology does not persuade, it usually jars). She wants to use the commandment to "love your neighbor" as a way to reorient the vision and the purpose of Christianity itself, and make it more attentive to the reality of human suffering and *malheur*. To those nonbelievers who are disinclined to pursue this perspective, Weil's moral doctrine may very well appear incomprehensible, unattractive, as "absurd" as the affliction she brings to light. The call to "project one's being" through the destruction of the "I," as Christ's benefactor to the afflicted, is likely to puzzle if not repel those who question Christian beliefs, not to mention religious faith itself. But this brings us to the second, and I think more accessible, way in which we might understand what Weil takes the "projection of being" to mean.

The second way is political. In this guise, Weil's concept of attention toward others takes the form of a moral argument embedded in the language of justice and a critique of "rights based doctrines," rather than in the language of *dépouillement*. Affliction is still of crucial importance, but in the context of this political language, Weil is led to ask "what is a person?" From there she proceeds to a critique of rights language, in search of a more compelling vision of justice.[25] Her argument is presented most systematically in the essay "Human Personality" (*HP*1962b:7–34), written in London in 1943.

## The Politics of Spirituality

The essay begins with a not-so-veiled attack on "Personalism," the influential philosophical doctrine of Emmanuel Mounier and the *Esprit* group active in Paris from the late 1930s until 1950. Although the Personalist movement never formulated a coherent and consistent ideology, it was distinguished by an unwavering commitment to the separation of the spiritual and the political orders, and by a concern for the human person "in its totality."[26] "In view of the depersonalizing nature of the contending ideologies of the 30s, 40s, and 50s, one scholar writes, "Personalism, a defense of the human person, seemed the fundamental ideal for many intellectuals, many of them of the Catholic Left" (Hellman 1973:387).

Weil is quite obviously at a far remove from the Personalists on the matter of the relation between the spiritual and the earthly realms, but in *HP*, her primary focus concerns their concept of the person.[27] She observes, no doubt in reference to their doctrine of the community as an affective bond among persons, that the conception of a person as "warmly wrapped in social consideration" misses the point. Rather uncharitably she adds, "That is why it was not in popular circles that the philosophy of personalism originated and developed, but among writers, for whom it is part of their profession to have or hope to acquire a name or reputation" (*HP*17). Even more precisely, however, she takes issue with the idea of person (*personne*) itself, as the *Esprit* group uses it, and offers a different, more comprehensive view:

> There is something sacred in every man, but it is not his person. Nor yet is it the human personality. It is this man; no more and no less. . . . If it were the human personality in him that was sacred to me, I could easily put out his eyes. As a blind man he would be exactly as much a human personality as before. I should not have touched the person in him at all. I should have destroyed nothing but his eyes (*HP*9).

The key to Weil's counterargument lies in her phrase, "this man, no more no less." What she means to suggest is that the idea of a "person" cannot be conceived but in relationship to the particular, concrete individual at hand, who is a distinctive blend of physical, psychological, spiritual, emotional, social—i.e., "personal"—characteristics. The "personality" of "this man" is simply one facet of a multifaceted being; thus what we must respect is not simply his personality but "[t]he whole of him. The arms, eyes, the thought, everything" (*HP*9). This radically comprehensive view of personhood leads Weil to another point, related to her rejection of "specimen thinking." It is impossible, she argues, for us to "define" in any abstract or universalist manner, what a person is. Any attempt to do so will succeed only in reducing distinctive, concrete, unique beings to a social category. That is to say, the attempt to define "person" or what is meant by "respect for human personality" undermines the very idea of "person" it wishes to preserve. Instead, we must eschew simple definitions or categories and be open and attentive to the person as a whole being, as well as to things we do not expect. In her *Notebooks*, Weil suggests that this sort of attentiveness has everything to do with justice:

> Justice. To be continually ready to admit that another person is something other than what we read when he is there (or when we think about him). Or rather: to read in him also (and continually) that he is certainly something other than what we read—perhaps something altogether different (*W*1956b:43).

Justice, then, is a form of attentive reading; it is the act of allowing another person to emerge as he or she really is. Or, to put it differently, it is a refusal to impose an "identity" or "personality" or a perspective upon the other. Any other attitude of mind is a submission to gravity, to "force," as Weil indicates when she writes: "To force someone to read himself as you read him (slavery). To force others to read you as you read yourself (conquest)" (*W*1956b:43).[28] The only way out of this trap of surface readings is through attention, the disposition that allows us to "read the world"—in this case other persons—more justly, with a deeper, more expansive, understanding and with a sensitivity that involves care. Attention like this requires great effort; we must be willing to forego attitudes or expressions like, "I know his type"; "Don't bother to explain, I already know what you'll say"; "Nothing she could do would surprise me"; "I can tell it all from first impressions." The very essence of attentiveness is quite contrary to such statements; it is a humility in the face of the incompleteness of one's own knowledge, a compassion which extends patience toward others, a recognition of the autonomy of others, a real effort to take in a reality beyond the self. When Weil speaks of attention as justice, then, she acknowledges the dimension of "care for others" that the concept sometimes holds for us. Those who are open to truth and proceed justly are far more worthy of respect, Weil observes, than are those of talent, personality, celebrity, or even conventional genius. In her typically disarming way, she declares: "A village idiot in the literal sense of the word, if he really loves truth, is infinitely superior to Aristotle in his thought, even though he never utters anything else but the supernatural virtue of humility in the domain of thought (*HP*25). For Weil, this supernatural virtue of humility is also the spirit of justice, and both consist "in seeing that no harm is done to men" (*HP*30).

We might understand Weil's own life—particularly her efforts as a factory worker and field laborer—and her political activities on behalf of the unemployed as exemplary of the attention she revered. Her politics both sprang from and were informed by precisely the sort of "supernatural humility" and "the faculty of pure and disinterested attention" she defends as justice.[29] Weil's message, of course, is not that we must work in the factory or labor in the field to achieve attention or to insure its authenticity. By our own efforts we can do so. But we must approach this task in the right way, without preconceptions or expectations. We must let another reading in, without presuming what it is. Above all else, Weil argues, we must avoid definitions or concepts of persons that rule out or narrow other possibilities. She also puts this idea in terms that recall her earlier argument in "The Power of Words," "a mind enclosed in language is in prison. It is limited to the number of relations which words can make simultaneously present to it . . . so the mind moves in a closed space of partial truth, which may be larger or smaller, without ever being able so much as to glance at what is outside" (*HP*26). In *HP*, Weil is concerned not only with how language as a whole logical system imprisons the mind and sets up barriers to the contemplation of "unformulable thoughts" but also with the way in which particular words, or definitions, or conceptual constructs can act as obstacles and prevent us from achieving a deeper reading of reality. When such a definition is set up "as a standard of public morality," she argues, "it opens the door to every kind of tyranny" (*HP*10). On this warning, she launches her critique of "rights."

Fundamental to Kant's precept to treat every person as an end and not merely a means and to seek principles of justice that embody it, is also the conception of rights. For the Kantian, the dignity of the individual must be understood in terms of the inviolability and primacy of rights secured by justice. Thus, intrinsic to human dignity and to justice itself is the idea of a person as the possessor of basic entitlements—as the bearer of rights. This prevailing liberal vision is the object of Weil's attack in *HP*. Her aim is not only to reveal the imprisoning quality the language of rights has for an understanding of what it means to be human, but also to break the bond between the "language of justice" and the "language of rights" liberalism has cemented.

What Weil holds, in essence, is this: the conception of rights upon which the liberal bases his argument for human dignity actually vitiates the precept that humans must be treated as persons and not as mere things. This is because, as she puts it, "The notion of rights is linked with the notion of sharing out, of exchange, of measured quantity. It has a commercial flavor, essentially evocative of legal claims and arguments" (*HP*18). The idea of "rights," in other words, is a part of a network of concepts that augment an exchange mentality as well as a cacophonous commercialism. This perspective actually fosters a conception of humans as "things with prices" rather than as persons with dignity. In one of her ironic turns, Weil points out that, in this sense, "the language of rights" does not reflect the dignity of the individual at all, but is instead closer to the behavior of the collective animal or brute force. "Rights are always asserted in a tone of contention," she notes, and "when this tone is adopted, it must rely upon force in the background or else it will be laughed at" (*HP*18).[30]

Weil actually locates the language of rights not in the origins of liberalism (about which she says little directly), but in Rome, where the *persona* was, for the first time, endowed with a juridical and legal identity, especially with regard to property. As she does with almost all things Roman, she condemns this development:

> It is singularly monstrous that ancient Rome should be praised for having bequeathed to us the notion of rights. If we examine Roman law in its cradle, to see what species it belongs to, we discover that property was defined by the *jus utendi et abutendi*. And in fact the things which the property owner had the right to use or abuse at will were for the most part human beings (*HP*20).

From the start then, the language of rights was tainted by force, and by a conception of humans as things. On Weil's telling, this Roman legacy was not in the least mitigated by later humanist and liberal arguments concerning the dignity of the rational individual. Kant's distinction between persons and things notwithstanding, the appeal to rights remains trapped in both a poverty-striken conceptualization of persons, and a language devoid of deep moral significance. If it is animated at all, the language of rights is animated by a destructive not an enriching vision of human sociability that comes, as Weil would have it, straight from the Romans.

Elaborating further on the difference of attitude or orientation that underlie various forms of language or conceptual frames of reference, she writes:

> If you say to someone who has ears to hear: "What you are doing to me is not just," you may touch and awaken at its source the spirit of attention and love. But it is not the same with words like "I have the right . . ." or "you have no right to . . ." They evoke a latent war and awaken the spirit of contention. To place the notion of rights at the centre of social conflicts is to inhibit any possible impulse of charity on both sides (*HP*21).

At times, Weil seems to be making a broad claim, that the "language of rights" is never appropriate, in any social context. For insofar as it is informed by some idea of a possessing "self" over and against other such "selves," rights talk encourages antagonism, divisiveness, conflictual relations, and the "shrill nagging of claims and counterclaims." None of these are conducive to the justice she associates with attending to others; they only exacerbate a confrontation with others. Or, in her terms, the "shrill nagging" of claims and counterclaims inhibits, perhaps even destroys, our capacity to ask "what are you going through?" The ethics of attention, then, is stifled by a mentality exclusively tied to "rights," and to a conception of self and other as calculating, self-interested marketeers.

Weil also offers a more narrow claim, however, when she implies that in some spheres of human activity the language of rights is defensible, while in others it is "ludicrously inadequate" (HP21). She grants that talk of rights may be appropriate in the economic marketplace, especially in relation to exchange values. But in other realms, when a person's dignity is threatened for instance, or her life is in jeopardy, an appeal to "rights" is at least morally insufficient, if not utterly bankrupt. She offers an example:

> If someone tries to browbeat a farmer to sell his eggs at a moderate price, the farmer can say: "I have the right to keep my eggs if I don't get a good enough price." But if a young girl is being forced into a brothel she would not talk about her rights. In such a situation the word sould sound ludicrously inadequate (HP21).[31]

By this I do not think Weil means that the issue of "rights" is unimportant or not relevant to the young girl's situation, but rather that to understand her situation solely as a denial of her rights is to fail to comprehend it fully or well.[32] We can imagine what she is getting at if we consider why a claim like "the pimp violated my right to control my own body" sounds reasonable but somehow incomplete. The claim does not capture the full extent of what it means to injure, harm, or violate a person, or to be so injured, harmed, or violated. Perhaps this is because one's "body" in such a locution is abstracted from the self and likened to a form of property. For Weil, with her radically complete picture of the person, this is tantamount to turning one's self into a thing. The claim therefore violates rather than vindicates human dignity.

But even if the young girl pursued her argument by elaborating upon her human rights and the pimp's attempt to deny her the dignity they reflect, Weil would have us conclude that there is still something missing in this account. To borrow her language, the appeal to rights cannot encompass the whole person; it may respect the legal entity and evoke legal claims, but it cannot pay tribute to "the radiance of the spirit" that is worthy of all human attention and respect. Put another way, the language of rights transforms all that is sacred—the uniqueness of the person, "the whole of him"—into the mundane. It encourages us to speak of ourselves and others in the "bargaining spirit"—as buyer, seller, possessor, owner, client, producer, product. As a result, we become imprisoned, closed off to a "deeper reading" of ourselves and others that passes through a conception of humans as autonomous "bearers of rights," and to a recognition of persons as complex, varied, richly diverse individuals who require our attention as concrete particulars. The latter, Weil informs us, is the essence of justice, and it is justice that is in jeopardy in a world of "rights."

Weil puts this same idea in other terms when she observes that the "cry we hear so often: Why has somebody else got more than I have?" refers to rights; the other cry, "Why am I being hurt?" raises the question of justice (*HP*30). In the modern age, the noise of rights arguments has all but drowned out the faint voices of those who require attention. But, not only that—the attentive silence necessary in order for the love of neighbor to bear fruit is compromised when the unafflicted are themselves caught up in the self-absorbed pursuit of rights. If the source of love of neighbor is our capacity to ask "What are you going through?" in all its depth and sincerity, then we must be able to listen. "To listen to someone," Weil notes, "is to put oneself in his place while he is speaking. To put oneself in the place of someone whose soul is corroded by affliction, or in near danger of it, is to annihilate oneself" (*HP*28). Amid the commercial contentiousness of rights however, listening is nearly impossible; hence attention cannot deepen, nor can the "ceaseless lamentation" of those who have suffered too many blows be heard.

This failure to listen, or to comprehend speech as anything other than the assertion of rights or as "freedom of propaganda" leads Weil to call for "a regime in which the public freedom of expression is characterized not so much by freedom as by an attentive silence in which the faint and inept cry can make itself heard," and for political leaders who are able and anxious to hear it (*HP*12). In contemporary democracies, where political parties are concerned first with their own propaganda, the words of the unfortunate, the poor, the unemployed, the disabled, the exiled, the oppressed, are so much "noise," and the noise is filtered, according to whether it contributes to or interferes with the platform of the party in question. "Tender and sensitive attention" Weil dryly observes, is not the *forte* of political parties. But neither, it seems, is it within the capacity of other organizations—trade unions, even churches—to listen with care to the voices of the afflicted. She would have us consider, then, what it would mean to live in an attentive polity, one in which justice is understood as the capacity to hear and respond to the cries of the unfortunate and listening, as attentive silence, is deemed as vital and important as speech.[33] For Weil, a polity such as this would revere and practice more than the general acknowledgement of rights; it would also entail the acceptance of an *obligation* on the part of citizens and institutions alike, to attend to those who are suffering—to "the stammering vagrant" as she puts it. "The name of this intense, pure, disinterested, gratuitous, generous attention," she proclaims, "is love" (*HP*28). Thus, her conception of justice is nothing less than a certain kind of attention raised to a public power, and understood as love. This is the new morality she offers, for both public and private life.

To make this new morality concrete, Weil might have pursued in *HP* the valuable issues her spiritual politics raises—the problem of human suffering, the politically moral response to it, the character of an attentive citizenry, and a conception of justice as love of neighbor. On many of these issues the tradition of Western political thought has been disturbingly silent—the glory of speech, but not the significance of listening, the autonomy of reason, but not the capacity to "attend," the possibilities of collective power, but not the value of compassion, have been more primary concerns. Most noticeably of all, perhaps, theorists have not introduced into their political orders the dimension of the human condition Weil refuses to ignore: the reality of human affliction. Even in the twentieth century, where *malheur* has assumed a proportion never before imagined and the very real possibility of global affliction confronts us, the refusal to think seriously about the political value of attention to others—especially radically different others—seems to mark the activity of political theorizing. Weil's concept of attention as justice provides a theoretical and practical antidote to this state of affairs, for it encourages us to rethink not only the meaning of human community, but also to confront our own uprootedness and the frame of human obligations this condition creates.

Despite the rich suggestiveness of her critique of rights, however, Weil herself does not pursue these issues in depth in *HP*. Instead of raising the difficult but potentially valuable discussion of the character of an attentive polity, she returns to a familiar theme that precludes any discussion of the polity at all—the notion of the collectivity ("We") as an infinitely dangerous thing. And instead of pursuing the question of who the attentive "self" is, she calls for the annihilation of the "I" or for what she also calls "impersonality" (a secular version of the theological *dépouillement*).

The achievement of impersonality is directly connected to overcoming the force of the collectivity and recognizing affliction. Weil says that insofar as the "I" glorifies personality, it is bound up with the Great Beast; therefore it too, like the collectivity, is "alien to the sacred" and cannot acknowledge the reality of *malheur*. As an example, she cites "those artists and writers who are most inclined to think of their ars2t as a manifestation of their personality"—Hugo, Wilde, Gide, the Surrealists—and she notes that these men are "in fact the most in bondage to public taste" (*HP*15). Thus, her conclusion: "the human being can only escape from the collective by raising himself above the personal and entering into the impersonal" (*HP*15).

"Impersonality," as Weil presents it in *HP* is a state of both physical and mental solitude. It can never be achieved, she warns, by "a man who thinks of himself . . . as part of something which says "We" " (*HP*14). Nor can it be realized by the man who clings to a "notion of respect for the person," by which she means the fixation upon the development of personality, the self, the ego. The only release from this sort of evil is found in solitude and silence—in the rooting of one's soul in the "impersonal good." Weil associates this disposition of the soul with a unique and demanding way-of-being in the world: "Every man who has touched the level of the impersonal," she writes, "is charged with the responsibility towards all human beings: to safeguard, not their persons, but whatever frail potentialities are hidden within them for passing over to the impersonal" (*HP*16). Those who have achieved "impersonality," then, are to bring others to recognize "the sacredness of the human being" and thereby assist them in transcending the "We" as well as the "I". In particular, those on the level of the impersonal have a responsibility to the afflicted, whose suffering brings them close to "supernatural good," but who may still need help to reach through their misery to something all humans deserve—a silence "in which truth can germinate and grow." "To ensure that they get it," Weil continues, "we can only count upon those who have passed beyond a certain barrier, and it may be objected that they are too few in number. Probably there are not many of them, but they are no object for statistics, because most of them are hidden" (*HP*32). Her point is that those who have achieved impersonality might serve as spiritual authorities, atten- tive to the afflicted but also aware of a more general obligation—never "to hold up for human aspiration anything but the real good in its perfect purity" (*HP*33).

In the end, then, attention as justice seems to resolve itself into a modified Platonism, only in Weil's vision those who have achieved the supernatural good are not philosopher kings but "impersonal" souls who attend to the afflicted and strive for a public life which is itself "impersonal and unrelated to any political form" (*HP*34).

Weil does not develop this vision of political leaders as "attentive souls" in *HP*. Indeed, she hardly appears convinced that such spiritual authorities are capable of transforming the dominant party politics of her time, if they are to be found at all. Despite her deep sympathies with the Platonic vision, this world is too much with her; she is not optimistic about the triumph of "perfection, truth, justice, and love" in the modern age. As I have tried to suggest, however, we might draw from *HP* a number of lessons of moral value—not only a critique of rights-based doctrines, but also an alternative conception of justice as compassion and of attention as a right way-of-being toward others. In the widest possible sense, the moral lessons Weil teaches are politically significant as well, for they hold implications not just for personal consciousness but also for citizenship, community, and democratic practice. Accordingly, those theorists currently engaged in the "communitarian turn" in political theory might find in her conception of attention an attitude or mentality compatible with the virtues community and egalitarian citizenship require. Feminists interested in alternatives to liberal individualist conceptions of the person and in compassion or care as virtues worth cultivating, would be well advised to consider her formulations on attentiveness and the love of neighbor as justice.

In a narrow sense, however, and despite their valuable implications for an alternative politics, Weil's reflections in *HP* are also politically problematic. Her continuing reluctance to find any sort of value in the collectivity prevents her from explicitly addressing any number of issues that her conception of attention could have informed—obligation, citizenship, the nature of community, patriotism as "love of country," the morality of national identity, etc. In *HP*, as in *RLO*, she is conceptually compelled to reject the possibility of a healthy collectivity because the only "We" is (still) a dangerous one. Indeed, in *HP* Weil goes even further, and denies any sort of healthy status to the "I" as well. If in *RLO* the antidote to the collectivity is to be found in individual methodical thinking, then in *HP* the problem is to find an antidote to both the collectivity *and* the individual—for neither society nor the self provide the starting point for a revitalized humanity. The only alternative is impersonality, wherein lies escape from both "We" and "I." And with this conclusion, she robs politics of almost all of its substance.

These frustrating features of Weil's later writings, replete as they are with (unfulfilled) promises of political insight, serve by way of contrast to make her most systematic work, *The Need for Roots* all the more remarkable. What we find there is that Weil suspends her hostility to the collectivity and follows a different impulse. She turns her full attention to the *metaxu*, "those earthly treasures" as the source of human roots. "Rootedness" now becomes the *presence*, not the absence of a place, and "roots" themselves are no longer affixed to the heavens, but brought back to the earthly ground, the "human milieu." With *The Need for Roots*, we might say that the exile "returns" to France.

## Notes

1. Among others, see Bramley (1967), Chaning-Pearce (1950–51), Davy (1951), Fischer (1979), Frenaud (1953), Jennings (1959), Krogmann (1970), Little (1970b), Marcel (1949), Teahan (1978), and Veto (1965).

2. See Ashcraft (1980), Blum and Seidler (1987), Dujardin (1975), King (1976), Pierce (1966), Rosen (1976), and Tomlin (1954).

3. Her impatience with Aristotle appears throughout her writings, and leads her to say some (characteristically) odd things. For example, "God in Plato"

begins with this remark: "Spirituality in Plato—that is to say, Greek spirituality. Aristotle is perhaps the only *philosopher*, in the modern sense in Greece, and he is quite outside the Greek tradition. Plato is all that we have of Greek spirituality" (W1968:90). One can make sense of this remark only if one remembers Weil's sympathy to all that is mystical in Greek thought, or under the influence of Pythagoreanism. Hence, in her eyes, Plato is far more "Greek" than the more worldly and empirical Aristotle.

4. Although I cannot pursue this theme in detail here, we must note that a distinguishing feature of Weil's thought is her attempt to integrate the Hellenic and the Christian traditions. She ends *TPF*, for example, by affirming the complementarity she finds in the two cultures: "The Gospels are the last marvelous expression of the Greek genius, as the *Iliad* is the first: here the Greek spirit reveals itself not only in the injunction given mankind to seek above all other goods "the kingdom and justice of our Heavenly Father," but also in the fact that human suffering is laid bare, and we see it in a being who is at once divine and human" (W1956:34). Most of the essays collected in *Intimations of Christianity Among the Ancient Greeks* (1957b) are concerned with developing the relationship between Hellenic and Christian myths, symbols, and ideas.

5. For a lengthier treatment of the Lord's Prayer, see her translation from the Greek and explication, "Concerning the Our Father" (W1951b:216–27).

6. For a suggestive interpretation of Beckett's play, based on Weil's mystical writings, see Cohen (1964). We should note, however, that *Waiting for God* is not *her* title but rather the title given to this collection of her letters and spiritual essays by Father Perrin, originally *Attente de Dieu* (1950a).

7. As for the "leap of faith" of the Christian existentialist, Weil wryly comments: "People who make athletic leaps toward heaven are too absorbed in the muscular effort to be able to look up to heaven; and in this matter the looking up is the one that counts" (W1968:157).

8. Perhaps nowhere is Weil's religious eclecticism or her unorthodox Christianity more obvious than in her emphasis on *dépouillement*. As many commentators have pointed out, her attraction to Catharism informs her doctrine of the surrender of the self. The Cathars allowed for a form of suicide by starvation, hence for renunciation of the world. That Weil finds Catharism a particularly compelling form of mysticism is evident in her letter to Deodat Roche (W1965:129–31).

9. We might recall here, of course, Weil's own self-loathing which leads her to consider herself mediocre, insignificant, and unworthy of attention, "the color of dead leaves like certain unnoticed insects," she tells Father Perrin (W1951b:101).

10. We might also think of Weil's doctrine of *dépouillement* in this way: renunciation of wordly evils entails a corresponding elimination of those evils not only *within* the self (as many other mystics have held) but *as* the self (Weil's more radical version). Thus to rid ourselves of "We" also requires us to rid ourselves of our "selves."

11. She also argues that affliction is not the province of the good or innocent alone: "God sends affliction without distinction to the wicked and to the good, just as he sends the rain and sunlight. He did not reserve the cross for Christ (W1952a:101).

12. Referring to the cross, the symbol that is at the core of her cosmic pessimism, Weil writes, "[the soul] has . . . to cross the infinite thickness of time and space in search of him whom it loves. It is thus that the soul, starting

from the opposite end, makes the same journey that God made toward it. And that is the cross" (W1951b:80).

13. As I suggested in Chapter 2, Weil's own death was deeply informed by this complex and difficult mysticism. Although much attention has been paid to her self-starvation, and numerous accounts have been offered to explain it, it seems to me that a truly meaningful one would have to confront her mystical belief that death is the ultimate detachment that closes the "infinite distance between God and God" (W1978:176). With the exception of J. M. Cameron's sensitive essay (White 1981) and a perceptive piece by Michele Murray (White 1981) no fully satisfactory accounts have yet been offered of Weil's death as a manifestation of her obsession with attention, affliction, and dépouillement. Although an analysis of this sort would require great care and sensitivity, evidence for the link between her self-imposed starvation and her conception of attention hardly needs manufacturing. The following observation from her notes, for example, is not an uncommon theme: "Man's great affliction, which begins with infancy and accompanies him 'til death, is that looking and eating are two different operations. Eternal beatitude is a state where to look is to eat" (W1952a:90). As I will suggest in Chapter 8, Weil's death cannot be fathomed (if fathomable at all) solely in terms of her mystical ideas. We must also consider the relationship she perceives between "self" and "country" in 1943, and perhaps understand her death as a self-sacrifice for the "nourishment" of France. Still, even these more political sensitivities are intricately intertwined with and informed by her mystical views, and particularly her conviction that "to look" rightly is "to eat" of the fruit of beauty and truth.

14. Although we must not use her mysticism as a rationalization, we might at least allow it to give some meaning to Weil's otherwise incomprehensible attitude concerning the Jewish question in the late 1930s and early 1940s. As McFarland and Van Ness (1987:17) note: "At the least it must be recognized that she perpetrated something perilously close to [a] "criminal error" by virtually ignoring and apparently distancing herself from Jewish suffering during this period." The source of Weil's attitude, as the above authors suggest, may be found in her lifelong revulsion toward identifying with any sort of collectivity. Or, more disturbingly, it could be that her blindness to the Jewish question emerged from her deep aversion toward what she perceived of as the religious tribalism of the "Hebrew race." Or we might understand her attitude in terms of a mysticism that accepts the reality of human affliction, and in turn leads her neither to regret nor to condemn the suffering of earthly beings, but rather to find *within* their suffering some meaning and hope, apart from the horrors of this world. Most likely, her attitude emerged from a complex combination of all three of these elements and, in the end, it is perhaps most accurately understood, as I argue here, as antipolitical rather than anti-Semitic. (For more on her problematical Jewish identity, see Chapter 1).

15. The words are those of Ignatius, Bishop of Antioch, shortly before he was thrown to the wild beasts in the public amphitheater of Rome (Pagels 1979:99).

16. The nature of affliction raises all sorts of complex psychological questions, and they are especially unavoidable given the physical and spiritual state of Simone Weil herself. She is quite clearly afflicted, and precisely in the terms she describes in *LGA*. In this sense we might understand her theology as the way in which she makes her reduced circumstances universally meaningful. Whether this means that she "cultivated" a sick psychology or fetishized her own misery is another matter, and a debatable one. At the least, it raises the issue that Erikson called "meaning it" and analyzed, in *Young Man Luther* (1958), in light

of Luther's argument for faith, not works. What is *within* the individual, so Luther had it, is what counts, not simply what the individual does external to his or her "self." He or she must therefore "mean" what he or she is and does. But what, Erikson asks, does this "meaning it" mean in a psychological sense? In Weil's case, we might ask, does affliction befall her, and does she transform it into a meaningful theology, or does she choose it, seek it out, and then use her theology to move toward even more extreme forms of personal evisceration? In other words, is her agony "authentic," or does she cultivate and pursue it with hidden purposes in mind? Is it her "secret triumph" over those who are stronger than she? I do not think there are any clear or easy answers to these questions. At the very least we must remember that Weil herself is suspicious of those who "take up" affliction, hence the argument that she fetishizes affliction would have to show how her practices can be turned against her own ideas. Although I will not attempt a resolution of these issues I think they are nonetheless worth facing, given the unavoidable affinities we can find between Weil's personal state and her doctrine of *malheur*.

17. I am grateful to Ann Smock for suggesting the significance of obedient "daily death" in Weil's mysticism.

18. On these matters, see also "Some Thoughts on the Love of God," where she notes: "A man works himself to exhaustion in order to eat, and he eats in order to get strength to work, and after a year of labour everything is exactly as it was at the beginning. He works in a circle. Monotony is only bearable for man if it is lit up by the divine. But for this very reason a monotonous life is much the more propitious for salvation" (W1968:152). As usual, she gives beautiful expression to the life of *animal laborans*, but in the questionable effort to reduce the human condition to it.

19. For an especially intelligent (and rare) discussion of this aspect of Weil's thought, see Teuber (1982).

20. This dimension of her argument goes some way toward checking the problem I noted earlier—that the emphasis on affliction might serve as a rationale for the evil doer. Quite clearly, Weil has a conception of criminality and criminal culpability that condemns those who afflict, even as it gives meaning to affliction itself.

21. Or, in the Eriksonian terms I suggested earlier (see note 16), Weil is addressing the issue of "the meaning of 'meaning it.' "

22. Weil is also similar to Kant in her emphasis upon the autonomy of the moral agent. Each of us, insofar as we possess the capacity for attention, constitute our own authority. Her mysticism, like Kant's moral theory, does not allow for Jesus to speak *as* a moral authority—we must wait for God and Christ, in our attentiveness as moral agents. It is through our attention that we find God and "Christ takes possession of us," not through Christ that we become moral agents. Thus, attention is a normative, moral concept, not simply a "description" of a state of "waiting."

23. This passage indicates the theological complexity of Weil's notion of "projection of being:" "To project one's being into an afflicted person is to assume for a moment his affliction, it is to choose voluntarily something whose very essence consists in being imposed by constraint upon the unwilling. And that is an impossibility. Only Christ has done it. Only Christ and those men whose whole soul he possesses can do it. What these men give to the afflicted whom they succour, when they project their own being into them, is not really

their own being, because they no longer possess one; it is Christ himself" (*LGA*191).

24. In some respects, at least, Weil's critique of the "derailment" of Christianity in the modern age shares much in common with the more recent writings of the late Eric Voegelin (1952, 1968) although one must hasten to add that she does not share his admiration for Aristotle, or his contempt for Gnosticism (which he uses as the symbol of all manner of modern Western developments he finds sectarian and dangerous), or his strident, cold-war, anti-Communism.

25. For a lengthy discussion of Weil's critique of rights, which attempts to situate her views within the broader context of "rights discourse" in Western thought, see Andrew (1986).

26. For further discussion of the features of the Personalist movement, especially in connection with the French Catholic left, see Hellman (1973).

27. As Hellman (1982) points out, Weil was initially drawn to the "ecumenical perspectives" of the young intellectuals around Mournier who were generally of left-wing political instincts, while convinced of the importance of spiritual values. She soon broke away from them, however, since she saw the connection between the political and the spiritual as a necessary rather than merely a possible one. The Personalists were far more flexible (or perhaps just ambivalent) on this score.

28. Weil's conception, at first glance, seems close to what Kant, in his aesthetics, called *eine erweiterte Dankungsart*, the "enlarged mentality" that requires a transcendence of the individual in order to "think in the place of" another. But for Kant, the enlarged mentality presupposes a particular sort of thought process (i.e., judgment) whereas for Weil a love of neighbor requires attention—a *suspension* of thought. Accordingly, even though they share a concern for a way-of-being that escapes the confines of narrow self-involvement, they have profoundly different notions of the attitude or mentality such a way-of-being requires.

29. For a different attitude on the Left, consider Herbert Marcuse (1964), who would have us view the workers as "one-dimensional" and blind to their "real concerns." For Marcuse, it is the workers who must gain awareness of "reality." Weil no doubt would find in Marcuse's view the mark of inattentiveness. To assume there is a "reality" that others need to know is to "force a reading" upon the other and thus to fail "to regard one's own reading and that of another person as equivalent" (W1956b:39). In her review of the Panichas volume, Joyce Carol Oates (1977:35) argues that despite Weil's theoretial concern for compassion and attention, "it is doubtful that she was at heart a very compassionate person." Oates appears to base this judgment only on a reading of Weil's critique of literature, perhaps revealing a lack of attention on her own part. Weil was not, it is true, a warm or particularly loving person, but she surely practiced her own form of attentiveness toward others, and lived her life constantly aware of the circumstances of others. For evidence, see her factory journal and her other essays on factory work in *La Condition ouvrière* (1951a), her essays on lost civilizations (1962a) and her numerous letters to her family and friends (1965) that occasion her reflections on her students, on the Spanish Civil War, the worker's condition, her family's hardship during World War II, and the plight of the French. Her letters to her mother and her father are particularly noteworthy for the depth of affection they reveal.

30. In addition to "rights," Weil argues that the notion of "person" and "democracy" tend to assume a similar tone of contention in everyday speech.

"Words of the middle region," she asserts, "such as *right, democracy, person,* are valid in their own region, which is that of ordinary institutions. But for the sustaining inspiration of which all institutions are, as it were, the projection, a different language is needed" (*HP*33). Her observation recalls the line of argument she pursues in "The Power of Words" (1962b) where she reveals the rigidity and thoughtlessness behind contemporary political discourse.

31. One is tempted to reply to Weil that, to the contrary, the "young girl" in this situation is quite likely to defend her "rights." In current political discourse, "rights language" rarely sounds inadequate; indeed, it extends quite easily to matters of the person, even among those who would be sympathic to Weil's reasoning. Note, for example, the readiness with which some feminists defend a woman's right to choose abortion as an extension of her "right" to control her own body, while those who oppose "abortion rights" defend the fetus's "right to life." Indeed, to imagine a concept of "person" that is *not* premised first upon rights is what sounds "ludicrously inadequate" to us—not as Weil would have it, the other way around. But then that is what she wants us to think about.

32. Despite this caveat, it is probably fair to conclude that Weil is most uncompromising on the matter of rights. A defense of rights, in any form, is not a part of her political thought. So, for example, she leaves "rights" out of her list of "needs of the soul" in *The Need for Roots* and stresses obligation instead. In fact, she argues that rights cannot be understood apart from obligations: "The notion of obligations comes before that of rights, which is subordinate and relative to the former. A right is not effectual by itself, but only in relation to the obligation to which it corresponds, the effective exercise of a right springing not from the individual who possesses it, but from other men who consider themselves as being under a certain obligation toward her. . . . A man left alone in the universe would have no rights whatever, but he would have obligations" (*W*1952b:3). She does not go on to develop and defend these claims in *TNFR*, but we can perhaps understand them in terms of what she writes in *HP*. An obligation, insofar as it is something that binds us morally to another, takes precedence over rights because it presupposes a moral attitude toward the other. (Of course, one might argue that rights also presume such an attitude, but Weil contests this). That is to say, acknowledging an obligation gives substance to a claim to rights. Or, to paraphrase Teuber, (1982) a sense of obligation toward a person helps to "bring home" the value of the person as a "bearer of rights." Without such a sense, we are reduced to a world of legal entities rather than persons, or a "system of claims" rather than one of values that give these claims meaning.

33. Theorists sympathetic to democracy, discourse, and the values of participatory citizenship have failed to attend to the sort of "silence" Weil emphasizes. But surely, any theory of democratic participation must include not only a concern for speech but also respect for what it means to listen. Weil's reflections on attention take on profound political importance in this sense, for she would have us consider what it means to be "communicative" as both a speaker and a listener as well.

# Part IV

## *The Need for Roots*

# 7

# The Crisis of France

Dᴜʀɪɴɢ Wᴏʀʟᴅ Wᴀʀ II, the civilian offices of the Free French Organization were located at 19 Hill Street in London. Simone Weil spent most of her time there after arriving in England from the United States in November of 1942.[1] With the help of Maurice Schumann, her former schoolmate from the Ecole Normale, and André Philip, the Commissioner of Interior and Labor in the FFO, she managed to obtain passage back to Europe and to secure a post in the Gaullist organization that was developing projects for the revitalization of France after the war. Among other things, Weil was directed to write a statement concerning the activities to be pursued in the course of such an event.[2] The Gaullists were thinking along the lines of an organizational policy paper with a dash of inspirational spirit, something that might establish anew the *Declaration des droits de l'homme* and, at the same time, set out some guidelines for re-establishing the institutions of the French government. From its inception, however, the assignment seems to have been intended primarily as busy-work for Weil, designed to keep her occupied and to free the officers of the Free French Organization for more immediate, "practical" tasks.[3] Simone herself seems to have been aware of the nature of her assignment. In a letter to her mother she observed: "When it is finished, I really wonder what they can do with me? . . . Naturally, I don't think there is the slightest reason to suggest that what I am writing will have any effect" (W1965:187). Nevertheless, she continued to work.

The result of her labors was *L'Enracinement*, or *The Need for Roots*, (*TNFR*1952b), which Weil called her "other *magnum opus*," the "Reflections Concerning the Causes of Liberty and Social Oppression" being the first. Their respective identifications are, however, about the only thing these two works have in common. In its theoretical structure, the *RLO* proceeds along a carefully outlined, methodical route, toward the approximation of an ideal of liberty. *TNFR* displays from the start a far more diffused intellectuality. As it develops, Weil offers both bold assertions and tentative intimations, reflections as well as directives; its three major sections are not explictly interrelated, nor does Weil suggest that they should be.

The respective standpoints of the two works are quite different as well. If the *RLO* is best described as a work of sociological critique, blended with an element of syndicalist utopianism, then *TNFR* is a work of political pragmatism with clear tones of Christian spiritualism. What is missing in the *RLO*—a programmatic rendition of the theoretical vision—is of major significance in *TNFR*. In the latter, Weil is concerned with actual practice as well as theoretical prescriptions, with the concrete enactment of her ideas as well as the ideas themselves. No doubt some of the differences between these two works can be explained by the circumstances that surround their writing—*TNFR* is a response to an immediate crisis, the fall of France. The reality of the political world bears down upon it. The *RLO*, although motivated by Weil's reaction to the oppressiveness of the modern world, has none of the pressing, concretely historical quality that characterizes *TNFR* and makes it "a work for the moment" as well as the object of theoretical concerns.

Were it simply the case, however, that in *TNFR* Weil renders the substantive theme of the *RLO*—individual liberty and methodical thinking—in an alternative, more historical and pragmatic mode, then perhaps the differences between the two would not be so striking. But what truly sets them at a great distance from each other are the different substantive themes each develops. For example, the idea of individual liberty, so fundamental to her argument in the *RLO*, virtually vanishes in *TNFR*. And methodical thinking, the keystone of her thought in her first "magnum opus," is completely absent in the second, where patriotism, country, and *enracinement*, "rootedness," are more central concepts. The most astonishing feature of *TNFR*, however, is the inspiration it draws from an idea Weil condemns and repudiates in almost all of her other writings, mystical and materialist alike: the collectivity as "nourishment" for the human soul. Except for the fact that so many other features of this text betray her hand, it would be tempting to conclude that Weil could not have written it, so devoid is it of encomia against the "Great Beast," the blind collectivity, and the wretched "We." In place of these (now familiar) attacks, Weil offers an alternative vision of "the first person plural," one that perceives of it as a basic human need. "We owe our respect to a collectivity of whatever kind," she writes, "country, family, or any other—not for itself, but because it is food for a certain number of human souls" (*TNFR*7). In her "Draft for a Statement of Human Obligations" (written alongside *TNFR*) she reiterates the vital importance of "natural human environments," and includes among them "a man's country, and places the language is spoken, and places with a culture or a historical past which he shares, and his professional milieu, and his neighborhood" (W1962b:226). Anything that uproots a person from such an environment she declares "criminal."

In *TNFR* she goes on to suggest three specific reasons why we must pay "the utmost respect" to collectivities: first, because of their respective uniqueness, the "food" of any given collectivity has no equivalent; once destroyed it cannot be replaced. Second, because of continuity: the food of the collectivity is for the souls of beings yet unborn, future generations, not just souls of the living. Third, a collectivity has its roots in the past, in "spiritual treasures" through which the dead speak to the living. Of all the collectivities she praises, however, it is "country" that Weil seems to think proves the truest medium of "Man's earthly needs" and the most vital source of unique identity and continuity across generations. With a decisive stroke, she thus reverses the hierarchy of values in her thought. What was in her mystical writings anathema to all that is pure and spiritual now becomes a vital need. What endangered the autonomous methodical thinker in her materialist writings—the collectivity—is now the primary nourishment of the human soul. Accordingly, in *TNFR* Weil sets out to determine what it means to belong to a collectivity and what a country requires in order for it to be a source of earthly roots. Conversely, she intends to confront the condition she thinks is most threatening to human souls in the modern world—*déracinement*—rootlessness.

## Affliction as a Political Condition

Weil begins *TNFR* by articulating what she thinks are "the needs of the soul," what we, as social and political beings, require in order to live a fully human life. Some of the needs she presents draw upon the oldest traditions of political theory: order, liberty, equality, security. Others bear the mark of modern preoccupations: obligation, punishment, private property, collective property, freedom of opinion. Still others reveal the distinctive perspective of Weil herself: responsibility, risk, hierarchism, honor, truth.[4] One "need", however, does not appear as part of the formal litany with which the book begins, but Weil nevertheless declares it "the mos important and least recognized need of the human soul": the need for roots. And it is the need for roots, rather than the others, that is the primary focus of her concern in *L'Enracinement*.

Although Weil notes that the need for roots is one of the hardest needs of the soul to define, she offers an approximate idea of what it entails when she writes:

> A human being has roots by virtue of his real, active and natural participation in the life of the community, which preserves in living shape certain particular treasures of the past and particular expectations of the future (*TNFR*43).

The natural sources of an individual's identity—family, home, vocation, religion, tradition, and the country that protects these selfsame "roots"—are what Weil thinks are the most valuable aspects of human communities. Her idea of community is not a contractual one of social life as an "artifice" wherein individuals live together but essentially go their own way, careful only to avoid (unnecessarily) harming others. Her sympathies, in this realm of thought at least, lie more with Edmund Burke. Like him, she perceives a community as a rich network of interrelationships within which we are born and to which we are inextricably bound. Its influences mold our habits, our values, our ways of thinking, just as our "active participation" shapes and creates the dimensions that distinguish our community from others.

For Weil, rootedness in community is spatial, territorial and multiple. In the deepest, most intimate sense (although she hardly develops this idea), our roots tie us to home and neighborhood. More widely, roots connect us to village or city, to the land or the factory, to pastoral serenity or urban intensity. More sweeping still, roots are political—since modern times, they have been found in ties to country or the nation.

Rootedness is also historical. Roots secure us to what Weil calls our "most valuable possession in the world of temporal affairs," to a sense of continuity in time (TNFR100). The community anchors us in the past and bears upon our future. As a part of it, we know familial as well as political ancestors and founders, the "treasure" as Weil puts it, of what has come before us. If we pay attention to our roots we know our "selves" more fully too—as social and historical beings who share a territory, a set of richly woven traditions, cultural inheritances, and a past in need of remembrance, retelling, and respect. For Weil, then, roots are both earthly ties to a place and they are "spiritual nourishment," a source of sustenance and meaning, identity and purpose extended over time.

The problem of modernity is that roots in collectivities of all kinds have nearly been destroyed. As Weil would have it, uprootedness is the paradigmatic condition of the modern age. Using her terms, we might conceive of it as affliction, rendered collective and political.

If one examines in detail the situations Weil ascribes to rootlessness, they turn out to be varied and diverse. For example, she associates rootlessness with literal uprootedness—with the actual physical displacement of persons from family, home, and country. Uprootedness may be forced (as in the case of deportations or military conquest) or "voluntary" (as in the case of refugees who flee in the face of potential danger), but in either instance it involves discontinuity, estrangement from one's natural birthplace or chosen habitat, from community, profession, land, and past. Rootlessness assumes other forms as well. It need not involve actual territorial exile or forced emigration, for a people can be rootless within its own homeland, she argues, as "when the conquerors are migrants who settle down in the conquered country, intermarry with the inhabitants, and take root themselves," and thus destroy, through social and cultural usurpation, the indigenous customs and traditions of the native population (*TNFR*44).[5] A still more complex form of rootlessness may exist amidst a people who have neither been conquered by some foreign power nor ravaged by war. This form of rootlessness Weil characterizes in terms of class domination and the alienation of labor. In a passage that recalls her Marxist sympathies as well as her thought in *La Condition ouvrière*, she observes that workers, "Although they have remained geographically stationary . . . have been morally uprooted, banished, and then reinstated, as it were on sufferance, in the form of industrial brawn" (*TNFR*45). Still more devastating is unemployment, "uprootedness raised to the second power" (*TNFR*45).

In the end, however, the core of Weil's understanding of rootlessness is not to be found in class analysis. Indeed, in striking contrast to her materialist writings, she gives the concept of "class" barely any attention at all, "it is not one of those notions," she argues, "which . . . are clear to the mind. It is even harder to conceive it or feel it without some definition than it is to define it" (*TNFR*126). The nature of *déracinement*, then, cannot be analyzed primarily as the alienation of labor, although the workers' condition is certainly a part of it. Instead, Weil offers a broader, political rather than social, vision of rootlessness. It hinges on her observation of "human collectivities" in general and one collectivity in particular, the one that has "come to replace all other bonds of attachment," the nation (*TNFR*99). This phenomenon is, in and of itself, a sign of rootlessness; smaller collectivities, the family, the village, the district, the region—those "little platoons" as Burke once called them— have been swallowed up and overcome by a "national sense." The nation, then, serves as the focus of *TNFR*, and the nation presents a paradox: it is the collectivity that is at once the most likely locus of membership and belonging in the modern age, and also the source of the deepest form of *déracinement*. Or, as Weil puts it, "just in this very period where the nation stands alone and supreme . . . we have witnessed its sudden and extraordinarily rapid decomposition" (*TNFR*100).

The "decomposition" Weil refers to, the deepest form of *déracinement*, might best be understood as the corruption of collective, public identity. In contemporary terms, her conception of rootlessness is akin to what contemporary theorists might call the "crisis of modernity," or "the *anomie* of mass culture." But we might also imagine that what she means is something closer to the condition the Greeks knew as *stasis*, and

Thucydides found in Athens during the Peloponnesian War. Rootlessness involves the breakdown of an ethos, the corruption of public spirit
and the shared understandings that lend a people or a "collectivity" its
identity and meaning. In one sense, then, rootlessness, like *stasis*,
involves the loss of a common past and common ancestors. If the human
collectivity (in whatever its various historical forms) "constitutes the
sole agency for preserving the spiritual treasures accumulated by the
dead," then rootlessness is the condition in which those spiritual
treasures have been forsaken and the past has slipped away. Weil
understands the decay of collective spirit literally, as the shrinking up
of those "treasures" that afford sustenance to a nation, the sort of
treasures Thucydides called to mind in the Funeral Oration, when he
had Pericles remind the Athenians of their indebtedness to the laws,
customs, and institutions of their ancestors (Thucydides 1954:143–51).
For him, the *stasis* of Athens was manifested in the Athenians' ultimate
failure to respect, protect, and perpetuate the gifts of the ancestors that
had made their city glorious, "the school of all Hellas." Weil thinks of
rootlessness in a similar way, hence she writes, "no one thinks nowa-
days about his ancestors who died fifty or even only twenty or ten years
before his birth; nor about his descendants who will be born fifty or
even only twenty or ten years after his death" (*TNFR*100). This is as true
of the nation as it is of the family; all sense of a national past or a
historical legacy, as well as a commitment toward future generations,
seems to have disintegrated.

In another sense, Weil's conception of rootlessness, like Thucydides'
idea of *stasis*, marks not just the decay of a collective communal spirit
but the decline of an expressly political one as well. If *enracinement*
involves "real active participation in the life of the community," then
*déracinement* is the corruption of democracy, citizenship, and politics
itself. Thus Thucydides revealed the decline of the Athenian ethos not
just as the abandonment of habits, values, and traditions, but also as
the gradual corruption of a certain kind of practice—political speech
and public participation—that resulted in the rule of demagogues and
finally in the complete collapse of Athens. Likewise, Weil thinks that
rootlessness manifests itself in the disintegration of democratic politics.
It is not just that the citizens of a nation lose sight of what unifies and
distinguishes them; it is also that they cease to act as political beings
and acquiesce to rule by politicians, charlatans, and most tragically,
dictatorial men.

Weil is aware, of course, that the political manifestations of rootlessness take different form in different nations. Democracies can disinte-
grate in very different ways. But her intention in *TNFR* is not to draw
the necessary distinctions among various forms of rootlessness in once
democratic citizenries. Rather, she wants to focus, not unlike Thucydi-

des, upon her own homeland and its citizens, in order to understand the *déracinement* indigenous to them and thereby shed light on the specific condition of the "human *milieu*" to which she belongs. Hence she writes:

> If France offered a spectacle more painful than that of any other European country, it is because modern civilization with all its toxins was in a more advanced stage there than elsewhere with the exception of Germany. But in Germany uprootedness had taken on an aggressive form, whereas in France it was characterized by inertia and stupor (*TNFR*49).

Only in the context of her immediate and concrete purpose—to confront the "inertia and stupor" of France—can we fully come to terms with Weil's theoretical enterprise in *TNFR* and thereby recognize what makes it both a remarkable and original work, an act of attention for the love of France.

## Diagnosing the Case: France and the Crisis of Patriotism

In the wake of the fall of France in 1940, there was no shortage of attempts, both intellectual and political, to come to terms with what Sartre later called the "strange defeat." Jacques Maritain, the Catholic philosopher, viewed it as the result of the collapse of the Cartesian tradition and as the final disgrace of "Rousseauism." Saint-Exupery wrote of the catastrophe as the unavoidable consequence of excessive individualism and a fall from spiritual values. Bernanos blamed the ideology of the Third Republic; de Jouvenal cited the inherent instability of democratic systems, and numerous social theorists and historians attempted explanations that drew upon specific economic conditions and social relations that may have contributed the vulnerability of the French state.[6] For Weil, the fall of France was more than a military debacle or the result of the ineptitude of political leaders. Neither could it be attributed solely to destabilizing class antagonisms, nor to some bad seed in the "national character." The catastrophe was the result of a much deeper and more malodorous, though less visible, political condition—the corruption of patriotism. "A tree whose roots are almost entirely eaten away falls at the first blow," she notes. The roots to which she refers are those connections that secure a people to their country and give life to what Tocqueville called "instinctive patriotism"—that undefinable, unpondered passion for the *patria* that "does not reason, but believes, feels, and acts (Tocqueville 1964:236–37). By 1940, that passion had ceased to exist in France; the political spirit that might have united French citizens was completely eroded. In its place was a disassociated mass in the grip of an apathetic stupor. The blow of 1940, Weil argues, must be understood accordingly:

The French people . . . were not a people waylaid by a band of ruffians, whose country was suddenly snatched from them. They are a people who opened their hands and allowed their country to fall to the ground. Later on—but only after a long interval—they spent themselves in ever more and more desperate efforts to pick it up again; but someone had placed his foot on it (*TNFR*101).

Weil perceives both the disaffection of the French and the desperate, and essentially empty, show of national feeling that followed the collapse, as more than momentary events or "moods," which would in time be overcome. The uprootedness that characterizes the transitory passions of the citizenry is not something that, left to itself, will disappear. The sort of roots that concern her do not grow naturally, nor does the disease of rootlessness run its course and then subside. More direct action is required to conquer the affliction that grips France. Thus, she writes, "The essential thing is to have rightly diagnosed the case, conceived a cure, chosen the right medicaments, and made sure the patient is supplied with them" (*TNFR*183).

Weil's "diagnosis of the case" proceeds from a historical sketch, a story, really, intended to reveal how the "love of Frenchmen for the kingdom of France" came to be poisoned.[7] She believes that a people's comprehension of its own past is essential to rootedness, hence the reconstruction of historical events is a necessary part of the recovery of meaning and identity. "Loss of the past," she tells her audience, "is the supreme human tragedy, and we have thrown ours away just like a child picking off the petals of a rose" (*TNFR*119). The recovery of the past is essential for at least two reasons: first, in order to bring to life those moments or traditions that might provide a people with renewed inspiration for the present, and second, in order to uncover certain truths that a nation may have distorted, evaded, repressed, or simply denied in the effort to make of itself what Weil calls an "absolute value." In a sense what Weil suggests in *TNFR* is that a healthy national identity presupposes a facing-up-to-the-past. Just as a truly mature self is one that has fully integrated his or her past by acknowledging that it survives, shapes, and is absorbed into the present, so the nation with "roots" is one that recognizes that it is deeply constituted by the realities of its past and encourages its citizenry to attend to them. When she tells France that it must feel it has a past but not "love the historical wrapper of the past," I think she is offering advice on political maturity in precisely this sense. For France to overcome its disastrous condition, it must work to restore a sense of identity that is rooted not in illusion and the distortion of history but in a patriotic spirit inspired by an attitude appropriate to full assimiliation of the past. In psychological terms, France's task is to become a "developed and fully integrated self" that "contains within it those aspects of the past which it values, and uses them to master and change its own impulses which it does not value."[8]

With something like this in mind, Weil urges the French to rethink their past, to reconsider the events that have molded them as a people, and to reassess these events in light of their present "inertia and stupor." In other words, she would have France face up to the shallow and sick spirit that passes for patriotism, discover its source, and set about a cure before it is too late. As physician to the sick body politic— or, more accurately perhaps, as psychologist to a psychically conflicted nation—Weil would assist the French in this enterprise. Her aim in *TNFR* is to provide a starting place, by directing the nation's attention to a story of its own past.

Weil begins her narrative with a brief account of the legacy of the French kings. That legacy, she argues, is not one of glorious conquest and territorial consolidation, but rather the story of a "state of despotism" to which the people of France were subject from the reign of Charles VI until the eighteenth century (*TNFR*104). This "first stage" of the decline of the French monarchy and the brutality that accompanied it, instilled within the people a suppressed hatred for the king, "a traditional hatred" that was never extinguished, and fully ignited at the end of the reign of Louis XIV. Weil attributes the decline of the monarchy to two general factors. First, she cites the oppressive policies the kings, *tout court*, enacted against the people, and that led other Europeans to look upon the French as enslaved, as "a people who could be treated like cattle by their sovereign" (*TNFR*105). Second, she recounts the brutality of the French kings' conquests of other lands and cultures: Breton, Corsica, Franche-Comte, Burgundy, and those lands south of the Loire annexed in the thirteenth century.[9] Her critique of the suppression of the "Romanesque civilization," in what is now the province of Languedoc and includes Toulouse, is both cultural and political. The kings' men not only obliterated the genuis of Languedocian art, literature, and moral values, they also destroyed a form of public, political life and a civic spirit that, in conformity with "the Greek ideal," loved liberty and obedience and detested force (*W*1962b:51). But her underlying point is about patriotism. What has passed in the history texts as a masterful assimilation of countries united as "France" was, in reality, a collection of uprooted peoples hostile to the French kings yet subdued by superior force and a dominant culture. This further weakened whatever bonds of patriotism might have tied the French people to their kings.

The gist of Weil's retelling of the monarchical episode of French history is not to deny that any attachment to France ever existed among the people; rather, she wants to suggest that whatever ties did give rise to an intensely conscious Frenchness had little or nothing to do with the kings. Perhaps her most radical claim is that, in the end, the event that welded together what were merely disparate territories under the monarchy was the Revolution of 1789. If, prior to that time, the French had some collective cultural identity, then after 1789 (for at least a brief moment) they had a political one inspired by their "enthusiasm for national sovereignty" (*TNFR*110). Thus in France, Weil says, patriotism seems to be founded not on love of the past, but on a most violent break with the past. She goes on, however, to suggest that this can be true only if the "past" is understood in terms of orthodox history, as the era of kings. In reality, if one tears away the "historical wrapper" and looks more closely, the Revolution appears to have had its own past and precedents in the "underground of French history." This underground past includes the freeing of the serfs, the liberties of the towns, social struggles, the revolts of the fourteenth century, the beginning of the Burgundian movment, the Fronde, and the establishment of a peoples' militia under François I (*TNFR*110). For Weil, truly to understand the French past—and patriotism—is to be aware of "the dynamic force thrusting beneath the surface" of the French people. Given this much of her historical narrative, her conception of patriotism is a decidedly political one that associates the emergence of a civic spirit with popular sovereignty, the dissolution of monarchy, the rise of republican institutions, and *liberté, égalité, fraternité*.

However, despite her assessment of the Revolution as the historical source and site for a healthy civic spirit among the French, Weil is not inclined to idealize 1789 or its aftermath. She views the Revolution as a paradoxical moment in French history, the moment when true patriotism was both realized and destroyed. Thus she writes:

> The Revolution melted all the peoples subject to the French Crown into one single mass, and that by their enthusiasm for national sovereignty. Those who had been Frenchmen by force became so by free consent, many of those who were not French wanted to become so. For to be French, thenceforward, meant belonging to a sovereign nation (*TNFR*110).

Yet at the same time the Revolution could not sustain this patriotic enthusiasm; it planted no roots.[10] Soon enough national sovereignty showed itself to be an illusion; in the absence of concrete associations and practices that might have made national sovereignty meaningful, and in the face of terror, patriotism changed its meaning. That is why Weil says that the date of 1789 awakens "a really deep echo," but all that is attached to it "is an inspiration, there are not institutions" (*TNFR*181). To put this in more expressly political terms, the Revolution created a public identity, that of the *citoyen*, but provided no way for citizenship to be practiced. Or, in psychological terms, the Revolution gave the French a new identity, but it offered no means for the authentic fulfillment of that identity.

## National Identity and the Failure of Public Imagination

Weil's historical narrative is yet more complicated than this, however. For it is not just that the Revolution failed to perpetuate patriotism or to create a sovereign nation and a political realm that would truly inspire it. If that were all, patriotism would simply not exist. But, Weil says, it does exist, though in perverted form, because the object to which it clings is itself a perversion of political life. That object is the State. So, to understand the problem of their patriotism, the French must not only break through the mythology of the Revolution but also examine an earlier event in the seventeenth century, when the notion of *patrie* was usurped by *étatisme*.

The rise of the State is, in essence, the focal point of Weil's historical narrative, and the episode toward which she directs her most critical powers. The emergence of the State marks what she calls the "second stage" of the decline of the French monarchy. Yet the State outlived the monarchy itself and has much to do with the subsequent uprootedness of France. The Revolution may have failed "to root" patriotism; the State assured its demise. The diagnosis is rendered in vivid metaphors—the State is a lifeless thing that is "blind, anonymous, and crushing," a "cold, metallic surface" (W1962b:94,114). Weil's mechanical descriptions recall the "collectivity," and suggest something sterile and artifical that can neither sustain roots or inspire love. The State suppresses everything that might be loved, she argues; it obliterates the *citoyen*, and levels public life.[11] When she does think of it as alive, Weil imagines the State as a parasite on the body politic: "the development of the State exhausts a country. The State eats away its moral substance, lives on it, fattens on it, until the day comes when no more nourishment can be drawn from it, and famine reduces it to a condition of lethargy" (*TNFR*120).

The political side of Weil's diagnosis focuses on the role of the State in the destruction of local and regional life, and real human roots, in family, village, and province. As the State expanded, she notes, France became ever more like "a dying man whose members are already cold, and whose heart goes on beating" (*TNFR*122). At the center of this drama, there is a villain, the man whose policy was "to kill systematically all spontaneous life in the country, so as to prevent anything whatsoever being able to oppose the State": the Cardinal Richelieu (*TNFR*116).[12]

Weil's contempt for Richelieu is matched only, perhaps, by her equally strong aversion for the imperial Romans, and it is not by chance that she directs similar criticism toward both.[13] Richelieu, like the Romans, stands as the symbol of a certain political tradition. He is the champion of the "inhuman, brutal, bureaucratic, police-ridden State," and a defender of its unbridled power and coercive potential in both foreign and domestic affairs. In TNFR, Weil's specific charge against Richelieu has to do with his complicity in creating the State and killing off public, political life. Quite simply, she says, "his devotion to the State uprooted France" (TNFR116). Expanding on this idea, she writes:

> the idea of making the State an object of loyalty appeared for the first time in France and in Europe with Richelieu. . . . It was he who first adopted the principle that whoever exercises a public function owes his entire loyalty, in the exercise of that function, not to the public, or to the king, but to the State and nothing else (TNFR115).

Under Richelieu's direction, the State developed as a centralized bureaucratic apparatus; it systematically destroyed the political life of the provincial towns and cities and replaced all public spiritedness with a "pall of ennui" (TNFR123). For Weil, this political situation is tantamount to the death of France:

> No other interest replaced the one lacking in public affairs. Each successive regime having destroyed at an ever increasing rate local and regional life, it had finally ceased to exist. France was like a dying man whose members are already cold, and whose heart alone goes on beating. Hardly anywhere was there any real throb of life except in Paris; but even there, as soon as you reached the suburbs, an atmosphere of moral decay began to make itself felt (TNFR122).

The moral decay she speaks of is, in essence, *political* decay—the disintegration of a public realm and political action in the regions and localities of the collectivity. Once the State took control of political life, "public affairs" were viewed with an attitude of contempt. "Frenchmen prided themselves on keeping away from all contact with what they termed la politique," Weil notes, "except on the day of elections, or even on that day, too" (TNFR122). In time, and as a result of expanding central power and impersonal institutions, the usurpation of local associations of action and order, and the rise of State sponsored political parties and politicians, political life itself became an object of disgust, just as the State was a target for derision. "The very word politics," Weil observes, "had taken on a profoundly perjorative meaning incredible in a democracy . . . 'All that, that's just politics'—such phrases expressed final and complete condemnation" (TNFR121).

Thus the story of patriotism in France, as Weil presents it, has revealed itself in familiar modern guise: as the gradual erosion of "real active natural participation" in the life of the community, at the hands of the autonomous, centralized State.

Despite its argument that the uprootedness of France has much to do with the monolithic powers of the centralized State, Weil's narrative does not absolve the French people from responsibility for their own *déracinement*. Her diagnosis is also a complex story of the alienated public consciousness that accompanied the disappearance of public life and the rise of the State. For this part of her "diagnosis," she goes back to "the need for roots," which she sees as a collective as well as a personal human requirement, a matter of importance to a people as well as to individuals. In the absence of a public, political life that would nurture collective roots, the need for roots and the desire to belong remain intense nonetheless. If there is no public realm, no local community of face-to-face associations within which a people's sense of identity might grow, then that loyalty will not die, but simply redirect itself toward something wherein it can find some identity and meaning. This political and psychological reality is precisely what Weil thinks confronted the French in 1789, and has been playing itself out ever since. The Revolution planted no roots; as a result, the French people's "love of sovereign nation" was an emotion in search of an object. But what could serves as an adequate source of political loyalty and the need for a national identity? The alternatives that did exist—international churches and political parties, class associations, professions, trades corporations—were either degraded, hopelessly inadequate, or themselves nearly extinct. Only one thing remained in France "to which loyalty [could] cling"—the State. Likewise, "the only form of sacrifice remaining in the public imagination was military sacrifice, that is, a sacrifice offered to the State" (*TNFR*127). The irony of this collective act of national identification cannot be ignored. The French, Weil suggests, found belonging and meaning in something that they in fact despised, and rootedness in the very source of their own alienation and *déracinement*.

The complexity of the French identity involves even more than this, however. The French do not simply profess allegiance to the State at one moment and have no qualms about robbing or cheating it the next, although that is indeed one manifestation of their destructive political identity (*TNFR*121). Another "strange spectacle" reveals itself in political life right up until 1940; a "loveless idolatry" commands the public consciousness and exists alongside hatred of the State. The idolatry is directed toward a political illusion that, in effect, is a *patrie* of the public imagination. The very inadequacy of the State as a source of political rootedness necessitated the manufacture of this illusion, which Weil sometimes refers to as the idea of "eternal France," sometimes as an image of "*ersatz* greatness."

Thus the true problem, in the end, lies not with Richelieu, but with the French themselves. Weil indicates that the French are complicit in their own uprootedness, in part because they have warped the meaning of country by perpetuating a dangerous illusion that masquerades as country and a destructive spirit that parades as true patriotism. She calls this spirit, variously, "national egoism" or "modern patriotism" or "loveless idolatry," but regardless of the description, this shallow but resilient sentiment bears no resemblance to the patriotism that is compatible with participation in public affairs. Indeed, rather than fufilling the need for roots, this national egotism perpetuates *déracinement*.

Behind this sentiment are a number of unexamined prejudices and emotions that fuel the public imagination and augment a perverse sense of solidarity. One that Weil suggests is the uncritical acceptance of the nation as an "absolute value" (*TNFR*130). "Present day patriotism," she notes, "consists in an equation between absolute good and a collectivity corresponding to a given territorial area, namely France" (*TNFR*144). What results is a pagan idolatry—the nation becomes an icon, an object of blind worship. This pagan idolatry is, in turn, both fed by, and feeds, a public pride that knows no bounds. Weil's discussion is reminiscent of Tocqueville's observation that patriotism is "most often nothing but an extension of individual egoism," only she thinks that egoism on a national scale is far more excessive:

> When it is a question of oneself, and even of one's family, it is more or less a recognized thing that one mustn't be too boastful; that one must beware of one's judgments . . . that one mustn't try to occupy the whole stage or think solely of oneself. . . . But when it comes to national egoism, national pride, not only is the field unlimited but the highest possible degree of it seems to be imposed by something closely resembling an obligation (*TNFR*140).

Thus the idea of "nation" as an absolute value makes legitimate a public mode of being and a collective attitude that is often deemed unacceptable in private. Furthermore, it seems that the checks that exist in the private realm to counter the excesses of individual behavior and encourage civility and fairness toward others, are cast off as hindrances in an uprooted public, where the more excessive one's pride in the nation, the better.

Weil's point, of course, is not merely that national egoism is an embarrassment, something like a lack of breeding or good manners. A people that conceives of itself as chosen by God, or a nation that thinks of itself as holy or "eternal" is both sacreligious and idolatrous. It labors under a profound misconception, one Weil wants vehemently to reject:

> It is easy to say, with Lamartine, "*Ma patrie est partout où rayonne la France . . . La vérité, c'est mon pays.*" Unfortunately, this would only make sense if France and truth were synonymous. France sometimes resorts to lying and commiting injustice; this has happened, is happening, and will happen

again. For France is not God, not by a long chalk. Christ alone was able to say, "I am the truth." . . . there is no such thing as a holy nation (*TNFR*147).[14]

What is truly at jeopardy within the "holy nation," is justice. National egoism puts the nation before justice, or at least collapses the distinction between them. Either way, it obliterates the significance of questions concerning the rightness or wrongness of a nation's acts. That is why Weil says, "in the modern form of patriotism, justice hasn't much of a part to play, and above all nothing is said which might encourage any relationship between patriotism and justice to be drawn" (*TNFR*134). National egoism and blind adherence to the idea that one's nation is beyond judgment or critique make it possible for the *collectivité* to evade responsibility for the nation's acts, and indeed, to rationalize the most unjust acts as necessary, even sacred duties, because they are in the interest of an "absolute good." A citizenry enthralled by such pride is open to "the manufacturers of sophistries inside it"—to the politicians and rulers who justify even the most outrageous policies in the name of the *patrie*, and under the assumption of its absolute value (*TNFR*144). In the grip of just such national egoism and under the spell of such politicians, Weil argues, France dispossessed the Algerians, the Polynesians, and the Vietnamese (*TNFR*199). Hence, one of the crimes of national eogism, itself a symptom of *déracinement*, is that it validates the *déracinement* of others.

Weil also refers to this national egoism in another way, as the "idolatry of self." And just as the State has its father in Richelieu, so the idolatry of self has an emblematic father: Corneille. In his *Horace* and *Polyeucte*, Weil says, Corneille handed down the legacy of national idolatry. Referring to Polyeucte's pursuit of a transcendent kingdom, she remarks sardonically, "Alexander wept, we are told, because he had only the terrestrial globe to conquer. Corneille apparently thought Christ had come down to earth to make up for this deficiency" (*TNFR*143). In Corneille's hands, "Christian morality" thus comes into disastrous contact with "the Roman spirit." She also notes that Corneille dedicated *Horace* to Richelieu, and appropriately so, for the guiding themes of his work, as she notes in "The Great Beast," are also those of Richelieu— the glory of conquest, "conquering, triumphing, dominating," and "delirious pride" (*W*1962b:134,143). A "Corneille-esque" conception of greatness can be found in the French attachment to empire, in the heroic glamour of military might, in the quest for national glory that ensures "prolonged existence in time and space," and in a continual boasting about the generosity and clemency of the nation, even after it has allowed "the most atrocious acts of repression or the most scandalous famines" to transpire in its conquered lands. The "cult of grandeur" is also evident in a culture before and after Corneille: in the *chanson de geste* that glorifies Charlemagne, in the heroes of Racine (with the exception of Phèdre), in Bossuet's deification of human grandeur, in the hymns of praise for Napoleon (*TNFR*134). For Weil, the idolatry of self, recapitulated in the numerous dimensions of "Corneille-esque" greatness, marks the ultimate failure of the public imagination. But even more seriously, the "idolatry of self" is a corrupt public morality, a slavish imitation of Rome.

Pushing Weil's diagnosis further than she does, we might conceive of French patriotism as deeply ambivalent and distorted: both idolatrous of the nation and loveless toward the State, at once obsessed with glory and filled with disgust for politics, enthralled by grandiose visions of self-sacrifice for country and contemptuous of the bureaucracy that demands it, transfixed by empty ideals but also pervaded by apathy and cynicism. The political consequences of such psychic trauma were evident in 1940; when it came time for the French to defend their country, there was no will to defend it. There was only, on the one hand, the State (which inspires nothing), and on the other the illusion of "eternal France," an empty abstraction that bears no real significance or meaning. Weil's analysis speaks to a nation so corrupted by false images and values that it could not find the spirit to move even against the threat of its own destruction.

Just as the failure of public imagination and morality must be revealed, however, so must an alternative set of images and a new morality be discovered. Thus, Weil asserts:

> The world requires at the present time a new patriotism. And it is just now that this inventive effort must be made, just when patriotism is something that is causing bloodshed. We mustn't wait until it has become once more just a subject for conversation in drawing rooms, learned societies, and open air cafes (*TNFR*147).

This "new patriotism" she proceeds to offer differs as much from the one that exists in France as love does from idolatry and virtue from vice. Weil intends for it to be the cure for a sick *collectivité*, a balm for the disease of uprootedness. Within this new patriotism, she hopes the political and the spiritual, the human and the divine, can be reconciled.

## Notes

1. Weil spent from June until November of 1942 in the United States. She lived with her parents in New York City.

2. She was also engaged in a number of other projects, not all of them for the FFO. Her essays during this period of her life include: "Are We Struggling

for Justice?" (1957a), "The Legitimacy of the Provisional Government" (1957a), "Essential Ideas for a New Constitution" (1957a), "Reflections on Revolt" (1957a), "Note on the General Suppression of Political Parties" (1950b), "Is There a Marxist Doctrine" (1973) and "Human Personality" (1962b). The titles alone lend credence to the notion that Weil's work is not best conceived of in terms of "early political" and "late spiritual" writings, but rather as a mixture of competing impulses and ideas.

3. The officers of the FFO, for many good reasons, wanted to dissuade Weil from her efforts to be parachuted into Occupied France, so that she could engage in espionage for the Resistance. The assignment, which became *L'Enracinement*, was intended to distract her from her determination to return to her country as a resistance fighter, and also to redirect her efforts away from her project for front line nurses. See "Plan for an Organization of Front Line Nurses," in her letter to Maurice Schumann (*W*1965:146–53).

4. I will return to the other "needs" Weil addresses in Chapter 8. But it is important to note that they are not as integrated into her reconstitution of France (i.e., Parts II and III of *TNFR*) as is the "need for roots." They appear in something of a manifesto form in Part I but do not feature prominently in the bulk of her discussion. This may be because she had "the needs of the soul" in mind as a separate text (it bears a strong resemblance to her draft document for a "statement of human obligations" (1962b)). Or perhaps she simply did not have the chance to reconcile all three parts of her manuscript to her satisfaction. It seems more likely, however, that she was primarily concerned with the discussion of roots and rootlessness—with, first, articulating the context or "natural environment" within which the needs of the human soul could be met, before going on to elaborate these needs in a more integrated way. At any rate, her failure to elaborate upon these needs is unfortunate, if for no other reason than that it is the section of her text which has, to date, drawn the most comment and (sometimes unwarranted) criticism.

5. Weil develops this idea more fully in her essay, "East and West" (*W*1962b:195–210).

6. See, in particular, the essay by J. H. King (1976) for an enumeration of various analyses of the fall of France, and for another view of Weil's relationship to them. Among the numerous general analyses of the Fall of France and the Vichy regime see Aron's magisterial study (1958), Paxton (1972), Paxton and Marrus (1981), and Hoffman (1963).

7. I characterize her analysis as "storytelling" because I think it is important to distinguish the narrative Weil presents in *TNFR* from a "professional history" that is guided by an orthodoxy of dispassionate reportage. She has often been criticized for her intemperate and "impressionistic" historical writings (usually by historians who distrust the use of narrative), but I think this charge misses the point of *TNFR*. Her aim there is not to present an empirically verifiable, "factual" explanation of a given set of events in French history, but rather to engage in an act of political education, through a reinterpretation of specific events and with particular political values in mind. Or, to put this another way, *TNFR* is best approached as an enterprise or a "realm of discourse" that is quite distinct from the realm of orthodox historical research and more appropriate to the genre of political theory. Thus the standards we should use in order to judge it most meaningfully are those more applicable to political theorizing than professional historical research. For an elaboration on what such standards entail see Wolin (1960, Chap. 1).

8. The phrase in quotes comes not from Weil but from Hanna Pitkin (1973:524). Weil, of course, does not use psychological language to discuss the crisis of patriotism and national identity; given her distaste for psychological literature in general she probably would recoil from the analogy between the political and the psychological I find in *TNFR*. Nevertheless, I think that the symmetry is an important one, and not only because the psychic component in *TNFR* helps us interpret her political thought in richer, more suggestive ways. We might also understand her coming-to-terms with the conflicted identity of her country as a coming-to-terms with her own "self"—the text is, in this sense, a personal struggle made political. I hope, by now, the reader understands that by saying this, I do not mean to suggest that *TNFR* is "really" about Weil's psyche, but rather that *only* Weil's psyche could have produced such a text and brought forth the valuable political insights on patriotism and national identity we find there.

9. Weil develops this idea and the importance of lost cultures in her essays "A Medieval Epic Poem," and "The Romanesque Renaissance" (W1962b:35–43).

10. For a complementary, although far more intensive critique of the political failure of the French Revolution, see Arendt (1963). Comparing the French experience to the American Revolution, Arendt notes (1963:92): "The direction of the American Revolution remained committed to the foundation of freedom and the establishment of lasting institutions, and to those who acted in this direction nothing was permitted that would have been outside the range of civil law. The direction of the French Revolution was deflected almost from its beginning from this course of foundation through the immediacy of suffering; it was determined by the exigencies of liberation not from tyranny but from necessity, and it was actuated by the limitless immensity of both the people's misery and the pity this misery inspired." For a compatible account, see also Sennett (1977).

11. Interestingly, in Weil's later work the state assumes many of the characteristics she earlier ascribed to the collectivity and, in *TNFR* at least, the collectivity is understood as a source of rootedness, particularly as one's country. For a similar, and equally damning critique of the French state, see Marx, "The Eighteenth Brumaire of Louis Bonaparte" (1978:606–7).

12. For a more extended commentary on Richelieu, see "Three Letters on History" (W1962b:85–88), where Weil acknowledges the Cardinal's accomplishments ("under his eye, things did get done") but also charts his crimes: "He deliberately and pitilessly fostered the wars in Europe . . . he prevented all hope of peace in Germany, . . . and it is impossible to exaggerate the horrors endured by that wretched country in the interminable war." His foreign adventures, she continues, reduced the French peasants "to such poverty as to have to eat grass."

13. And her hatred of Rome is matched by her contempt for "Hitlerite" Germany, which she thinks apes all things Roman. At least this is the crux of her argument in "The Great Beast" (1962b), where she writes: "the spirit of the two systems seems to be very nearly identical and to merit praise or execration in identically the same terms" (131). She fears that France is susceptible to the same Roman influences.

14. On this score, the "Hebrews" take the brunt of her criticism. Weil is unrelenting in her attack upon the notion of a "chosen" people or a sacred nation. In *Gravity and Grace* (W1952a:146–47) she observes: "Rome is the Great Beast of atheism and materialism, adoring nothing but itself. Israel is the Great

Beast of religion. Neither the one nor the other is likeable." And she notes, "Perhaps there was only one ancient people absolutely without mysticism: Rome. By what mystery? It was an artifical city, made up of fugitives, just as Israel was." Weil's views on the Israel of the Old Testament have been taken as anti-Semitic, but this perhaps misstates their nature. Without doubt, she displayed an intemperate narrow-mindedness on all things Hebrew (but on things Roman and "Hitlerite" as well). In "The Great Beast" (1962b) her commentary is directed against tribalistic, nationalistic, forms of collective belonging, not against a people as a people.

# 8

# Refashioning the Soul of a Country

IN TURNING FROM Weil's diagnosis of the malady that afflicts France to her understanding of truly moral patriotism, we turn from a fallen state to one that brings hope of political redemption, from rootlessness to, as she puts it, the "growing of roots." The "cure" she offers in this final work, in its final pages, might best be conceived as "attention raised to a public power" in the form of both spiritual patriotism and patriotic spiritualism. To understand the spiritualism behind this new patriotism, we must recall what Weil rejects, and what her therapeutic politics is meant to uncover—the mystique of *étatisme* that uproots political life, and the "idolatry of self" that at once corrupts public morality and is also a sign of its corruption.

All of these things were deeply entrenched in the national identity of the French, so Weil argues, before the fall of 1940, but now there is also the pathology of war itself at work. War, she observes, has further ravaged an already sick nation: "Victory is going to liberate a country in which everyone will have been almost exclusively occupied in disobeying, from either good or bad motives" (*TNFR*156). Victory also brings with it a blood lust—what Weil calls "diffused terrorism"—that results from a people's urge to exact revenge for its defeat and humiliation. And it brings as well a "mendacity complex," a general desire to possess and consume what has been denied and give nothing back in return. So the citizens of France are doubly diseased, beset by both a degenerating identity and by the ravages of war, which push their degeneration still further. Responding to this situation, Weil acknowledges a "terrible responsibility"—it is imperative "to give the French people something to love; and, in the first place, to give them France to love" (*TNFR*157). The "cure" she has in mind addresses both of these concerns. In "The Growing of Roots," Weil considers what is worth loving in a healthy collectivity and, even more importantly what it would mean for the French to "love France."

168

## Conceiving a Cure: A New Patriotism

At the heart of Weil's recommendations on patriotism is her conviction that a "new inspiration" must be breathed into the citizens of France, into the nation she calls the "dying man." If the crisis of France is, in part, a failure of public imagination, then the French must be encouraged to reimagine the idea of country in a way that will inspire them. Also at the heart of her analysis is an implicit acknowledgement that facing up to the past is a necessary task that prepares the way toward a new patriotism, but it is not, in and of itself, sufficient. For the French are beset by more than a distorted sense of their own history. They are also in thrall to a conception of country that is dangerous and destructive. "The love of good will never spring up in the hearts of the population in general, as it is necessary it should do for the salvation of the country, so long as people believe that in no matter what sphere greatness can be the result of something other than the good" (*TNFR*237). Part of Weil's project is to have the French recover "the good" and reconceptualize country so that they might rid themselves of the destructive identity that promotes nothing but a loveless idolatry. Let us look first, then, at what she has to recommend regarding the recovery of the good, and then at her alternative conception of "country."

Reflecting upon the numerous symptoms of France's disorder, Weil concludes that the most serious defect of all, from the viewpoint of national identity, is the false, "Corneillesque" conception of greatness that pervades the public consciousness. In particular, she blames the official repositories of culture, especially historians and literary figures, for promoting distorted values and ideals. Throughout *TNFR* there are comments upon history—not just upon the mythologized history of France—but also upon the way in which histories are written, to whom they are addressed, and what purposes they serve. She asserts, with characteristic boldness, "History . . . is nothing but a compilation of the depositions made by assassins with respect to their victims and themselves." And historians, who look at such depositions, too often forget to "read between the lines," or fail to "pierce through the paper to discover real flesh and blood." Hence they miss or ignore, among other things, the vanquished but truly valuable cultures and peoples from whom we might draw inspiration (*TNFR*224–25).[1]

Furthermore, when these histories based on depositions of victors and assassins are made publicly accessible, a part of the "orthodox education" of a nation, they become even more far removed from the truth. Indeed, for schoolchildren, the victors and assassins are all to often glorified and established as the font of cultural values and collective identity. The result is what Weil calls "the transmission of spurious greatness" and a contempt for morality and the good. With respect to the young, she asks: "How should a child who sees cruelty and ambition glorified in his history lessons, egoism, pride, vanity, passion for self-advertisement glorified in his literature lessons . . . how should he be expected to learn to admire the good?" (TNFR234).

Weil believes that such an expectation is not reasonable. Instead of "admiration of the good," this education in "spurious greatness" ends in the presumption that greatness has little or nothing to do with the good, and that talent ("which has nothing to do with morality") is something worthy of adulation. Far from being "amoral," history lessons embody both explicit and implicit appeals to values and all too often to the worship of ersatz greatness in particular. At best, such lessons offer unworthy examples for emulation ("Who can admire Alexander," she asks, ". . . whose soul is not base?"). At worst, these lessons create a value system of the most self-deluding kind, and are a threat to civilization itself.

Weil sees Hitler (and Nazism in general) as an example of such a value system made real in the world. Hitler is the youth "athirst for greatness," the "wretched uprooted wanderer," who found sustenance in the idea of being great. He is an example of the worship of ersatz greatness, and by seizing such greatness "with both hands" instead of merely worshipping it, he has gone one step further (TNFR226). Hitler is living proof of how the meaning of true greatness has nearly vanished from the world, and how its loss can result only in a civilization that is corrupt, criminal, beyond salvation. In Nazism, the "idolatry of self" triumphs in history and recapitulates Rome; the total abasement of a people is realized.

Weil's concern is not limited to delegitimizing Hitler however. She also sees a political imperative in cultural transformation—to deter "little boys thirsting for greatness" from viewing him as an example worthy of emulation (TNFR227). In this respect, her lesson must be read as more than a message for the Germans. Everyone, she suggests, is equally capable of succumbing to the lure of false greatness. More directly, she tells the French:

> Our conception of greatness is the very one that has inspired Hitler's whole life. When we denounce it without the remotest recognition of its application to ourselves, the angels must either cry or laugh, if there happen to be angels who interest themselves in our propaganda (TNFR219).

Later, drawing upon the inspiration of the New Testament, she counsels: "in order to have the right to punish the guilty, we ought first of all to purify ourselves of their crimes, which we harbor under all sorts of disguises in our own hearts" (TNFR241).

Despite the enormity of the problem, Weil does not hesitate to confront head-on the issue of how to transform the meaning of greatness and educate citizens toward the good. Some of her suggestions for instilling respect for "perfect beauty, perfect truth, perfect justice" are more than a little reminiscent of Plato's directives in *The Republic*. And her overall approach to the matter of educating rightly would no doubt endear her to moral absolutists. In her essay "The Responsibility of Writers," she states quite flatly: "I believe in the responsibility of writers of recent years for the disasters of our time." She then goes on to criticize the "unbelievable degradations" in the literature of the twentieth century (W1968:166–67). What is most obvious is the "disappearance of the idea of value," and any reference to the good. "Words like virtue, nobility, honor, honesty, generosity," she notes, "have become almost impossible to use or else have acquired bastard meanings. . . . The fate of words is a touchstone of the programmatic weakening of the idea of value." Furthermore, when words begin to lose their meanings one cannot help but place responsibility upon writers, since, after all, "words are their business" (W1968:168). But the crux of Weil's thinking on this matter lies in this remark: "When literature becomes deliberately indifferent to the opposition of good and evil it betrays its function and forfeits all claim to excellence" (W1968:169). Her recommendations for a "cure" in *TNFR* build on this charge.

In general, her recommendations run to matters of culture, especially concerning poets, philosophers, painters, composers, and writers who deserve to be revered for their "true greatness," and whose works should be studied as examples of "genius revealing truth, heroism, and holiness" (*TNFR*234). She mentions, among others, the painters Giotto and Velasquez, the tragedies of Aeschylus and Sophocles, Racine's *Phèdre*, also *King Lear*, and Monteverdi, Bach, and Mozart. As for French literature in particular, there is the poet Villon, also Maurice Scève, D'Aubigné, and Théophile de Viau ("a great poet and in several respects an inheritor of the Languedocian tradition") (*TNFR*235:W1962b:51). Also, Mallarmé, Rabelais, Montaigne, Descartes, Retz, Port Royal, and "above all" Molière. In the eighteenth century, she mentions Montesquieu and Rousseau, then adds, "that is perhaps all" (*TNFR*236). Weil is not unaware of the personal sensibilities that underlie this breathtaking litany of "truly great" figures; it is the "Christian and Hellenic" genius, far more than things specifically French, to which the French themselves must attend. The idea is to "drink in torrents of absolutely pure beauty from every point of view" (*TNFR*236). Thus a part of her educative intent is to open history, especially cultural history, to the classics that deserve to be revered, and thereby counter the "cruelty, ambition, and pride" that are the food of pagan patriots.

When she writes as the creator of a culture of the good, Weil is not at her best. Her judgments, although perhaps not "charged with self-righteous zeal" as one critic has complained, (Oates 1977) are character-istically demanding and highly idiosyncratic, even arbitrary. The figures she leaves out of her list of "pure beings" seem as important as those she admits—what of Pascal, Lamartine, Renard, La Fontaine, Zola? Or Beethoven, Brahms, Milton, Michelangelo, Leonardo? And some of those she does admit seem odd choices indeed as examples of "purity" (at least of personal "purity")—Rousseau, for instance, or Mozart. Of course, her basic point is true and important; the "classic works" of the West and East bring human beings face to face with the deepest questions of human existence and, if taken seriously, can inspire, uplift, and elevate. Yet it hardly bears noting that there is also much that is excessively idealistic (not to mention undemocratic) about her conviction that selected works of poetry and literature, painting and architecture, can infuse the hearts of a people with a love of the good, and others must be suppressed. In the twentieth century sentiments such as these—noble as they may be—seem at best embarassingly náive, at worst politically threatening. For who shall decide precisely which works shall inspire would-be citizens, and lead them toward the good? At times it seems that the dilemmas and debates of liberal societies have completely by-passed her—it is as though she writes from a different era, to an audience that has never troubled over the deep complexities of morality and education, or forced her to do so.

Fortunately, however, there is more to her conception of a "cure" for France than these Platonic sentiments. A stronger and more compelling part of her vision is her alternative conception of "country," and how, precisely, the French should love it. The alternative conception she offers draws upon the notion of a "vital medium," and the organic metaphor of roots. The appropriate attitude toward country she recom-mends is akin to compassion. Both of these ideas—the organic one of roots, and the moral one of compassion—are in opposition to the "metallic" notion of the State and the idolatry that distinguishes it. Together, they form the basis of Weil's new patriotism.

By reimagining country, Weil introduces a new ethos into the lan-guage of patriotism that directly challenges not only Corneille, but the entire patriotic ethic of the West, from the Romans to Rousseau, Hegel, Nietzsche, and beyond. As we should now expect, Rome is the symbol of the political pathology of the West. In Weil's telling, it is not only the great exemplar of the State and the will to dominate (which Hitler madly imitates), but also the very image of a "tough, unshakable, impenetra-ble, collective self-satisfaction" that so many nation-states have slavishly nutured and taken for patriotism. She writes:

> The Romans really were an atheistic and idolatrous people; not idolatrous with regard to images made of stone or bronze, but idolatrous with regard

to themselves. It is this idolatry of self which they have bequeathed to us in the form of patriotism (*TNFR*141).

Weil wants France to recognize how, to paraphrase Marx's famous words, "the ghosts from the days of Rome have watched over its cradle," and left their traces in the dreams of Richelieu and Corneille, Robespierre, and Napoleon, and in the structure of the modern State, "which in so many ways resembles the political structure evolved by Rome" (*W*1962b:136). Her intention is to demythologize the Romans and to wrest the imagination and the ethos of the Gallic nation from the grip of an utterly destructive, politically and psychically ruinous identity. Her assessment of ancient Rome is, in this sense, an attack upon the entire patriotic ethos of the West. By exposing the base origins of French patriotism, Weil would have the nation repudiate its Romish forebears, and turn instead to the spirit of Christianity and ancient Greece.[2]

She begins by affirming the reality of the nation. Although her commitment to the idea of regional and local forms of cultural and political life is obvious, she does not allow it to deny the "givenness" of nationhood. In taking up her redefinition, she writes:

> Just as there are certain culture beds for certain microscopic animals, certain types of soil for certain plants, so there is a certain part of the soul in everyone and certain ways of thought and action communicated from one person to another which can only exist in a national setting and disappear when a country is destroyed (*TNFR*159).

Drawing upon organic images, Weil conceives of the nation as a fertile ground that provides nurturance and sustenance for a distinctive form of life. Belonging to country is not, therefore, a mere matter of contractual relationship, or sheer happenstance—nor is it simply a "given" unworthy of careful reflection (although the French, she suggests, seem to have taken it as such until France fell). Rather, a country is a "life-giving nucleus" (*TNFR*163), a source of identity, purpose, and meaning. Just as a plant without roots withers and dies, so it is with a people who have no appreciation of their country as the home or habitat on earth that envelops, encloses, and unites them by virtue of their common history, and shared habits, traditions, and values. It may be, Weil acknowledges, (no doubt thinking of the Languedoc) that this "vital medium" evolved "at the expense of some other combination richer in vital properties," but past events cannot be undone, only recognized, and the medium that does exist, such as it is, must nevertheless be guarded "like a treasure" for the good it contains (*TNFR*162).

Weil does not want this "treasure" to be mistaken for an "absolute value," however. There is a vast difference between imagining one's country as a "vital medium" or a "culture bed" that sustains a unique way of life, and as something that is glorious and beyond evil. Her advice on history is intended to rectify the moral obtuseness that accompanies the notion of country as "absolute value"; her conception of the vital medium is meant to challenge the Corneillesque conception of glory, and replace it with an idea of country as "something beautiful and precious, but . . . imperfect, and . . . very frail and liable to suffer misfortune" (TNFR176). If a nation is perceived in the latter sense, Weil suggests, it is very difficult to commit the Roman error and make pride and glory the prevailing ethos of patriotism. The idea of imperfectibility checks pride, just as the idea of frailty counters glory, and neither accommodate the "cult of grandeur" that fuels so much of modern patriotism. Or at least that is Weil's hope.

There is another dimension to this reconceptualization of country as well—we might call it a "populist" one. For the unfortunate, greatness in the Roman manner is a mockery; it refuses to be touched by the reality of human suffering. Weil thinks the notion of a precious and fragile culture-bed in need of care-taking is an image of country particularly accessible to ordinary people, to those who "have a monopoly of a certain sort of knowledge . . . the reality of misfortune; and for that very reason . . . feel all the more keenly the preciousness of those things that deserve to be protected from it" (TNFR177). The people themselves, she suggests, have never "[felt] themselves at home" in a patriotism founded upon pride, pomp, and glory. These things are as foreign as "the salons of Versailles," and far removed from the realities of everyday life. A vision of country that speaks more directly to the experiences of "the people," as opposed to "certain Frenchmen who have covered themselves in glory" would provide a far better stimulant for the reconstruction of France and also serve as a "genuine inspiration" for others (TNFR176,197).

In many respects, Weil's conception of country recalls the anticontractarianism of Burke, and prefigures the "ecological" vision of human society favored by Michael Oakeshott. Like Burke, Weil thinks the nation is an elaborate and complicated web of relationships, but also fragile and easily destroyed. She could have easily said, with Burke, that a country is "a treasure of inestimable value," passed on and inherited from one generation to the next, requiring the care and preservation of those who live within it.[3] Like Oakeshott, Weil recognizes that a society (or a country) is a complex living whole—that vital system from which the individual derives his or her origin, growth, life, vigor, and support. Yet despite her affinities with Burke and Oakeshott, Weil is ultimately and more profoundly influenced by Christian ethics rather than conservative ones. And in her discussion of the attitude the true patriot should take toward country, this Christian influence appears most powerfully and challenges the spectre of loveless idolatry and "pagan" patriotism.

There are many ways in which Christian ethics can be used as a standard for judging the secular world. Weil's way is unique to her, and very much centered upon the problem of belonging to country. Or, to put this otherwise, in order to achieve some compatibility between politics and morality, she recommends something like a spiritual patriotism, grounded in Christian compassion. There are, she says, "two distinct ways of loving" one's country—one that is fueled by false images of glory, eternal strength, or unquestionable rank and power, and another that is inspired by a "poignantly tender feeling for some beautiful, precious, fragile and perishable object" (*TNFR*171). She no doubt has in mind something close to what Augustine called *cupiditas* and *caritas*, and described as the "two loves" that distinguish the earthly city and the city of God. The first sort of love we already know; it is the real adversary in Weil's theory, not truly love at all, but a "loveless idolatry" and self-aggrandizement of Roman origin "incapable of creating any real, ardent sense of fraternity" (*TNFR*175). The only true alternative, and the sole spirit that can unite the French, is of the second kind, a fellow-feeling born in the recognition of collective suffering and misfortune. Weil suggests the inspiration of Jesus and Jerusalem:

> In the Gospels, there is not the least indication that Christ experienced anything resembling love for Jerusalem and Judea, save only the love which goes wrapped in compassion. . . . He wept over the city, foreseeing as it was not difficult to do at that time, the destruction which should shortly fall upon it (*TNFR*170–71).

In their reverence for the example of Jesus and in awareness of their own country's misfortune, the French people should cultivate "that species of love which can be given the name of charity" and then collectively direct that love toward their country (*TNFR*172). Compassion alone "suits the situation in which the souls and bodies of Frenchmen actually find themselves," Weil writes, "and possesses the humility and dignity appropriate to misfortune" (*TNFR*173). It is, in other words, a way of facing misfortune without either succumbing to or mystifying it. As she also says, "Compassion for France is not a compensation for, but a spiritualization of, the sufferings being undergone" (*TNFR*174). Her point is not that the *collectivité* might use patriotism to erase or offset the reality of the nation's misfortune, but rather discover, through patriotism, the depths of France's misfortune as well as the strength to overcome it. And the only sentiment adequate to this is compassion. Drawing once more upon psychological terms, we might conceive of compassion as the sublimation of defeat. It is the "healthy side" of national humiliation, a way of converting potentially debilitating sentiments into a vital solidarity, at once informed by the fragility and destructability of country, and intent upon protecting it from harm.

In Weil's moral psychology, then, compassion is the richest source of political belonging for the nation. She does not mean to limit her recommendation, however, to those under the dominion of force and defeat. Happiness is as much an object for compassion as unhappiness, she writes, "because it belongs to this earth, in other words is incomplete, frail and fleeting" (TNFR172). There is yet another earthly reality that renders compassion the truest sort of patriotism for all nations—it has to do with the unavoidable evils of politics itself:

> such a love can keep its eyes open on injustices, cruelties, mistakes, falsehoods, crimes, and scandals contained in the country's past, its present, and its ambitions in general, quite openly and fearlessly, and without being thereby diminished. . . . Thus compassion keeps both eyes open on both the good and the bad and finds in each sufficient reasons for loving (TNFR173).

Understood this way, Weil's compassionate patriotism simply is the sort of healthy self-love—critical yet forgiving, demanding yet protective—that accompanies a genuine acknowledgment of the past. Or, to put this in Augustinian terms, compassion is a humility born of the recognition of past sinfulness and a capacity to learn, to forgive, and to go on loving. For Weil, as for Augustine, the paradigmatic example of such compassion is Jesus. Conformity to the compassionate Christ is above all the model of absolute love. Yet unlike Augustine, Weil does not conclude that "Christ is our native country," or (as does the "mystical Weil") direct the attention of compassionate souls to an other-worldly realm.[4] Her commitment in TNFR is secular as well as spiritual; thus she would have Jesus' compassion serve to exemplify the love of citizens for their earthly country, not for a realm outside the political world.

Lest she be taken as recommending a patriotism that is "coddling and weak," however, she says, "Let no one imagine that compassion for one's country excludes warlike energy" (TNFR171).[5] She commends the Carthaginians, for example, for their determined defense and protection of their country against all odds. Her vision of patriotism surely includes the idea of military heroism, although not the so-called heroism of adventurers, militarists, and conquistadors. Rather, what Weil has in mind is something more like the heroism that distinguishes a man who protects his "young children, aged parents, or a beloved wife" (TNFR172) from danger—a watchful and tender concern than can give rise to fierce defense and courageous battle.[6] Implicit in this is the idea that citizens have an obligation toward their "culture-bed." She also says it explicitly: "Every individual in the population owes his country the whole of his strength, his resources, and his life itself, until the danger has been removed" (TNFR164). Later she adds, "Those who don't want to defend their country should be made to lose, not life or liberty, but purely and simply their country" (TNFR164). She does not maintain a lucid distinction between false appeals about the nation's security and real threats to country that truly merit a citizen's participation in its defense. (Although it is clear from her critical remarks about the nation as "absolute value" that she does not condone a conception of duty as unlimited or unquestioning allegiance).[7] Nevertheless, she seems generally inclined to assume that the very transfiguration of the idea of country—from "absolute value" to "vital medium"—will bring about a shift in the way a citizenry conceives of the defense of country and their obligation to it.

The notion of compassionate patriotism also has implications for the way in which citizens should understand the State and, likewise, for the State's duty toward citizens. In essence, Weil imagines the State as (ideally) the protector of the culture bed of country, not something to be taken as synonymous with country. Hence, its duty is to keep watch over the security of national territory, but more importantly "to ensure that the people are provided with a country to which they really feel they belong," and "to make the country, in the highest possible degree, a reality" (*TNFR*167, 165). More specifically, the State must in various ways encourage "progressive associations"—not "wheels within wheels" of bureacracy, but public organizations in contact with public affairs (*TNFR*165,167). It must also continue to foster the regionalist identities and local differences—Brittany, Lorraine, Provence, Paris— that make France what it is. Part of a compassionate patriotism involves recognizing all sorts of special attachments as "treasures of infinite value and rarity" worth tending like the most delicate plants. The State must deepen, not uproot or distort these connections.

But if the State has a duty to provide and protect a country with a myriad of culture and social roots, then the citizens have a reciprocal duty, and that is obedience to the State, "because obedience is essential for the country's preservation and tranquility" (*TNFR*178). Weil offers the following analogy:

> We must obey the State, however it happens to be, rather like loving children left by their parents, gone abroad, in the charge of some mediocre governness, but who obey her nevertheless out of love of their parents. If the State happens not to be mediocre, so much the better . . . but whether mediocre or not, the obligation of obedience remains the same (*TNFR*179).

Although she stresses that what she has in mind is not an "unlimited obligation," Weil nevertheless says that disobedience to the authorities is "more dishonorable than theft" and that public order, the result of obedience, is more sacred than private property (*TNFR*179). Now, this may seem an astonishing set of claims for a thinker who is otherwise so suspicious of the State and deeply critical of the injustices of State power. But before we conclude that her argument is, at best, confused, we must remember to whom she is writing—a nation on the brink of chaos and disorder, with no coherent political structure to lend it purpose and direction. With this in mind, we may view her emphasis on obedience to the State as, in part at least, an attempt to reconstitute some respect for authority in a people increasingly (and understandably) inclined to view their political authorities as no different from the enemy who occupies their villages, countryside, and cities.

Faced with the very real dilemma of having to relegitimize the State, Weil chooses first to redefine it and disassociate it from country, and second, to make its capacity to preserve the country contingent upon the good will and obedience of the citizens of France. By refusing to make the State the core of French identity, but nevertheless establishing it as vital to country, she both affirms and minimizes its authority. She grants it legitimacy but also diminishes its centrality. Drawing upon a religious metaphor, she observes: "The State is sacred, not in the way an idol is sacred, but in the way common objects serving a religious purpose, like the alter, the baptismal water, or anything else of the kind, are sacred" (TNFR182). The State's majesty, then, is to be understood in terms of its service to the country; it is not an "ironbound machine" but the vital protector of a sacred, earthly, treasure.[8]

If we assume a broader, external perspective on this new patriotism, we might view Weil's project as an attempt to resolve or reconcile any number of antinomies: the political and the ethical, the secular and the spiritual, the State and country, and even, perhaps, France and God. That is to say, Weil's political theory of patriotism is not simply informed by one side of a series of dualisms—the ethical, spiritual, and Godly— but is rather something more complex, an attempt to render the political spiritual and to place spirituality in the service of politics.

Perhaps we can best understand the spirituality of Weil's politics and her attempt to resolve the above antinomies if we turn to one final emblematic figure, the Christian (and female) alternative to the pagan (and male) Richelieu and Corneille. As I have already suggested, Jesus is the most striking example of the compassion Weil has in mind, but she offers another for our consideration as well: Joan of Arc, "the virgin fighting on behalf of justice" (W1956b:195).[9] Although Weil refers to Joan only fleetingly, the spirit of the Maid of Lorraine nevertheless suffuses her discussion of the new patriotism. Hers is not the Joan "dictated by contemporary public opinion," (W1956b:195), the symbol of both Vichy and de Gaulle, a nationalist inspiration. Instead, Joan embodies the right way of loving country; she is military prowess mediated by a love of things fragile and earthly, and valor reconciled with humility and grace. Or so, at least, would Weil have us imagine her.

The significance Joan bears to Weil's conception becomes all the more interesting once we realize that the history of the Maid in modern French mythology is one of continuously shifting and seemingly irreconcilable symbols. Marina Warner has compared the French heroine to an "ecotype," "a plant that travels, adapts itself, and develops differently in different surroundings" (Warner 1981). By the nineteenth century, an ambivalent perspective had taken root in France. Joan was hailed as both a potent political figure by nationalists, and as a religious inspiration by Catholics and monarchists. The story of the posthumous Joan is, in and of itself, an example of the deep fissure within France. Not only is there the partisan fissure between "the red and the black," but also the psychological fissure between a national identity driven by secular and nationalistic sentiments on the one hand, and one informed by the spiritual doctrine of the Catholic Church on the other. Seen in this light, we might understand Weil's patriotism, and her own mythology of Joan, as an effort to reconcile the secular and spiritual sides of these two identifications by ridding the first of its crass nationalistic aspects, and the second of its doctrinal Catholicism. The "new patriotism," like Weil's Joan of Arc, thus embodies a "Christian secularism," or a "spiritual patriotism" free of both "Corneillesque greatness" and religious orthodoxy. It replaces the cult of grandeur with Christian compassion and care-taking, yet reaffirms the country, as a culture-bed, over and above all other collectivities, including the State and the Church. As Weil would have it, then, Joan would vanquish Richelieu (who embodies both State and Church) and serve as the emblematic inspiration for a new patriotism rooted in the firm ground of a new and reconciled France, a healthy *collectivité*.

## The Spirituality of Politics

Reflecting upon the condition of France in 1940, Stanley Hoffman has observed that the search for personal survival, plus collective hero worship in the midst of the ruin of the old alignments and beliefs, meant that for a while France was no longer a nation of citizens (1963). His observation echoes a truth that Weil perceived clearly and early on. Indeed, one of the great contributions of *TNFR* is that it renders the loss of citizenship in France palpable by embarking upon a voyage to rediscover patriotism and refashion the soul of the nation. In so doing, Weil not only deepens the meaning of the crisis of France; she also presents a more generally applicable conception of "belonging to country" upon which all citizens can draw in ways unique to their own history and geography, and constitutive of their own traditions, customs, and inheritances.

Without doubt, we can learn much about patriotism from her. At the very least, she exposes the delusion inherent in blind devotion to the idea of national glory. The "new patriotism" rejects the nationalistic idolatry and the xenophobia that attend the idea of the nation as an absolute value, and replaces them with a conception of self and country that is both dignified and humane. Weil's critical reflections force us to reconsider the nature of patriotism but not to abandon it. She does not prefer the language of internationalism, universal humanism, or socialist solidarity; she simply wants to restore the language of patriotism to health. In the course of this project, she also gets us to see how, as another theorist puts it, "the word patriotism is a member of a family of words and largely takes its meaning from its membership" (Schaar 1981:286). Accordingly, she reconstructs the language of patriotism by giving new life to the family of words around it—roots, belonging, loyalty, caretaking, country, citizenship, obligation, compassion, and love. Or, to carry the idea a little further, Weil seeks to distinguish between the rightful members of the word-family of patriotism and its "bloody relatives"—glory, grandeur, conquest, superiority, force, State, and idolatry.[10] By exposing patriotism's bloody relatives, and demystifying the idolatry of State, she would create a healthy "We"—a coherent and moral patriotism—as an alternative to a sick and deracinated one.

The sort of patriotism Weil imagines has contemporary relevance as well. The idea of country as something fragile, precious, and in need of protection, finds its analogue in contemporary feminist discourse, particularly in the "ethic of caring," and in various attempts to apply the idea of maternal thinking to the political realm. Her conception of belonging and rootedness is surely compatible with an ecological outlook that emphasizes land stewardship and preservation of the environment as well as respect for diverse cultures, traditions, and localities. And her idea of patriotism as a protective but not aggressive, vigilant but peace-loving attitude of mind that rejects greatness as "force of arms," holds meaning in a nuclear age where the ideas of loyalty to the nation and supremacy in weaponry are made synonymous, and need to be disconnected and examined more attentively. In short, Weil's vision of compassionate patriotism embodies a perspective appropriate for the times we live in and a language that responds to real human needs.

We should also note the significance Weil's new patriotism has within the contours of her own thought. Because it presents a vision of *collectivité* as a necessary and meaningful aspect of human existence and, moreover, links such a *collectivité* to the terrestrial realm of the nation, *TNFR* goes a long way toward correcting some of the imbalances we noticed in both her materialist and her mystical thought. Here, for example, she does not fix the achievement of human dignity solely within the reach of the autonomous, rational thinker, but rather imagines "country" as the context within which the individual can develop most fully. Nor does she reject this world as a source of roots, but rather attempts to locate within this world a spiritual morality. In one sense, then, *TNFR* is Weil's most focused attempt to reconcile the tension between the individual and the collectivity, and in another it is her most focused attempt to reconcile the human and the divine.

Weil's recommendations for France and her more general pronouncements on patriotism have not always met with appreciative acknowledgment, however. *TNFR* has been read critically, and received both as a "proto-totalitarian" document by Phillippe Dujardin (1975), and as the mark of a profoundly "antipolitical" thinker by Conor Cruise O'Brien (White 1981:95–110). Dujardin draws his evidence largely from Weil's conclusion that the State (despite its secondary status to country) merits "the obligation of obedience" and from her argument that the members of the FFO must be made the leaders and the "spiritual voice" of France. O'Brien draws his charge from what he identifies as Weil's warnings against "loving country too much" and from her revulsion for associations of all kinds. He offers this view of her "reconstructive sketch" of France, based on her (extremely sketchy) discussion of the "needs of the soul":

> A France reconstructed on Weilian lines . . . would have no political parties, no trade-unions, no freedom of association. It would have a rigid, primitive, eccentric form of censorship . . . it would be organized on hierarchical lines, although we are not told just what these lines would be. There would be liberty or something so described, coming second after "order" and just before "obedience" among the needs of the soul (White 1981:96).

Regardless of the ambiguities embedded in Weil's programmatic view of the reconstructed French state and the role she assigns the leaders of the FFO (especially de Gaulle), neither Dujardin's nor O'Brien's claims are wholly convincing. Dujardin's charge seems misguided in the extreme. Aside from her own denunciations of totalitarianism, and her outright rejection of idolatry in a nationalist form "composed of a man acclaimed as leader and as his stage the ironbound machine of State" (*TNFR*182), we must remember that Weil's intention in *TNFR* is to condemn precisely the sort of politics Dujardin suggests she emulates. The State that uproots local and regional life, the bureaucratic machine that numbs true politics, corrupt and demagogic leaders, and the mindless idolatry of the mass public that follows them, are all manifestations of the political *déracinement* she abhors. And if we consider, for instance, that language regulations in the Third Reich combined the organic and the mechanical (the ideal German was like steel (*stahlern*), lived in an organic community (*organische Volksgemeinschaft*), charged with power (*aufgeladen*), then Weil's idea of country as a vital medium or culture bed in need of caretaking seems to constitute a direct challenge to the Nazi conception. She is determined to break apart the bond between the organic and the mechanical, and have us reject the assimilation of State and country, machine and citizen, force and community. Finally, we must remember that her rejection of all things Roman is not simply a commentary on the past, but a condemnation of the Reich and its appropriation of the symbolic accoutrements of the Roman Empire. In short, Weil is as definitive in her opposition to Nazi Germany as she is in her reappraisal of France, and her condemnation can rightly be analyzed as, among other things, "anti-totalitarian." In even the most general sense of the (very ambiguous) term, "totalitarian" is an unfitting adjective to apply to her and to her prescriptions in *TNFR*.

O'Brien's charge stems from an altogether different perspective. He thinks Weil is profoundly antipolitical, in both a broad and narrow sense. Among other things, he writes, she is a "rigorous enemy of the first person plural," disdainful of human beings in any corporate entity, certainly in the body politic (White 1981:98). More narrowly, she is an enemy of political involvement, critical of all forms of political association and collective action. As I have previously indicated, charges such as these are valid as a critique of Weil's mystical writings. The mystical Weil's antipolitical disposition comes close to precisely what O'Brien describes as an antipathy to the "first person plural." We can even find a similar suspicion of "We" in her materialist writings, especially *RLO*. How puzzling, however, to find that his critique is not directed against the mystical or the materialist, but rather against *TNFR*. And in this context, I find his claims unpersuasive.

O'Brien is wrong to argue, for example, that Weil condemns loving country too much. To the contrary, she warns against loving country *in the wrong way*—like idolaters. Compassionate patriotism places no limits on attachment, only upon absolute and unconditional adoration; it is about loving, but loving rightly. Moreover, the "first person plural" O'Brien says Weil denigrates is the mass society of atomized and alienated beings who have no roots in the life of the community and no healthy identity to bind them together.[11] Far from devaluing political associations and collectivities, Weil despairs over their demise in France, and over the rise of a State that has corrupted the "national sense." Her aversion is not for all political associations, but only for those, as she says in *TNFR*, that have become "single, compulsory, professional organizations," obliged to toe the line in public affairs. What she regrets is not democracy, but the sham institutions that render democracy meaningless, "an object of disgust, derision, and disdain" (*TNFR*121). These "sham institutions" include political parties, which Weil argues should be abolished. Thinking of Germany, she writes:

A democracy where public life is made up of strife between political parties is incapable of preventing the formation of a party whose avowed aim is the overthrow of that democracy. If such a democracy brings in discriminatory laws, it cuts it own throat. If it doesn't, it is just as safe as a little bird in front of a snake (*TNFR*28).

Leaving aside the questionable nature of her assumption that the abolition of parties would resolve a classic problem for democratic states that protect free speech, we might nevertheless view her critique of parties not as another example of her "bias" against the first person plural, but rather as a defense of an alternative vision of politics. Noting that a public life without parties is a practical goal, she adds: "In the eyes of the people of 1789, there was literally no other possibility. A public life like ours has been over the course of the last half century would have seemed to them a hideous nightmare" (*TNFR*28). Her aim, then, is not to condemn all forms of collective life, but rather to suggest that a public realm free from the ravages of party strife is a better form of collective life, and one well worth pursuing. On this score, she returns to Rousseau: "Rousseau clearly demonstrates how party strife automatically destroys the Republic. He had foretold its effects. It would be a good thing just now to encourage the reading of the *Contract Social*" (*TNFR*28). (Since O'Brien's sympathies are rather more with Burke, he is not overly inclined to be attentive to Weil's views on these matters). In the end, I think the very "We" O'Brien claims Weil dismisses is what she is actually attempting to recover—it is what compassionate patriotism is supposed to nurture and protect.

Despite the fundamental wrong-headedness of Dujardin's and O'Brien's arguments, however, they do nonetheless raise some problematical issues surrounding Weil's vision in *TNFR*. Dujardin is right, for example, to notice Weil's excessive emphasis on the role of the FFO as the political and spiritual inspiration for France, as well as her strange capitulation to the authority of the State. Undeveloped although they are, her comments on the FFO as the spiritual leader of France's regeneration suggest strong Gaullist sympathies (which, had she lived, she no doubt would have tempered). At any rate, in these passages her conception of politics seems to center more upon leadership, authority, and "founding," than upon democracy, popular sovereignty, and public participation.

O'Brien, for his part, is not completely amiss to charge that Weil fails to pay sufficient attention to the idea of political involvement. I would suggest, however, that these problems do not stem from antipolitical sensibilities on her part; they are rather the consequence of a conception of belonging to country that is compelling, but ultimately inadequate as a foundation for political life. Or, to put this another way, Weil is political but, in the end, she is not quite "political" enough. Although in *TNFR* she finally affirms what the *RLO* denies—that a political collectivity is a vital source of identity and meaning—she nevertheless stops short of imagining political life as democratic politics, or of conceiving of patriotism as an active engagement in the public realm. What I want to suggest is that Weil's limited "politicalness" stems from two theoretical problems: first, from her reliance upon a metaphor that diminishes the meaning of "belonging to country," and second, more importantly, from a patriotic ethic that is informed by a private, spiritual, morality rather than a public, political one. These two theoretical problems lead almost inexorably to the "medicaments" she offers in *TNFR*, of which Dujardin and O'Brien are so critical. Let us consider, then, each of these theoretical problems in turn.

Earlier, in examining the failure of Weil's first "magnum opus" to account for the possibility of a healthy "We" as opposed to an oppressive one, I suggested that her argument was damaged by the "spectre" of the metaphor of the collectivity. There is perhaps a similar sort of problem in *TNFR*, a metaphor that obstructs rather than assists understanding—only this one allows for the possibility of collective life but at the same time diminishes the possibility of political action. It is the organic metaphor of "roots" itself, as well as its satellite images of "culture bed" and "vital medium."

In some respects, Weil's organic metaphor of rootedness does exactly what a metaphor should do. By extending our imaginations, it gives us a richer, more fully developed conceptualization, in this case, of a human society. Her metaphor specifically gets us to recognize ourselves as creatures who need stability, permanence, and security in order to grow and flourish, and as collective beings whose societies are complex and dynamic living wholes, cultural "root-systems," as it were. Thus, just as the principles of nature involve growth, nourishment, root-fixing ground, andecological balance (or so Weil implies in her metaphor), so the most healthy societies emerge amid a flourishing culture, a fixed territory, and harmonious social relationships. In particular, Weil's metaphor works to remind us of what humans share with nature, of the life-cycle of the species as part of the perennial process of birth and death, growth and decay. Like plants, our societies are at once sturdy and fragile; we can escape neither the rhythm of the seasons nor the forces of disintegration, whether natural or human. We are, Weil reminds us, both vital and vulnerable organisms that come to life, and inevitably must pay "the tribute due to nature."

But there is something incomplete about this metaphor, and, accordingly, about a political perspective that takes its inspiration from the literal idea of roots and rootedness. For despite what they share with the natural realm, human societies are also vastly different from the culture-bed of plant forms or the vital mediums of organic life. Among other things, as Aristotle taught us, human beings and their societies are, "by nature," political animals, *zoon politikon*. Thus, to ascribe organic characteristics to humans as political beings, or to analyze political matters in terms of biological metaphors, is to diminish, if not altogether destroy, the special meaning and distinctiveness of the political itself. And this is precisely what metaphors are not supposed to do. When Weil discusses country as a "culture bed" and a "vital medium," and citizenship as the "growing of roots," however, she is making just this sort of mistake. Ironically, by ascribing biological characteristics to political phenomena, she fails to plumb the depths of the very political phenomena (such as "politics," "country," and "citizenship") she is intent upon preserving. Indeed, if we were to push her organic metaphor to its farthest limit, we might be inclined to view politics, country, and citizenship as parts of a causal and cyclical life-process that, somehow, determines human life and can neither be radically altered nor rearranged. But politics is not solely or best understood as part of the rhythms of nature, nor is a country best conceived of as a nutrient bed, nor is a citizen merely a species of organic being. This is not to say, of course, that human agents and their creations are so utterly different in kind from biological organisms with caused behavior that metaphors such as Weil's hold absolutely no meaning. As another theorist has pointed out, we are creatures who can be seen in, and in fact see ourselves in, "seemingly incompatible ways"—as organic beings with caused behavior, and also as free agents who continually transform our world.[12] My point here is that Weil's metaphor of roots and rootedness plays too much to the former and not enough to the latter. In other words, the images she offers, inviting as they are, leave too much out. The idea of country as a "culture-bed" or of patriotism as the right sort of love toward the "roots" that sustain us, do not sufficiently emphasize that human beings are actors and creators of the world, not simply organic objects in it.

In one sense, of course, Weil recognizes this last point as clearly as anyone. In fact *TNFR*, as an act of political theorizing, is meant to clarify how humans as political beings might best revitalize, preserve, and protect their nation. Weil does not expect this to come naturally; if anything, she sees the opposite course, the systematic destruction of public life, as being the more "natural" proclivity of human beings in the modern world. What she wants to do is advance a conceptualization of patriotism that will reverse that destructiveness and give rise to a new public spirit and political life. One might question, however, the extent to which patriotism as an "organic" idea of "rootedness" in country meets this end, especially given its theoretical inadequacy as vision of political participation and public action. What her organic metaphor gets us to see, in other words, is "country" as a fragile ecosystem but not "country" as a collectivity of participatory citizens. Likewise, her conception of patriotism would have us revere "rootedness," but not as the actual *activity* of citizenship. Quite simply, the latter is something that the metaphor of roots—whatever else it evokes—cannot evoke very well at all. Indeed, what the metaphor of roots most vividly captures is the notion of security and fixity, rather than the notion of political change and action, the attributes of the *zoon politikon*. As vitally important as "security and fixity" are in any political society, they are not, in and of themselves, sufficient conditions for a fully political society. Despite her intentions, then, Weil's conception of politics and patriotism is diminished by her commitment to a limited metaphor that, in turn, reduces the power of her political vision.

As central as the organic metaphor is, however, it is not the decisive feature of Weil's limited politicalness. For that, we must turn instead to the patriotic ethic she propounds, and to a different set of metaphors which convey the conception of patriotism as an moral attitude and of the nation as the locus of identity. The metaphors are personal and familial ones; they transform patriotism into compassion, country into a loving "parent," and citizens into obedient children. Under the force of these conceptions, the personal and the political, the familial and the public, become one and the same; thus, the special distinctiveness of that which is public and political is lost.[13] This is the second, more problematical, theoretical feature of *TNFR*, and we might now consider how it works itself out in Weil's thought.

At the basis of *TNFR* is a problem that reaches far back to Plato and the ancient Greeks, and reappears throughout Western political thought. Can politics be made virtuous, and if so, how? Weil asks a question like this, only with special attention to patriotism, and drawing upon both Greek and Christian inspirations, she answers (at least a qualified) yes. Accordingly, she offers an ethic of compassion as the basis for a revitalized patriotism. Or, to put this otherwise, despite her often clear-eyed recognition of the inherent imperfectibility of the political world and the inevitable evils of politics itself, she ultimately envisions a patriotic citizenry as an ethical, spiritual, self—a compassionate person, who cares rightly for a fragile and imperfect country. To this end, she is fond of quoting the New Testament, "A good tree cannot bring forth evil fruit, neither can a corrupt tree bring forth good fruit" (Matthew 7:16–18). This scriptural lesson, and others, guide her conception of the French as an ethical self, a "good tree" (*TNFR*200).

Earlier, in drawing a psychic component from Weil's argument, I suggested that a moral psychology like the one she offers has significant implications for politics. There is something valuable and true, for instance, about her analogy between the egocentric individual and the nationalistic collectivity. And, in many respects, the "fully integrated" compassionate self serves as an instructive model for a healthy national identity, especially if we understand that a nation, like an individual, has a history that is integral to its identity and in need of right remembrance. What I am contending, then, is not that Weil's conception of patriotism as a spiritual attitude is wholly irrelevant to or inappropriate for politics. To the contrary, it speaks very much to the point, and is a reminder of just how deeply integrated our moral and political values are or, at least according to Weil, should be.

At the same time, however, this perception of a nation or a citizenry as a moral "self" can take us only part of the way toward an appropriate conception of patriotism. As helpful as moral psychology or some notion of "ego identity" is, the situation France faces is not finally and best understood as a "self" in identity crisis that must learn to "love" rightly, but rather as a body politic with no public sense of solidarity, one that must revitalize its political life. The problem of patriotism, that is, has to do with the decline of the *citoyen*, not just with France's distorted sense of identity. To fail to reckon with the former is to risk overlooking the things that are distinctive and important to political life—democracy, justice, freedom, citizenship—things that the psychological language of the self and the private language of love and compassion can neither fully capture nor fruitfully illuminate.

There is a viewpoint in Western political thought, from Aristotle to Machiavelli, and Tocqueville to Arendt, that upholds precisely the argument I am making here, and contends that the confusion of the private and the public realms is both conceptually problematical and practically dangerous. To presume the applicability of personal virtues (or psychological attributes) to the political realm, so this view goes, is to deny the uniqueness of politics, and perhaps even to forget or to erase those virtues specific to politics that are in need of remembrance and defense. By conceiving of the French as a "self" and patriotism as a spiritual attitude *toward* country rather than a particular sort of activity—the exercise of freedom—*within* country, Weil loses sight of precisely the sort of political virtues Aristotle, Machiavelli, Tocqueville, and Arendt in their very different ways defend.[14] Not by chance does the language of liberty play such an insignificant role in *TNFR* (as compared to the *RLO*). The language of the ethical person—of compassion, love, and tender care—overtakes the political language of liberty, and displaces the idea of patriotism as active citizenship in favor of a more privatized way of thinking about belonging to country. And nowhere is this subordination of political to personal more evident than in some of the analogies Weil offers regarding patriotism. In a (telling) simile, she advises the French to love naturally, and not for prestige, "as a mother whose son is first in the competition for the Ecole Polytechnique loves something altogether different in him" (*W*1957a:26). Similarly, in calling upon another familial metaphor, she offers the example of "loving children" who obey their governess (the State) out of love for their parents (the country) (*TNFR*179).

The difficulty these familial images pose for a conception of patriotism should be obvious; citizens are neither "loving mothers" nor "obedient children," and a country is not their parent.[15] Citizens stand in a special, distinctive, *political* relation to each other (one that familial metaphors cannot capture), and rather than being "parental," one's country is perhaps better conceived of as the site of, or the context for, this special relationship or activity. By failing to emphasize this, Weil again diminishes the meaning of politics, even as she rightly reminds us of patriotism's moral dimension. Since the familial metaphors she invokes and the patriotism of compassion she expounds do not counsel a love of a different sort—of the exercise of liberty, self-governance, democratic values—she is left with a conception of politics and power that is at once virtuous and radically incomplete.

The irony in Weil's discussion of patriotism as a spiritual ethic rather than a political activity is that, in effect, it excludes precisely the sort of politics and patriotism she herself defends when she presents her historical narrative, and writes of France's "underground past," the corruption of democracy, and of rootedness itself as "active, natural participation in the life of the community." When she conjures up the image of town liberties, the Burgundian movement, the Frond, and most of all, 1789—that brief, bright, spark of patriotism—she envisions precisely the sort of politics that distinguish participatory citizenship from State government. When she criticizes the French for having a corrupted understanding of democracy and an unhealthy cynicism toward public affairs, she intimates that a reconstructed France must not only change its attitude toward country, but also revitalize its political life. And when she says that for France to become a reality, "it must become, *in fact*, a life-giving agent, really . . . good, root-fixing ground . . . a favorable setting for participation in and loyal attachment to all other sorts of environmental expression," she offers up a distinction between patriotism as a spiritual attitude and patriotism as the sort of concrete practice that makes political freedom a reality (*TNFR*165). Quite clearly, in her reconstructed history, Weil conceives of national sovereignty as well as the resuscitation of local and regional associations as major aspects of French identity. Equally apparent is her concern (implicit in her discussion of the State) that democratic politics has nearly disappeared in the nation. But when she turns to her "cure" for France's diseased condition, these acute democratic sensibilities fall away, and in their place emerges a patriotic ethic informed by things spiritual, familial, and private, rather than public and political.

## Worldlessness and Death

In Simone Weil's case, the consequences of collapsing the personal and the political are evident not only in the substance of her political thought; they also color her life and death. By way of conclusion, we might now briefly return to the difficult circumstances of her death, and see if we can draw some connections between her thought and her identity that might allow us to make some sense of it.

She was taken to Middlesex Hospital in April 1943, "debilitated, dreadfully thin, feverish, and exhausted," as a chaplin who was asked to visit her wrote (Pétrement 1976:521). There is no question that her physical condition was deteriorating rapidly. Overwork, despair about her failure to receive permission for her mission to France, her voluntary and persistent refusal of nourishment, all contributed to her state of weakness and decline. By August, when she was moved to Grosvenor Sanatorium at Ashford in Kent, tuberculosis had been diagnosed, and she was even more lethargic from the strain of the disease and her lack of food, which aggravated it. It seems there was little the doctors could do for her, since she would not—or could not—eat. Thus, a few weeks after her arrival at Grosvenor, on August 24, she died in her sleep. Near the end, she said her refusal to eat had to do with her determination to have no more than did her fellow French, especially the children, who were on rations. While still at Middlesex, she is said to have remarked, "I cannot be happy or eat to my satisfaction when I feel that my people are suffering" (*P*525). Clearly, she linked this condition to the larger political crisis as well; in *TNFR*, for example, she wrote, "Today every Frenchman knows what it was he missed as soon as France fell. He knows as well as he knows what is missing when one is forced to go hungry" (*TNFR*159). Most accounts of her death have taken these expressions as the key to understanding her behavior and her ultimate demise. As persuasive as these accounts are, however, they nevertheless seem to be, to put it in Weilian language, "surface readings." A deeper reading may be possible as well. I wonder, that is, if we cannot also find something more behind Weil's death than an immediate political gesture born of her (characteristic) identification with those who suffer in the world. In particular, we might look one final time at what she attempts on a theoretical plane in *TNFR*, and consider the relationship her political thought bears to her personal vocation.

No one who encounters *L'Enracinement* can fail to notice the predominant images that inform it—images of bread, food, sustenance, nourishment, and nuturance, and, alternately, of hunger, starvation, poisoning, famine, disease, and death—all of which the author mobilizes in her argument for the revitalization of her country. Thus "needs" are to the soul as food is to the life of the body (*TNFR*9); collectivities must serve not to "devour" souls but as food for them; the same respect that one owes to food, Weil says, "is owed to any collectivity" (*TNFR*9). Likewise, all forms of oppression "create a famine," (*TNFR*22), and none more so than forced uprootedness which is a "mortal disease" (*TNFR*44). France itself is a "dying man," "reduced by famine" to a "condition of lethargy," and the French are "poisoned" and being "starved of greatness" (*TNFR*174) in much the same condition as the "devoured and digested" lands they once conquered (*TNFR*144). The State "appeared as an inexhaustible horn of plenty" but, in reality, it has exhausted the country and "eats away at its moral substance, lives on it, fattens on it, until the day comes when no more nourishment can be drawn from it" (*TNFR*120). The "nourishment" the country requires includes a true love of beauty—"it is a food" (*TNFR*93). Hence also the "need for root-fixing ground" and those life-sustaining connections that transmit food and assure the health of the living organism (*TNFR*165).

Surely these images and metaphors do not have to be distorted beyond recognition to have them call up the self and psyche of their author. Yet what, exactly, might we make of all this? Perhaps that Weil, in her own self-starvation, sees herself and France as one? Does she, in fact, go beyond the mere solidarity with her fellow French that her biographers suggest and, in essence, identify with France the nation, exacting upon herself the same starvation and weakness, the same "lethargy," she thinks plagues her country? This reading is tempting, and not only because, in a narrow sense, Weil's physical condition and her political metaphors in *TNFR* are of such a piece. In a wider sense, we might understand the physical decline she inflicts upon herself, with France in view, as a way of finally reconciling the opposition between "I" and "We" that so preoccupied her. If, as Nietzsche said, all theory is autobiography, then we might imagine the cure Weil proposes for France—rendering the personal virtues political—as also the means through which she attempts to cure her own "dilemma of worldliness." By "becoming" France, by taking the starvation of the nation upon herself, she resolves the tension between "I" and "We".

Another reading presses here, however. For Simone Weil's openness to death reveals her ultimate failure to reconcile "I" and "We" in any meaningful way. Instead of a resolved or even a still-unresolved worldliness, she followed another impulse and left the world behind. To understand her identification with France more deeply, then, we need to return to her mystical thought, and its possible relationship to her death. We must move, in other words, beyond the dilemma of worldliness and consider that other constant in Weil's life and thought, her mystical impulse toward worldlessness and the divine.

To better grasp how Weil's mysticism bears upon her political thought, we might consider something else she writes in *TNFR*, to those who would love France:

> Whoever feels cold and hunger, and is tempted to pity himself, can instead of doing that, from out of his own shrunken frame, direct his pity toward France; the very cold and hunger themselves then cause the love of France to enter into the body and penetrate to the depths of the soul (*TNFR*174).

If we consider this observation closely, and recall the condition Weil was in when she wrote it, we might see her as not so much struggling to become France, but rather as attempting to engage in an act of true attention toward France. From what she writes, it seems that the love she counsels is one that sees the nation as the "afflicted other," into whom those who themselves suffer, and would pity France, must "project their being." Crucial to this reading are the mystical ideas we encountered earlier, particularly attention, affliction, and *dépouillement*. But now, in *TNFR*, these mystical ideas are enlisted for political ends, and guide the way toward nourishment of the *metaxu*, those "earthly treasures" which "warm and nourish the soul" and make a fully human life possible. Thus, patriotism becomes a form of spiritual attention: an act through which the "I" is directed toward country, and the compassionate soul is projected into it. Those who have suffered the "cold and hunger" of uprootedness should transform their personal sufferings toward political ends, Weil suggests, thereby finding within themselves the warmth and nourishment their bodies lack.

On one level, Weil's counsel can be read as a simple patriotic appeal in a time of national crisis: it is better to love or pity one's country, or ask what you can do for your country, rather than remaining preoccupied with yourself. But knowing what we do of her death, we must also see in her directive to attend to France something much more than this. Her counsel to "pity France" becomes, in the end, her own private, spiritual calling rather than a collective, public one. In order to "cure" France, she clearly sets for herself an act of attention that (as she so often characterizes it) "is the same as eating." We might recall that the act of attention, or compassion toward the afflicted, requires a "projection of being" into the other that presupposes destruction of the "I," and that this act is one of her most visceral impulses. Thus, the more miserable or afflicted, "cold and hungry," her own condition, the more likely it is that she will be able to engage in attention and achieve true *dépouillement*. Remembering these elements of her mysticism, perhaps we can appreciate both the awful folly of her patriotic convictions, and the courage it took for her to follow them.

In sum, the patriotism Weil sets for herself is obviously not a political one that demands her continued engagement in public affairs; nor is it even a sublimation of self that renders itself as total devotion to country.

What her patriotic *dépouillement* requires is neither political action nor psychological sublimation, but a literal self-sacrifice—the death of the "I." Within this spiritual politics, France becomes the "afflicted," in need of attention and compassion if it is to be saved. The compassion is one that Weil, as "benefactor," or "care-taker" of her country, would extend. Her own wretchedness sets the stage for it; the "cold and hunger" she experiences make possible a genuine compassion toward France that is also, in her words, "universal" and "nonexclusive," able to "extend itself over all countries in misfortune" (*TNFR*174).[16] Paradoxically, however, this compassion requires of the benefactor a personal renunciation of this world, and an abandonment of "the wretchedness of our human condition" (*TNFR*174). Or, to put this a little differently, the "food" Weil is determined to offer her starving collectivity can be given only through a "looking" that she conceives of as nourishment of the most elevated sort. She is prepared for such a giving, as this passage from her notebooks makes clear: "Man's great affliction, which begins with infancy and accompanies him till death, is that looking and eating are two different operations. Eternal beatitude is a state where to look is to eat" (*W*1952a:90). In transforming these mystical thoughts into a conception of patriotism, Weil creates for herself a terrifingly personal task. In compassion for France, she prepares herself to "look" in a way that would enable her to surmount man's great affliction and await eternal beatitude. Perhaps therein she also sought the "truth" that always eluded her—the reconcilation of the human and the divine.

In reflecting upon Simone Weil's death, we cannot easily forget her heroines, Joan of Arc and Antigone, who also died identifying with their collectivities and in profound allegiance to the divine. For many, it is tempting to read in Weil's death, as we read in the myth of Joan and the drama of Antigone, a special kind of nobility, a spiritual commitment to the world that manifests itself in a personal denial of the world, for the love of a "transcendent kingdom." Many have indeed found this spiritual nobility and purity within her, hence her reputation as a "saint." But in an age where such sacrifices are also viewed as terribly bizarre, it is perhaps equally tempting to read her death as a pathetic and wasted act—a vain gesture brought about by a strange confusion of the personal, the mystical, and the political. Many have found this in Weil as well, hence her reputation as an oddity, a "tragic buffoon." Or, as J.M. Cameron has more sympathetially put it, "Either this is madness or it is obedience to a vocation few are called to" (White 1981:46).

Whatever we choose to make of it, Simone Weil's death is not easily understood, and certainly not easily reduced to a simple choice between saint or buffoon. Whatever its meaning, her worldlessness and her lonely death will continue to transfix and to repel. In the end, we might at least take it as a necessary and urgent reminder of the tragedy, personal and political, of *malheur* and *déracinement* in the modern world. Perhaps her death should also serve to strengthen our resolve not to do as she did, but rather to attend to the problems she posed and ponder the solutions she offered, however best we can.

## Notes

1. This insight once prompted Weil to note, "The highest piety is a patriotic attachment to a dead country" (W1962b:45).

2. Her writing is, among other things, a study in the symbolic tension between Greece and Rome, an attempt to have the former triumph over the latter. The "Manichaean dualisms" we have found in so much of her thought, between oppression and liberty, gravity and grace, force and attention, is recapitulated again in her dyad Greece/Rome. If the Greeks were the creators of spiritual bridges, then "spiritual life in Rome was hardly anything more than an expression of the will to power" (W1962b:116). If the Greeks were endowed with the spiritual force that allowed them to avoid self-deception, then the Romans "were unsurpassable in the art of perfidy" (W1962b:103). If the Greeks were contemplative, then the Romans were propagandists, and so on. "With the possible exception of Tacitus," Weil writes in "The Great Beast," "the [Romans'] inferiority when compared to the Greeks is overwhelming" (W1962b:116). She also says: "In a general way, the word purity, which can so often be legitimately used in praising Greece in every sphere of spiritual creation, is hardly ever applicable in the case of Rome" (W1962b:120). When it comes to Rome, then, her powers of attention—or "Homeric impartiality"—are quite obviously stilled.

3. It is worth noting, of course, that Weil uses this conservative conception in an innovative way—to induce some radical changes in France.

4. Quoted in Bouswma (Erikson 1978:90).

5. The phrase in quotes is Nietzsche's (1955:151). He continues: "Compassion . . . as I said before, there are problems higher than any pleasure and pain problems, including that of the pain of compassion; any philosophy which seeks to culminate here is a náiveté" (151–52). The "compassion" Nietzsche goes on to defend in *Beyond Good and Evil* is precisely the opposite, a transvaluation, of the one Weil later recommends.

6. Her recommendations for a warlike energy born of compassion are intriguing, not only because they attempt to fuse combat and caring. These views also mark a break from her earlier pacifism. Indeed, she is perhaps one of those rare characters who pacifism ends *after* a spiritual conversion.

7. In *TNFR* (179) she writes: "No criterion can be offered indicating exactly what this limit [on obligation to country] is; it is even impossible for each of us to prescribe one for himself once and for all; when you feel you can't obey any longer, you just have to disobey. But there is at least one necessary condition, although insufficient of itself, making it possible to disobey without being guilty of crime; this is to be urged forward by so imperious an obligation that one is constrained to scorn all risks of whatever kind."

8. In many ways Weil's reformulation of the State runs parallel to her assessment of the Roman Catholic Church. The Church "protects" and pre-

serves religious practice but is not to be confused with it. To Father Perrin she writes: "I love the Catholic liturgy, hymns, architecture, rites and ceremonies. But I have not the slightest love for the Church in the strict sense of the word, apart from its relation to all these things that I do love" (W1951b:50). Like the Church, the State, in Weilian terms, is best conceived of as "in relation to" or protective of what is truly worth loving. Thus it is necessary to clarify the distinction between the "common object" (State, Church) and what is truly sacred (love of country, love of God).

9. Further psychobiographical investigations would no doubt uncover a number of similarities between Joan of Arc (as the mythology presents her) and Weil. Both were decisively religious but held nonorthodox (even heretical) views; both were inclined toward an almost anorexic asceticism, androgynous dress, and toward what Marina Warner (1981) has called "mysticism's metaphor for angelic purity"—chastity. And, of course, both were singularly devoted to France and sacrificed their lives for their country, though in significantly different and historically constituted ways.

10. The phrase patriotism's "bloody relatives" is John Schaar's (1981:285).

11. On a more general level of analysis, I hope I have shown why reading Weil simply as "anti-human" is one-sided and incomplete. Although an aversion to the "collectivity" does indeed mark some of her work, it is not characteristic of it in any "final" sense, just as none of her other impulses are characteristic of her thought in any final sense. Here it bears repeating that her suspicion of human collectivities is rather one of a number of conflicting impulses in her work, not the least of which is her commitment to collectivities.

12. See Pitkin (1976:301–17).

13. Those who are familiar with Arendt's distinction between public and private, and her argument against "moral goodness" as a criterion for judging action in the public realm, will recognize her influence in the critique of Weil's concept of patriotism that follows (Arendt 1958). Of all of Arendt's distinctions, the one between public and private has perhaps generated the most criticism, especially (directly and indirectly) in much current feminist political thought. I cannot undertake to defend that distinction here, but I have attempted to defend it elsewhere, particularly in response to those "maternal thinkers" who would have the family and the private realm serve as ethical and practical models for the political and the public. See Dietz (1985).

14. Nowhere is the influence of Plato and Rousseau more evident than in this dimension of Weil's thought. Like Plato, she is inclined to view a citizenry as a single soul or, as I have suggested, a single "self." Like both Plato and Rousseau, she is inclined (most of the time) in TNFR to view virtuous politics as in some way analogous to virtuous personhood. Thus my criticism of Weil's blending of the personal (or spiritual) and the political may also be taken as a criticism of this perspective in Plato and Rousseau. The alternatives to this approach in the history of ideas are varied and diverse, and this is not the place to engage in a lengthy discussion of them. The theorists I mention—Aristotle, Machiavelli, Tocqueville, Arendt—are not to be taken as uniform "bloc" but merely as an "alternative set of visions" in opposition to the ones embodied (again differently) by Plato and Rousseau. Arendt is especially critical of compassion as a political attribute; in On Revolution she argues that, as a private virtue made a public vice, it contributed not only to the downfall of Robespierre, but to the unhappy fate of the Revolution itself (1963:79–95). In a complex argument in The Human Condition (1958:241–43) she contends that love is "not only apolitical

but antipolitical, perhaps the most powerful of all antipolitical human forces." Here she appears to forward two claims: first, that love, by reason of its passion, actually destroys the very condition of separation and relatedness that politics requires; and second, that love can flourish only in a "narrowly circumscribed sphere"—when it is transformed into a political quality, *it* is destroyed. Thus, Arendt suggests, the appropriate virtue for political life is not love, but rather respect, a "kind of "friendship" without intimacy and without closeness" that preserves the condition politics requires. For all practical purposes, Weil stands at the other end of this argument, and defends love and compassion as appropriate virtues of the political world.

15. The great exception to this view, of course, is Socrates who, in the *Crito*, compares the laws and constitution of Athens to a kind of "superparent" and has them ask in imaginary dialogue: "since you have been born and brought up and educated, can you deny, in the first place, that you were our child and servant, both you and your ancestors? . . . Are you so wise as to have forgotten that compared with your mother and father and all the rest of your ancestors your country is something far more precious, more venerable, more sacred, and held in greater honour both among gods and among all reasonable men?" (Plato 1954:91–91). The other great exception is Burke, who likens the "faults of the state to the wounds of a father" and revolutionaries to children who are "prompt rashly to hack that aged parent to pieces" (1955:109). At least on the metaphorical level, if not on matters of concrete particularity, Weil would seem to agree with both. What is most troubling about these metaphors is not just that they turn country into a parent, but that they would make children of citizens and, in Weil's case at least, render patriotism a matter of "respectful obedience."

16. Keeping in mind that Weil often speaks of country as a "parent," we might also find in her call for a compassion that is nonexclusive and universal the triumph of the resourceful, "obedient child" who preserves the virtues of her protective, caring mother and rejects the vices of her idolatrous one (i.e., the one who exclusively worships André).

# Bibliography

Alain. 1950. "Simone Weil." *La Table Ronde* 28 (April): 47–51.

Anderson, David. 1971. *Simone Weil*. London: SCM Press Ltd.

Andrew, Edward. 1986. "Simone Weil on the Injustice of Rights-Based Doctrines." *Review of Politics* 48 (1): 60–91.

Arendt, Hannah. 1968. *Between Past and Future*. New York: Viking Press.

———. 1963. *On Revolution*. New York: Penguin.

———. 1958. *The Human Condition*. Chicago: University of Chicago Press.

Ariès, Phillipe. 1962. *Centuries of Childhood*. New York: Vintage Books.

Arnold, G.L. 1951. "Simone Weil." *Cambridge Journal* 4 (6): 323–38.

Aron, Raymond. 1958. *The Vichy Regime*. Boston: Beacon Press.

Ashcraft, Richard. 1980. "Petty Bourgeois Radicalism and Marxism: Reflections on the Political Thought of Simone Weil." Unpublished manuscript, UCLA.

Augustine, St. 1960. *Confessions*. John K. Ryan, ed. New York: Doubleday and Company.

Bainton, Roland. 1971. "Psychiatry: The Examination of Erikson's *Young Man Luther*." *Religion in Life* 40 (Winter): 450–71.

Beiner, Ronald. 1983. *Political Judgment*. Chicago: University of Chicago Press.

Bendix, Richard and Seymour Martin Lipset, eds. 1974. *Class, Status and Power*. New York: Free Press.

Benrubi, Isaac. 1926. *Contemporary Thought of France*. Ernest B. Dicker, trans. London: Williams & Nargate.

Berger, Peter. 1967. *The Sacred Canopy*. Garden City: Doubleday.

Berki, R. N. 1979. "On the Nature and Origin of Man's Concept of Labor." *Political Theory* 7 (Fall): 35–56.

Berrigan, Daniel and Robert Coles. 1970. *The Geography of Faith*. Boston: Beacon Press.

Blanchot, Maurice. 1969. *L'entretien infini*. Paris: Gallimard.

Blum, Larry and Vic Seidler. 1987. *A Truer Liberty: Simone Weil and Marxism*. Unpublished manuscript.

Blumenthal, Gerda. 1952. "Simone Weil's Way of the Cross." *Thought* 27 (105): 225–34.

Bramley, J.A. 1967. "A Pilgrim of the Absolute." *Hibbert Journal* 66 (August): 10–14.

Buber, Martin. 1960. *The Prophetic Faith*. New York: Harper and Row.

———. 1952. *At the Turning*. New York: Farrar, Straussard Young.

Burke, Edmund. 1955. *Reflections on the Revolution in France*. Thomas Mahoney, ed. New York: Bobbs-Merrill.

Byrnes, R. F. 1950. *Anti-Semitism in Modern France*. New Brunswick, N.J.: Rutgers University Press.

197

Cabaud, Jacques. 1957. _L'expérience vécue de Simone Weil_. Paris: Librarie Plon.
———. 1967. _Simone Weil à New York et à Londres_. Paris: Plon.
Camus, Albert. 1965. _Essais_. Paris: Gallimard.
Chaning-Pearce, Melville. 1950–1951. "Christianity's Crucial Conflict, The Case of Simone Weil." _Hibbert Journal_ 14: 333–40.
Chiari, Joseph. 1975. _Twentieth Century French Thought_. New York: Gordian Press.
Cobban, Alfred. 1964a. _Rousseau and the Modern State_. Hamden, Conn.: Archon Books.
———. 1964b. _The Social Interpretation of the French Revolution_. London: Cambridge University Press.
Cohen, Robert. 1964. "Parallels and the Possibility of Influence between Simone Weil's _Waiting for God_ and Samuel Beckett's _Waiting for Godot_." _Modern Drama_ 6 (4): 425–36.
Coles, Robert. 1987. _Simone Weil: A Modern Pilgrimage_. New York: Addison-Wesley.
Cuddihy, John M. 1974. _The Ordeal of Civility_. New York: Basic Books.
Davy, Marie-Magdelene. 1951. _The Mysticism of Simone Weil_. Boston: Beacon Press.
Dietz, Mary. 1985. "Citizenship With a Feminist Face: The Problem with Maternal Thinking." _Political Theory_ 13 (1):19–37.
Dinnerstein, Dorothy. 1977. _The Mermaid and the Minotaur_. New York: Harper Colophon.
Dujardin, Philippe. 1975. _Simone Weil, Idéologie et Politique_. Grenoble: Maspero.
Dunaway, John M. 1984. _Simone Weil_. Boston: Twayne Publishers.
Erikson, Erik, ed. 1978. _Adulthood_. New York: W.W. Norton and Co.
———. 1968. _Identity: Youth and Crisis_. New York: W.W. Norton.
———. 1959. _Young Man Luther, a Study in Psychoanalysis and History_. London: Faber and Faber.
———. 1950. _Childhood and Society_. New York: W.W. Norton and Co.
Fiedler, Leslie. 1951. "Simone Weil, A Prophet Out of Israel." _Commentary_ 11 (January): 36–46.
Fischer, Clare Benedicks. 1979. "The Fiery Bridge: Simone Weil's Theology of Work." Unpublished thesis. Graduate Theological Union, Berkeley, Calif.
Fitzgerald, David. 1965. "Simone Weil: A Note on Her Life and Thought." _Dublin Magazine_ 4 (Spring): 30–41.
Fraisse, Simone. 1975. "Révolte et obéissance chez Simone Weil." _Esprit_ 43 (October); 530–43.
Frenaud, Georges. 1953. "Simone Weil's Religious Thought in the Light of Catholic Theology." _Theological Studies_ 14:349–76.
Friedman, Maurice. 1967. _To Deny Our Nothingness_. New York: Delacourt.
Godman, Stanley. 1950. "Simone Weil." _Dublin Review_ 114th year (October–December): 67–81.
Gramsci, Antonio. 1971. _Prison Notebooks_. New York: International Publishers.
Guerard, Albert. 1957. _Fossils and Presences_. Stanford: Stanford University Press.
Hanson, Norwood Russell. 1958. _Patterns of Discovery_. Cambridge: Cambridge University Press.
Hardwick, Elizabeth. 1977. "Simone Weil." _New York Times Book Review_ (January 23): 1–2, 14–16.
Hauerwas, Stanley and Alasdair MacIntyre. 1983. _Revisions: Changing Perspectives in Moral Philosophy_. Notre Dame: University of Notre Dame Press.
Hellman, John. 1982. _Simone Weil: An Introduction to Her Thought_. Waterloo: Wilfrid Laurier University Press.

———. 1981. *Emmanuel Mournier and the New Catholic Left, 1930–1950.* Toronto: University of Toronto Press.

———. 1973. "The Opening to the Left in French Catholicism," *Journal of the History of Ideas* (July–September): 381–90.

Hobbes, Thomas. 1969. *Leviathan.* Michael Oakeshott, ed. New York: Collier Books.

Hoffman, Stanley, ed. 1963. *In Search of France.* Cambridge: Harvard University Press.

Homer. 1951. *The Iliad.* Richard Lattimore, ed. Chicago: University of Chicago Press.

Horkheimer, Max. 1974. *Critique of Instrumental Reason: Lectures and Essays Since the End of World War Two.* New York: Seabury Press.

Hughes, H. Stuart. 1968. *The Obstructed Path.* New York: Harper and Row.

———. 1958. *Consciousness and Society.* New York: Knopf.

James, William. 1958. *The Varieties of Religious Experience.* New York: Mentor.

Jennings, Elizabeth. 1959. "A World of Contradictions." *The Month* 22 (December): 349–58.

Jonas, Hans. 1958. *The Gnostic Religion.* Boston: Beacon.

Kateb, George. 1984. *Hannah Arendt: Politics, Conscience, Evil.* Totowa, N.J.: Rowman & Allanheld.

Katz, Steven, ed. 1978. *Mysticism and Philosophical Analysis.* New York: Oxford University Press.

Kazin, Alfred. 1955. "The Gift." *The Innermost Leaf: A Selection of Essays.* New York: Harcourt, Brace.

King, J.H. 1976. "Simone Weil and the Identity of France." *Journal of European Studies* 6:125–43.

King, Preston and B.C. Parekh. 1968. *Politics and Experience.* Cambridge: Cambridge University Press.

Kohut, Thomas. 1986. "Psychohistory as History." *American Historical Review* 91 (1):336–54.

Krogmann, Angelica. 1970. *Simone Weil.* Hamburg: Rowohlt.

Kuhn, Thomas. 1962. *The Structure of Scientific Revolutions.* Chicago: University of Chicago Press.

Lichtheim, George. 1961. *Marxism: an Historical and Critical Study.* London: Praeger.

Little, J. P. 1977. "Albert Camus, Simone Weil, and Modern Tragedy." *French Studies*, 31, January): 42–51.

———. 1970a. "Society as Mediator in Simone Weil's Venise Sauvé." *Modern Language Review* 65 (2): 298–305.

———. 1970b. "The Symbolism of the Cross in the Writings of Simone Weil." *Religious Studies* 6 (June): 177–82.

———. 1969. "Heraclitus and Simone Weil: The Harmony of Opposites." *Forum for Modern Language Studies* 5 (1): 72–79.

McFarland, Dorothy. 1983. *Simone Weil.* New York: F. Ungar Publishing Company.

MacIntyre, Alasdair. 1981. *After Virtue.* Notre Dame: University of Notre Dame Press.

———. 1966. *A Short History of Ethics.* New York: Collier Books.

Marcel, Gabriel. 1949. "Simone Weil." *The Month* 2 (July): 9–18.

Marcuse, Herbert. 1964. *One Dimensional Man.* Boston: Beacon.

Maritain, Jacques. 1941. *A travers le désastre.* New York: Éditors de la Maison Française, Inc.

———. 1940. *Scholasticism and Politics*. New York: Macmillian.

Marrus, Michael and Robert D. Paxton. 1981. *Vichy France and the Jews*. New York: Basic Books.

Marx, Karl. 1978. *The Marx-Engels Reader*. Robert C. Tucker, ed. New York: Norton.

———. 1967. *Writings of the Young Marx on Philosophy and Society*. Lloyd D. Easton and Kurt H. Gudat, eds. New York: Doubleday.

———. 1959. *Basic Writings on Politics and Philosophy: Karl Marx and Friedrich Engels*. Lewis S. Feuer, ed. New York: Doubleday Anchor.

Massachusetts Institute of Technology, Seminar on Culture and Technology. 1975–1976. "Simone Weil: Live Like Her?" Unpublished manuscript, Cambridge.

Merton, Thomas. 1968. *Faith and Violence*. Notre Dame: University of Notre Dame Press.

Meyerhoff, Hans. 1957. "The Reading of Reality." *The New Republic* 146 (January 21): 18–19.

Mitzman, Arthur. 1964. "The French Working Class and the Blum Government (1936–1937)." *International Review of Social History* 9: 363–90.

Mueller, Claus. 1973. *The Politics of Communication*. New York: Oxford.

Murdoch, Iris. 1956. "Knowing the Void." *The Spectator* 197 (6697): 613–14.

Nicholl, Donald. 1950. "Simone Weil, God's Servant." *Blackfriars* 31 (365): 364–72.

Nietzsche, Friedrich. 1964. *Beyond Good and Evil*. Marianne Cowan, trans. Chicago: Henry Regnery Co.

Oates, Joyce Carol. 1977. Review of *The Simone Weil Reader*, George Panichas, ed. *The New Republic* (July 2): 33–37.

Pagels, Elaine. 1979. *The Gnostic Gospels*. New York: Random House.

Panichas, George, ed. 1977. *The Simone Weil Reader*. New York: David McKay Company.

Paxton, Robert. O. 1972. *Vichy France: Old Guard and New Order, 1940–1944*. New York: Knopf.

Perrin, Father Joseph and Gustave Thibon. 1953. *Simone Weil As We Knew Her*. London: Routledge & Kegan Paul.

Pétrement, Simone. 1976. *Simone Weil: A Life*. Raymond Rosenthal, trans. New York: Panthenon.

———. 1949. "The Life and Thought of Simone Weil." *Politics* 6 (42):13–19.

Peyre, Henri. 1961. "Contemporary Feminine Literature in France." *Yale French Studies* (27):47–65.

Pierce, Roy. 1966. *Contemporary French Political Thought*. New York: Oxford.

———. 1962. "Sociology and Utopia: The Early Writings of Simone Weil." *Political Science Quarterly* 77 (4): 505–25.

Pitkin, Hanna Fenichel. 1984. *Fortune is a Woman*. Berkeley: University of California Press.

———. 1976. "Inhuman Conduct and Unpolitical Theory." *Political Theory* 4 (3): 301–17.

———. 1973. "The Roots of Conservatism." *Dissent* 20 (4):496–525.

Plato. 1975. *Phaedrus*. W.C. Helmbold and W.G. Rabinowitz, trans. Indianapolis: Bobbs-Merrill Company.

———. 1959. *Timaeus*. Francis M. Cornford, trans. New York: Bobbs-Merrill Company.

———. 1951. *The Symposium*. Walter Hamilton, trans. New York: Penguin.

———. n.d. *The Republic*. Benjamin Jowitt, trans. New York: Modern Library.

Powys, John Cowper. 1938. *The Enjoyment of Literature*. New York: Simon and Shuster.

Rees, Richard. 1966. *Simone Weil, A Sketch for a Portrait*. Carbondale: Southern Illinois University Press.

————. 1959. *Brave Men*. Carbondale: Southern Illinois Press.

Ricoeur, Paul. 1969. *The Symbolism of Evil*. Boston: Beacon Press.

————. 1965. *History and Truth*. Evanston: Northwestern University Press.

Rosen, Fred. 1979. "Marxism, Mysticism, and Liberty: The Influence of Simone Weil on Albert Camus." *Political Theory* 7 (3): 301–19.

————. 1973. "Labor and Liberty: Simone Weil and the Human Condition." *Theoria and Theory* (7):33–47.

Rousseau, Jean Jacques. 1972. *The Government of Poland*. W. Kendall, trans. Indianapolis: Bobbs-Merrill.

————. 1968. *The Social Contract*. Maurice Cranston, trans. Baltimore: Penguin.

Rustan, M.J. 1953. "La Notion de limite chez Simone Weil et chez Albert Camus." *Terre Humaine* 3 (February): 32–43.

Sandel, Michael. 1982. *Liberalism and the Limits of Justice*. Cambridge: Cambridge University Press.

Schaar, John. 1981. "The Case for Patriotism," in *Legitimacy in the Modern State*. New Brunswick: Transaction Press.

Sennett, Richard. 1977. *The Fall of Public Man*. New York: Knopf.

Smith, Colin. 1964. *Contemporary French Philosophy*. New York: Barnes and Noble.

Sontag, Susan. 1963. "Simone Weil." *The New York Review of Books* 1:22.

Spitz, Lewis. 1973. "Psychohistory and History: The Case of Young Man Luther." *Soundings* 56: 182–209.

Staal, Frits. 1975. *Exploring Mysticism*. Berkeley: University of California Press.

Stein, Maurice R., Arthur J. Vidich, and David Manning White. 1960. *Identity and Anxiety: Survival of the Person in Mass Society*. Glencoe: The Free Press.

Taplin, Oliver. 1986. "Homer Comes Home." *The New York Review of Books* 33: 4.

Taylor, Mark. 1973. "History, Humanism and Simone Weil." *Commonweal* (August): 448–52.

Teahan, John. 1978. "Renunciation of Self and World: A Critical Dialectic in Thomas Merton." *Thought* 53 (109): 133–50.

Teuber, Andreas. 1982. "Simone Weil: Equality as Compassion." *Philosophy and Phenomenological Research* 43 (2): 221–37.

Thomas, Keith. 1981. "A Working Girl." *The New York Review of Books* 28 (June 28).

Thompson, David. 1969. *Democracy in France Since 1870*. 5th ed. New York: Oxford.

Thucydides. 1951. *The Peloponnesian War*. Rex Warner, trans. New York: Modern Library.

Tillich, Paul. 1967. *A History of Christian Thought*. Carl E. Bernstein, ed. New York: Simon and Schuster.

Tocqueville, Alexis de. 1966. *Democracy in America*. J. P. Mayer and Max Lerner, eds. New York: Harper and Row.

Tomlin, E. F. 1954. *Simone Weil*. New Haven: Yale University Press.

Voegelin, Eric. 1974. *Order and History*. Vols. 2, 4. Baton Rouge: Louisiana State University Press.

————. 1968. *Science, Politics, and Gnosticism*. Chicago: Henry Regnery Co.

————. 1952. *The New Science of Politics*. Chicago: University of Chicago Press.

Vetö, Miklos. 1965. "Simone Weil and Suffering." *Thought* 40 (157): 275–86.

———. 1962. "Uprootedness and Alienation in Simone Weil." *Blackfriars* 43 (September): 383–95.

Warner, Marina. 1981. *Joan of Arc: The Image of Female Heroism*. New York: Knopf.

Weber, Eugen. 1962. *Action Française*. New York: Stanford University Press.

Weil, Simone. 1987. *Formative Writings*. Dorothy Tuck McFarland and Wilhelmina Van Ness, eds. Amherst: University of Massachusetts Press.

———. 1978. *Lectures on Philosophy*. Hugh Price, trans. London: Cambridge University.

———. 1974. *Gateway to God*. David Raper, ed. Glasgow: William Collins Sons and Co.

———. 1973. *Oppression and Liberty*. Arthur Wills and John Petrie, trans. Amherst: University of Massachusetts Press.

———. 1968. *On Science, Necessity, and the Love of God*. Richard Rees, ed. London: Oxford University Press.

———. 1965. *Seventy Letters*. Richard Rees, trans. London: Oxford University Press.

———. 1962a. *Pensées sans ordre concernant l'amour de Dieu*. Paris: Gallimard.

———. 1962b. *Selected Essays 1934–1943*. Richard Rees, trans. London: Oxford University Press.

———. 1960. *Écrits historiques et politiques*. Albert Camus, ed. Paris: Gallimard.

———. 1957a. *Écrits de Londres et dernières lettres*. Paris: Gallimard.

———. 1957b. *Intimations of Christianity Among the Ancient Greeks*. Elisabeth Geissbaahler, ed. London: Routledge & Kegan Paul.

———. 1956a. *The Iliad or the Poem of Force*. Mary McCarthy, trans. Wallingford, Pa.: Pendle Hill.

———. 1956b. *The Notebooks of Simone Weil*. 2 Vols. Arthur Wills, trans. London: Routledge & Kegan Paul.

———. 1955. *Venise Sauvé*. Paris: Gallimard.

———. 1953. *Letter to a Priest*. Arthur F. Wills, trans. London: Routledge and Kegan Paul.

———. 1952a. *Gravity and Grace*. London: Routledge & Kegan Paul.

———. 1952b. *The Need for Roots*. Arthur F. Wills, trans. Boston: Beacon Press.

———. 1951a. *La Condition ouvriére*. Paris: Gallimard.

———. 1951b. *Waiting for God*. Emma Craufurd, trans. New York: Harper.

———. 1950a. *L'Attente de Dieu*. Paris: La Colombe, Edns de Vieux Colombier.

———. 1950b. *La Connaissance surnaturelle*. Paris: Gallimard.

———. 1950c. "Note sur la suppression générale des partis politiques." *La Table Ronde* 26 (February): 9–29.

———. 1946a. "Essai sur la notion de lecture." *Etudes Philosophiques* 1 (January– March): 13–19.

———. 1946b. "Words and War." *Politics* 3 (March): 69–73.

———. 1945. "Reflexions on War." *Politics* 2 (February): 51–55.

West, Paul. 1966. *The Wine of Absurdity*. State College: Pennsylvania State University Press.

White, George Abbott. 1981. *Simone Weil: Interpretations of a Life*. Amherst: University of Massachusetts Press.

White, James Boyd. 1984. *When Words Lose Their Meaning*. Chicago: University of Chicago Press.

Wolin, Sheldon. 1960. *Politics and Vision*. Boston: Little, Brown and Co.

# Index